Game Writing:
Narrative Skills
for Videogames

GAME WRITING: NARRATIVE SKILLS FOR VIDEOGAMES

EDITED BY
CHRIS BATEMAN

CHARLES RIVER MEDIA
Boston, Massachusetts

Cover Design: Tyler Creative

CHARLES RIVER MEDIA
25 Thomson Place
Boston, Massachusetts 02210
617-757-7900
617-757-7969 (FAX)
crm.info@thomson.com
www.charlesriver.com

This book is printed on acid-free paper.

Chris Bateman. *Game Writing: Narrative Skills for Videogames.*
ISBN: 1-58450-490-0

Library of Congress Cataloging-in-Publication Data
Game writing : narrative skills for videogames / edited by Chris Bateman. -- 1st ed.
    p. cm.
  ISBN 1-58450-490-0 (pbk. : alk. paper)
 1. Video games--Authorship. I. Bateman, Chris Mark.
  GV1469.34.A97G36 2006
  794.8--dc22
                        2006017150

Printed in the United States of America
06 7 6 5 4 3 2

CHARLES RIVER MEDIA titles are available for site license or bulk purchase by institutions, user groups, corporations, etc. For additional information, please contact the Special Sales Department at 800-347-7707.

Contents

4   Nonlinear Game Narrative   71
Mary DeMarle

5   Keeping the Player on Track   85
Chris Bateman

6   Game Characters   103
Andrew S. Walsh

Acknowledgments

The authors would like to extend their grateful thanks to Nick Adams, Duke Clement, Richard Cobbett, Emma Cowie and ELSPA, the entire DeMarle crew (and most especially Ann), Phil Drinkwater, Sean Dromgoole at GameVision Europe, Patti Durr, Jonathan Evans, Judith M. Jacobs, Zoe and Noah Jacobs, Jonathan Kray, Andrea Kuehnel, Eddie Kuehnel, Michael Kuehnel, Nick Laing, Cheri Langdell and the entire worldwide Langdell team, Marty O'Donnell, Katie Pagliara, Kyle Peschel, Lynne Ransom, Jason Della Rocca, Mark Rudolph, Mike Seifert, Tom Sloper, Adria Smiley, Alice Taylor and the BBC Creative Research & Development department, Raison Varner, Chris Viggers, Scott West, the Writers Guild of America (West), and the Writers' Guild of Great Britain.

We would also like to offer grateful thanks to the people at Moby Games (*http://www.mobygames.com*) for their invaluable record of videogame details, to the people at the Killer List of Videogames (*http://www.klov.com*) for the comprehensive list of arcade games, and to everyone at the IGDA, and especially in the IGDA Game Writers' Special Interest Group, for their tireless assistance.

About the Authors

GAME WRITING:
NARRATIVE SKILLS FOR VIDEOGAMES

Edited by Chris Bateman

This book is written by a group of authors with extensive backgrounds in game writing, including Ernest Adams, Chris Bateman, Richard Boon, Richard Dansky, Mary DeMarle, Matt Entin, Stephen Jacobs, Ed Kuehnel, Tim Langdell, Rhianna Pratchett, Coray Seifert, James Swallow, and Andrew S. Walsh.

Subedited by Richard Boon, Neil Bundy, Richard Dansky, Wendy Despain, Beth A. Dillon, Stephen Jacobs, Tim Langdell, Ahmad Saad, Coray Seifert, Ben Serviss, and James Swallow.

ABOUT THE EDITOR

Chris Bateman is managing director of International Hobo, a specialist company in the field of market-oriented game design and narrative, and a noted game designer and writer. Games he has both written and designed include *Discworld Noir*, *Ghost Master*, *Heretic Kingdoms: The Inquisition*, and *Play with Fire*. He has two published novels *Downtime* and *Dreamtime*, and is co-author of *21ˢᵗ Century Game Design*, a guide to the practicalities of game design put into the context of meeting the needs of the audience. He sits on the executive panel of the IGDA's Game Writers Special Interest Group. His blog can be found at *onlyagame.typepad.com*.

ABOUT THE CHAPTER AUTHORS

All the authors of this book are members of the IGDA's Game Writers' Special Interest Group and are renowned in their field.

Ernest Adams

Ernest Adams is an independent game designer, writer, and teacher, working with the International Hobo design group. He has been in the game industry since 1989 and is the author of two books, *Andrew Rollings and Ernest Adams on Game Design*, with Andrew Rollings, and *Break into the Game Industry: How to Get a Job Making Video Games*. Ernest was most recently employed as a lead designer at Bullfrog Productions on the *Dungeon Keeper* series, and for several years before that, he was the audio/video producer on the *Madden NFL Football* product line. He has developed online, computer, and console games for everything from the IBM 360 mainframe to the PlayStation 2. He is the founder of the International Game Developers' Association and is a frequent lecturer at the Game Developers' Conference. His professional Web site is at *http://www.designersnotebook.com*.

Richard Boon

Richard Boon has written dialogue scripts for a dozen games while working for International Hobo Ltd, a UK-based game design and dialogue scripting company. He also dabbles in game design, is co-author of the book *21ˢᵗ Century Game Design*, and teaches design and videogame theory as program leader for Salford University's Computer and Video Game course.

Richard Dansky

Richard Dansky is the head writer at Red Storm Entertainment in charge of the Tom Clancy properties and has been involved in games for more than a decade. Richard Dansky is the Central Clancy Writer for UbiSoft, and has been with Red Storm Entertainment for more than six years. He has written, designed, or otherwise contributed to numerous games, including *Far Cry*, *Ghost Recon: Island Thunder*, *Rainbow Six: Raven Shield*, and the upcoming revival of the *Might & Magic* series. A published novelist, Richard is the author of *The Trilogy of the Second Age* and has also worked extensively in the role-playing game field. Richard sits on the executive panel of the IGDA's Game Writers' SIG. You can find him online at *http://www.snowbirdgothic.com.* He lives in Durham, North Carolina, with his wife, writer Melinda Thielbar, and their two inevitable cats.

Mary De Marle

Mary De Marle has worked in the game industry as both a freelance contract writer and a full-time narrative game designer for more than 10 years. Her work has crossed genres and play styles, including such titles as *Myst III: Exile* (an AIAS finalist for Original Character and Story Design Achievement in 2001), *Myst IV: Revelation* (a Gamespot finalist for Best Story in 2004), and *Homeworld II*. She is currently employed as a Narrative Designer on Ubisoft Montreal's *Splinter Cell* license. In addition to the work she does on games, Mary has been actively involved in teaching others how to make better ones: in 2004, she was one of the primary designers behind a 4-year undergraduate curriculum on Game Development that is currently being offered at Champlain College, Vermont.

Matt Entin

Matthew Entin has worked in the videogame industry since 2002. He wrote his first comedic title, the freeware graphic adventure OCKERS, while still an undergrad at Syracuse University. He then co-wrote *Leisure Suit Larry: Magna Cum Laude*, for which he was nominated for a Game Developer's Choice award in the category of Best Writing and a Game Audio Network Guild award for Best Dialogue.

Stephen Jacobs

Stephen Jacobs is an Associate Professor of Information Technology at the Rochester Institute of Technology, where he teaches graduate courses in Game History, Writing, World Design, and On-Line Community and Identity. He also heads the Lab for Technological Literacy, which focuses on using media and games for informal science and technology education. He's been a contributing editor to *Videomaker*, *Television Business International*, *Television 2.0*, and CNET. He is happily married to Professor Patricia Durr of the National Technical Institute for the Deaf, and the father of Zoe, 10 (who monopolizes his DS for her *Nintendogs*) and Noah, 8 (who's a *Super Smash Brothers Melee* kind of guy).

Ed Kuehnel

Edward Kuehnel has been a writer/game designer for more than five years. His first comedic effort, *Leisure Suit Larry: Magna Cum Laude*, earned him a Game Developer's Choice nomination for Best Writing and a Game Audio Network Guild nomination for Best Dialog. He invites you to visit his Web site at *http://www.wrestlevaniaproductions.com*.

Tim Langdell

Tim Langdell is an early founding member of the games industry having formed one of the first companies, EDGE Games, which at one time was effectively Electronic Arts Europe and Sega Europe as well as being a top five European game publisher. At EDGE he devised and developed the brand name (which is well known through the very successful *EDGE Magazine*) and has more than 180 games to his credit. He has been involved in founding numerous organizations, including the American Academy of Interactive Arts & Sciences (AAIAS) and the British Academy of Interactive Arts & Sciences (BAIAS). He currently serves on the Board of AAIAS, is Chairman of BAIAS, and is Vice Chair of the Writers Guild of America (West) New Media Caucus. Tim taught at the University of Southern California where he instigated the interactive media and game classes in 1992 and had more than 500 students attend his game design, production, and testing classes in the past three years. He recently became the Chair of the Department of Media at National University. Tim has also written a number of books on video games, most recently the first ever book on games testing (*Game Testing All In One*, Thomson, February 2005) which he co-wrote. His first book, *The Spectrum Handbook*, reached number five in the *London Times* Best Seller List.

Rhianna Pratchett

Despite wanting to be a mermaid when she grew up, the inability to locate a suitable fish tail in the depths of rural Somerset meant that Rhianna Pratchett instead decided to embrace the scaly hands of journalism that had long been reaching out for her. After many years working in the videogames press, Rhianna left the security of full-time employment to pursue the flexible hours and pajama-based life of freelance writing. For the past three years, she has also been giving talks, consulting, and working on scripts for videogames. Rhianna is currently working on several projects for Firefly Studios, Blitz, Nokia, and Larian Studios; while also fulfilling the role of chief writing ninja for Sony's PS3 title *Heavenly Sword*. Rhianna lives in London where she accidentally collects cats and lives in fear that she will one day be crushed by her precarious mountains of books, DVDs, and videogames. Her email address is *rhiannapratchett@blueyonder.co.uk*.

Coray Seifert

Coray Seifert is an associate producer at Kaos Studios, a THQ development house nestled in the heart of midtown Manhattan. Coray has developed games as a writer, designer, and voice-over director for companies such as Large Animal Games, Creo Ludus Entertainment, and the US Department of Defense. He is also a coordinator of the New Jersey chapter of the International Game Developers Association and serves as a committee member for the IGDA's Game Writers' Special Interest Group. In addition, Coray teaches game design at the New Jersey Institute of Technology and has appeared on gamasutra.com, Xbox Exclusive, CNBC, and NY1; in *Game Developer Magazine*; and at numerous game industry events as an editor, panelist, lecturer, or host.

James Swallow

James Swallow is an author, journalist, and scriptwriter. His work in the games industry includes licensed titles based on the *Star Trek* and *Battlestar Galactica* franchises, as well as original IPs such as *Killzone* and *Maelstrom*. The author of 14 books and several audio dramas, Swallow's writing features tie-ins based on *Star Trek: Voyager*, *Doctor Who*, *Warhammer 40,000*, *Judge Dredd,* and *Stargate Atlantis*, as well as the original *Sundowners* series and the nonfiction title *Dark Eye: The Films of David Fincher*.

Andrew S. Walsh

Andrew Walsh's professional writing credits span theatre, radio, animation, television, film, and videogames, which he finds scary and amusing and hopes that one day this experience will help him take over the world. Aside from work with Granada, HTV, Zenith North, Risk, Diamond, and Yorkshire Television on shows such as *Byker Grove, Emmerdale,* and *Family Affairs*, as well as radio work for the BBC, Andrew has worked extensively in the videogames industry with 20 games under his belt so far. Alongside his work as a writer, Andrew is also a theatre and vocal director as well as an active figure in the Writers' Guild of Great Britain. He likes beer, motorbikes, oddity, and talking. His latest adventures can be found at *http://www.andrewwalsh.com* which makes him sound much more sensible than he ever feels.

About the Sub-Editors

In addition to the writers and editor, each chapter was also reviewed by a number of volunteers from the IGDA Game Writers' SIG who contributed their time and experience to individual chapters.

Neil Bundy has worked on many of the International Hobo game projects (including *Ghost Master, Heretic Kingdoms: The Inquisition, Air Conflicts,* and *Play with Fire*) as a game design assistant, usability and playability consultant, and general troubleshooter.

Sande Chen is a game writer, producer, and consultant, and has been active in the game industry since 1998. Her past game credits include 1999 Independent Games Festival winner *Terminus, Scooby Doo,* and *JamDat Scrabble.* She is the co-author of the book, *Serious Games: Games That Educate, Train, and Inform.*

Wendy Despain worked for seven years with a major media company experimenting with combining Alternate Reality Games with television. Now she is a freelance writer working with traditional videogames as well as ARGs, pushing the boundaries of interactive narrative.

Beth A. Dillon is a graduate of the innovative Writing program at Portland State University in Oregon, where she served as an editor for Ooligan Press. Her publications and conference presentations relate to digital games, interactive storytelling, and cultural studies.

Ahmad Saad is a junior game designer in the industry. He is striving to perfect his knowledge in the field of storytelling by surrounding himself with the experts from the IGDA Game Writers' SIG.

Ben Serviss has written on the design side of the game industry as well as the games press, including feature articles for the avant-garde game site gamebrains.com and the trade publication *IEEE Multimedia Magazine.* He is also a co-founder and managing editor of the IGDA's Game Writers Special Interest Group Quarterly Newsletter. Ben is currently a designer/writer at Creo Ludus Entertainment.

About the IGDA

The International Game Developers Association is a nonprofit professional society that is committed to advancing the careers and enhancing the lives of game developers by connecting members with their peers, promoting professional development, and advocating on issues that affect the developer community. For more information on the IGDA, visit *http://www.igda.org* or email *info@igda.org.*

About the IGDA Game Writers' Special Interest Group

This volunteer organization within the IGDA framework exists to support, promote, and improve the situation of writers working in the games industry, and also to enhance the quality of narrative in games. The SIG began in 2002 when Chris Bateman and Raphael van Lierop realized a growing number of writers were working in interactive media, but there was very little community, cooperation, or even communication among them. The IGDA provided the perfect foundation to build upon. A mailing list was started immediately, and members of that list gradually self-assembled into a functioning SIG with big-picture objectives and specific initiatives. Membership has grown steadily, and in 2005, a constitution was formed and monthly online committee meetings began.

The Game Writers Special Interest Group focuses on the following:

- Building a community of game writers
- Promoting the art and craft of game writing to the industry as a whole
- Educating game developers about writers, and educating writers about game development
- Identifying and addressing those issues of importance to the community
- Fostering better narrative in games

Preface

The relationship between videogames and narrative is constantly evolving. Professional game development is too young a discipline for a coherent narrative language to have fully emerged, and as a result, considerable opinions exist on how game stories should be implemented. We are still a comparatively young media, but increasing commercial interest forces those who make videogames to deal with the problems of game narrative as they are discovered, rather than solving the problems in advance.

Despite the publication of many books on the subject of narrative in games, very little attention has been paid to the actual skills used by people working in the field of game writing. As a result, most discussion tends to be in fairly abstract terms, and the pragmatic skills required to construct game narrative and dialogue are frequently overlooked entirely. In the absence of continuity of knowledge regarding the skills being used, the craft of game writing has lacked clear definition.

The creation of this book was largely motivated by this lack of discussion of technical game-writing skills. There seemed a definite need to capture a snapshot of the way stories make their way into games, and it seemed equally important that this process be presented as the synthesis of many different writers' experiences, rather than a description from a single perspective. Partly, this reflects the immense diversity in the field of games. A game writer can create narrative situations within a game in many ways, and the methods used for an action game, an adventure game, a sports game, and so on are all significantly different.

The IGDA's Game Writers' Special Interest Group, also known as the Game Writing Special Interest Group, was founded with the express purpose of building a community of game writers to promote the art and craft of game writing, to educate about the field, and to identify and address those issues of importance to the community of game writers, as well as to foster better narrative in games in more general terms. Within this remit, it quickly became apparent that a book that could serve as a skills-based reference to the field of game writing would rapidly become essential.

Building a coherent reference book for a field that is still effectively in its infancy has not been easy, not least of which because there are still many areas that are ill defined. The clearest indication of this is that there is still no single script format because different game projects have radically different requirements regarding scripts. A Hollywood-style screenplay is arguably suitable for cut scenes (the short noninteractive sequences in games) but not for the bulk of dialogue and text that is used in a typical game. This situation makes the definition of a common script format an exceptionally tricky proposition, which could prove even more difficult than presenting a summary of the skills currently used by writers working in the field of games. If and when such a common script format evolves, it will likely not be a static text-based format at all, but some form of markup language that can encode additional data in a seamless fashion. The ultimate game script format should be able to transform between a general script, a programmer script, an artist and animator reference, a voice actor script, and a translator script at will. This will require careful thought and application, not to mention tremendous industry cooperation, if such a format is to become standardized.

Additionally, games are difficult to adequately compare to other media, primarily due to their interactive nature. Whereas the concept of genre has a clear meaning in the context of a novel or film, it is less clear in the context of a game. Games with narrative elements represent genre in a multidimensional manner because they consist of a narrative genre on the one hand and a gameplay genre on the other. Games often share a common gameplay genre but have different narrative genres (two adventure games may share similar gameplay, but one might be a fantasy comedy and the other a tale of swashbuckling action). Similarly, two games can share the same narrative genre but have radically different gameplay (a First Person Shooter (FPS) and an adventure game may both be rendered in a film noir style, for instance). This only adds to the complexity of the issues involved in dealing with game narratives.

Another problem has been the lack of clear examples of great game narratives. Although people who work in games have many examples they like to cite, these fall somewhat below the highest standards of work in other media—perhaps this is only to be expected in such a young medium. The problem in this regard is that we have yet to solve even a fraction of the key issues in game design, and this limits the kinds of stories that can be told. We can tell a great monster story, and we can tell a heroic quest story quite well too, but the essential tension between the freedom of the player and the constraints of narrative places severe limits on what can be achieved at the present time. This is not to say that there are not some hugely talented people working on game narratives. Rather, it means that the best that we have achieved thus far can only really be appreciated in comparison to other games; whereas narrative comparisons to the best novels, films, and plays often leaves games seeming slightly deficient.

A severe problem in this regard is the absence of a stable and supported underground game development community. Without a framework to support "art house games," artistic freedom is lacking. When the vast majority of games (and certainly any that are developed on a reasonable budget) are purely intended for entertainment, it is hard for the artistic aspects of game narrative to be fully explored. Just as underground films drive innovation and creativity in the movie industry, so, too, we need a similar engine of artistry for games.

Despite these problems, there are still hundreds of game writers working in the field of videogames, all of whom are trying to do the best job they can under severe and sometimes restrictive limitations. There is much to praise in their achievements, especially when placed against the context of unravelling the Gordian knot of presenting narrative—traditionally a static form—via games, which are at their heart dynamic interactive systems. The incompatibility here seems irreconcilable; the fact that we have any game stories of any quality at all is testament to the skill and creativity of pioneers in a largely unrecognized field.

It cannot be overstressed that whereas the narrative language of theatre, novels, films, and television has become largely codified and consensually agreed, the narrative language of games is still very much in a state of evolutionary flux. We do not know what the final narrative language of games will be like—likely we will not know until all the technology pertinent to games has been developed, and this could take decades or even centuries. Therefore, everyone working in the field of game writing strives toward an ideal that lies somewhere beyond the horizon.

This book captures a snapshot of the narrative skills employed in the modern games industry. If it successfully teaches a wider audience about these skills and how to employ them to create game narratives, it will have served its purpose. If it also contributes in any significant manner to the larger goal of constructing the foundations of a coherent narrative language for this emerging art form, it will have been especially worthwhile.

Chris Bateman
Editor

1 Introduction to Game Narrative

Richard Dansky

What is *game narrative*? It's a question that developers, writers, reviewers, and publishers have been trying to answer for years with only limited success. Like many other things in this still-young industry, narrative is an area where definitions are still being stretched, formulated, and tried on for size. It is crucial, however, to formalize a definition of game narrative before attempting to create one. Otherwise, you're trying to hit a moving target with an entire development team waiting for you to make the perfect shot, with a limited chance of success.

To begin with, it is helpful to define what we mean by *narrative*, which is itself a term replete with ambiguity. For the purpose of this book, we define narrative as the methods by which the story materials are communicated to the audience. We'll return to this definition and pursue it in more depth in a later chapter.

Some game genres are more narrative-friendly, by definition, than others. A multiplayer strategy experience such as *Battlefield 1942* (Digital Illusions, 2002) doesn't have or even need much of a narrative. The game takes a familiar context (World War II) and situation (here's a battle—go win it) and turns the players loose. Fighting games are also light on narrative. After the central conceit of beating the snot out of the other guy—whomever or whatever he may be—has been established, the narrative exists simply to string the series of bouts together toward the ultimate goal.

On the other hand, some genres of game are heavily dependent on narrative. Adventure games are almost entirely narrative-driven, and platformers and First Person Shooters (FPSs) often have strong narrative components as well. Computer Role Playing Games (cRPGs) are yet another category that depends almost entirely on narrative—the play experience through the game corresponds precisely to the character growth through the course of the narrative. To put it another way, without narrative, Sora, the protagonist of *Kingdom Hearts* (Square, 2002), stays on the island, sparring with his friends and eating fruit forever. It may be an idyllic existence, but is really fun to play?

The greatest mistake that is made in defining game narrative is the attempt to reduce it to story and story alone. Story is a good start for the narrative, but if story were all there were, then we would be discussing fiction, not games. The story is a launching point for the narrative, not the narrative in toto. By the same token, elements cannot be excised from the narrative as a whole simply because they don't appear to fit in at first blush. Backstory may often be viewed as nothing more than content to splash on a Web page to create buzz, but a good, coherent backstory may be necessary to support and contextualize the narrative as a whole. Which game feels like it has a stronger narrative, a generic fantasy hack 'n' slash or one derived from *The Lord of the Rings*? The answer to this, unlike the question of what is narrative, is comparatively obvious.

Ultimately, narrative comes down to one simple question: What happens? That is the heart of game narrative—what happens in the game? What story do the players create through their actions as they advance through the challenges, decisions, and rewards laid out for them by the development team? All the other questions—what is the world like, who are the characters, why is the player doing this—are secondary to that essential query. Understand what happens, and you understand narrative. Understand how to create a good answer for that question, and you understand how to create good game narrative.

Numerous techniques underpin this quest to create a narrative, including—cut scenes, character, dialogue, and more. All of these are useful tools for creating the overall construct of the narrative, but they cannot and should not be confused with the narrative itself. They're part of the process, not the process itself.

DEFINITION OF TERMS

To explore the meaning of game narrative, let's consider the definitions of some basic terminology.

Story

In the context of game development, *story* is often confused with *design*. The story is what happens, the flow of the game that can be separated from the game mechanics and retold as a narrative. For example, the story in *Grim Fandango* (LucasArts, 1998) can be summed up as "The adventures of a travel agent for the dead named Manny, who uncovers corruption in the afterlife and sets out to do something about it." The story in *Godzilla: Save the Earth* (Pipeworks Software, 2001) can be described as "Aliens come to earth to steal Godzilla's DNA, and he fights a bunch of monsters in order to stop them." Of the two, *Grim Fandango*'s story takes considerably longer to tell, but they both serve essentially the same purpose.

Character

Characters are the actors (or in the case of player characters, avatars) who exist in the game world and perform the in-game actions. Lara Croft is a character. So is the loathsome Morag from *Neverwinter Nights* (BioWare, 2002), the friendly hench-hippo Murray from *Sly Cooper and the Thievius Raccoonus* (Sucker Punch, 2002), and the gabby but not terribly bright guards from *Far Cry* (Crytek, 2004). Every character in a game should be designed to serve a purpose. Lara Croft is someone you want to be as you move through the world, whereas the guards are enemies to shoot and sources of information to eavesdrop on.

The character or characters the player controls are sometimes referred to as *player characters* (PCs), although the term *avatar* is becoming standard. Everyone else in the world is referred to as NPCs (*non-player characters*), or occasionally as AI (artificial intelligence), although this technically refers to the algorithms controlling their behavior rather than the characters themselves.

Setting

The *setting* defines the world that the action of the game takes place in, including character races, languages, laws of physics and metaphysics (do you have spells, blasters, or both?), and pretty much everything else necessary to define the game world. For an overtly "realistic" game such as *Tom Clancy's Splinter Cell* (Ubisoft, 2002), much of the setting goes without explanation, as we all have a pretty good idea of the real world. For a steampunk extravaganza such as *Arcanum: Of Steamworks & Magick Obscura* (Troika Games, 2001), the equation expands to include something much broader because a world of dwarves, zeppelins, and tech needs more detailed and specific explanation for players to feel comfortable in this more esoteric setting.

Backstory

Backstory is the history leading up to the events of the game, the explanation of what has produced the situation that will be played through. Related to setting, it can be defined as "who did what to whom, and what does the player have to do in order to fix it?" The backstory of *Tom Clancy's Rainbow Six 3: Raven Shield* (Ubisoft, 2003) includes World War II bank looting, the deportation of an elderly businessman from his home in South America, and the fascist Ustache regime. None of these are things that the player will interact with directly in the game, but they frame the game's narrative and action, giving the player the information he needs to immerse himself in the fiction and move forward with the action.

Cut Scenes

Cut scenes refer to in-game movies—sections of noninteractive footage that the player watches. Some are prerendered for a high level of visual polish, whereas others are produced with the in-game engine to provide visual continuity. Either way, cut scenes refer to events or conversations that the player sits back and watches with (usually) no interaction. They can be used to reward the player with a spectacular visual, provide an opportunity for conversation or exposition that would get lost in gameplay, or contain events—such as the death of a character, the pillaging of the main characters' equipment, or a villain's escape—that can't be left up to chance. At best, the player can look around during a cut scene, but more often than not, they have a theatrical presentation the player watches.

When many cut scenes are collected together, the result is a noninteractive sequence known as a *cinematic*. Game introductory sequences are generally cinematics, as they provide a perfect opportunity to explain setting and backstory before the player needs to use any of the information.

Scripted Events

A *scripted event* is a part of the game where control of some aspect is taken away from the player. Although related to cut scenes, they are distinctly different both in how they are made and how they are experienced. A single scripted event can be as simple as quickly pulling the camera angle around to show a looming surveillance camera (also known as a *camera case*) or as complicated as setting up a sequence of events involving multiple NPCs to illustrate a game point. Stealth games frequently use the former technique. *Half-Life 2* (Valve, 2004) made good use of the latter, letting the life-or-death struggles of NPCs in the game world illustrate environmental perils to the player vividly.

In-Game Artifacts

In-game artifacts are rather self-explanatory; they are objects in the game world that serve to advance the narrative. They can roughly be defined as narrative that the character, not the player, finds. Frequently, in-game artifacts take the form of documents of one sort or another—diaries, letters, books, and the like. By reading these, the player gains valuable information about what's going on and the world the player's moving through. The answering machine message the player overhears in *Max Payne 2: The Fall of Max Payne* (Remedy, 2003) is another example, as are the radio broadcasts in *Far Cry* and the emails Sam Fisher hacks into in *Splinter Cell*.

In-game documents are not the only way for artifacts to move the game narrative along; sometimes an object has symbolic significance. An example is the Tsortese Falchion in *Discworld Noir* (Perfect Entertainment, 1999) around which the plot of the game revolves. Players have seen their avatar slain in the opening cinematic with this very weapon, so when it is discovered during the course of the game, it has especial significance. It cannot be used as a weapon or a useful item for solving puzzles and exists in the game solely for its symbolic value.

WHAT IS THE PURPOSE OF GAME NARRATIVE?

On the most basic level, narrative strings together the events of the game, providing a framework and what can alternately be called a justification, a reason, or an excuse for the gameplay encounters. At its best, narrative pulls the player forward through the experience, creating the desire to achieve the hero's goals and, more importantly, see what happens next. At its worst, narrative merely sets up the situation and turns the players loose to do as they see fit. It achieves these goals through three important techniques: *immersion*, *reward*, and *identification*.

Immersion

The term *immersion* is frequently heard in the context of games, although it is seldom defined. In general terms, immersion refers to the state of mind where a person is completely absorbed in what they are doing. It has been related to the psychological state of "flow" [Csikszentmihalyi91] and also to the notion of suspension of disbelief [Coleridge1817]; to some extent, the term covers both of these otherwise unrelated notions. The important thing is, when players are immersed in a game, the real world ceases to exist, and the game world becomes their reality.

Narrative provides context for game events, and a sufficiently believable context provides immersion. At their most basic level, most First Person Shooters (FPSs) are the same. Move the targeting reticule onscreen, press a button, and hit the target—that's the center of the gameplay. Yet the genre has produced wildly divergent games, from the gore-spattered action of *Doom* (id, 1993) to the gritty historical realism of *Brothers in Arms: Road to Hill 30* (Gearbox, 2005) to the gloom-shadowed fantasy of *Thief: The Dark Project* (Looking Glass, 1998). The distinctions between these games lie partly in the differences in game mechanics but also in their significantly distinct narrative content. The story provides a way to believe in those mechanics and to give the player a reason to accept the need to perform them.

For example, in *Tom Clancy's Ghost Recon* (Red Storm, 2001), the player guns down innumerable enemies in a broadly realistic fashion. However, the narrative explains who these enemies are (Russian ultranationalists intent on doing bad things to Eastern Europe), who the player is pretending to be (American soldiers fighting aggression), and what he's supposed to do (shoot the bad guys). All of this combines to immerse the player in the fantasy and to tell him it's appropriate and reasonable to do some serious damage to the hostile AI. The narrative contextualizes the situation and the player objectives—"move and shoot" becomes "secure the downed aircraft," and "stay in one location for a certain length of time without getting shot" becomes "hold Red Square against the last desperate effort of the enemy troops." Because the action is now attached to the fantasy the narrative presents, it's a more appealing goal and something the player is more interested in achieving— and willing to work harder to obtain.

Reward

Narrative can also serve as a reward to the player. The narrative events can be revealed gradually, delivered as rewards for achieving in-game goals. When this has been done frequently enough inside the same game, the player will expect to receive another chunk of narrative after winning a boss fight or overcoming a particularly tough challenge.

For example, in *God of War* (SCE Studio Santa Monica, 2005), the backstory is revealed gradually as play progresses. After players clear out a chapter, they receive another chunk of backstory explaining how the protagonist, Kratos, came to be in such dire straits (that is, engaged in the action of the game) in the first place. These lengthy cut scenes give players no in-game advantage. They give no extra powers, no hints as to how to defeat enemies or unlock hidden advantages. Instead, they just give narrative information—who Kratos is, why he is so obsessed with killing Ares, and how he came to be in the middle of a war between the Olympian gods in the first place. They are rewards, pure and simple, each chapter ending with a cliff-hanger that exists to pull the player forward through the gameplay to the next one. In principle, these cliff-hangers drive players to want to know what happens next and thus motivate them to continue to persevere with the game.

Identification

The third major role that narrative serves is that of identification. It lays everything out for the player, telling him what's what, who's who, and what the state of the world around him is. By doing so, it gives the players context for their actions, and this in turn provides justification for game actions: when a game asks you to shoot things, it's helpful to know that the things you are shooting are dangerous terrorists, flesh-eating zombies, mutated lawyers, or something else that you have little or no moral qualms about dispatching into digital oblivion. By laying out clearly what the elements of the world are, the narrative establishes the players' place in it and the actions they are expected to take as a result. The players, in turn, can take those actions in confidence, knowing it's what they're supposed to do, instead of asking "Why am I doing this?"

The narrative provides identification in another sense as well, namely the sense of kinship and desire to become the central character. Players are invited to identify directly with a game protagonist (even more so than when they are invited to identify with the protagonist of a film or novel) because they will actually get to influence or control the game's lead role. The course of a game narrative should be designed, in general, to make the fantasy of being the lead character more appealing, and to make the lead character more sympathetic. Giving the protagonist a chance to act heroically, behave admirably (in whatever sense of the word you choose), and achieve ever-more impressive victories might be the key to making the player want to be—and therefore want to play—that protagonist.

WHAT MAKES GAME WRITING UNIQUE?

Videogame writing is unlike any other form of writing. There is some relation to screenplay writing, some relation to writing fiction, some technical writing, and other elements both diverse and esoteric. Furthermore, the expectations of what will be delivered in a videogame script change more rapidly than in other media, because of changes originating in advanced technology and corresponding changes in audience expectations.

Game writing has very real expectations, limitations, and codes that are unique to the medium. Screenplays, novels, and short stories all present a single path through the material; all are media that are received passively by the reader. Videogames, on the other hand, are all about player choice and action. This is extremely rare in other media.

Tabletop RPGs (whose influence on modern videogames cannot be underestimated) involve player choice, but they're written to be open experiences, offering plot hooks and possibilities so the players and gamemasters (the player in charge of the narrative and mechanics of the game) can run with the possibilities. The players construct the narrative experience in an ad hoc fashion.

In a videogame, the narrative experience must be completely defined in advance. The players will chart their way through the game, each making their own decisions so that no two players have an identical experience. It is vitally important that game writing takes into account anything and everything the player might decide to do in the world. Videogame writing is a closed system wherein the writing must lead the player to stay within the confines of the anticipated action. Everything in the world is already in the world, and there's no gamemaster who can insert content or improvise on the fly. This means a videogame script must be both flexible enough to cover the player's likely actions and sufficiently constrained to be less than infinite in scope.

There are simple and clear differentiations between game writing and other forms. Traditional scriptwriting involves a single narrative that doesn't allow for choice or variance. In addition, there's the question of scale—television dramas run at approximately 44 minutes per show whereas films are generally between 90 minutes and 3 hours. Games risk being pilloried for being too short if they clock in at fewer than 10 hours. The basic structure of scriptwriting may be applicable to game narrative, but it's not an exact fit.

Fiction writing is just as straightforward, and offers the author the opportunity to change narrative viewpoint without asking the programmers if that feature is available. Fiction also makes the protagonist the center of the action, not the player, and doesn't have to deal with interactive elements.

Tabletop RPG writing might be the closest to videogame writing, but even then there are major differences. RPGs are about open-ended experience and adjusting things on the fly, whereas videogame writing is a closed experience, focused on keeping the player satisfied with the options and actions available.

That being said, being able to draw on techniques from these types of writing is invaluable, as all of them can and do inform game writing. Writing dialogue and cut scenes is a process that draws heavily on traditional scriptwriting. Establishing setting and creating in-game artifacts, as well as basic storytelling techniques, can be drawn from traditional fiction. And an understanding of writing to support the game experience, not to mention working with mechanical limitations and world building, is a natural derivative of tabletop RPG work. But videogame writing is all of these and none of them, and anyone relying too heavily on another medium's techniques as a panacea will doubtless run into difficulties sooner or later.

There are some areas of parallel with other media. When film screenwriters write a script, they know that the director, cinematographer, set builders, prop makers, wardrobe, actors, stunt people, and effects personnel will help realize the script. Similarly, when game writers compose a script, they know the producers, concept artists, modelers, animators, programmers, game designers, and voice actors will have to find ways to integrate the script into the game. In many ways, game writing is sometimes geared as much toward ease of implementation as anything else. This means writing to expected length and count, getting across key game information to the player, and making sure the writing matches the design, assets, and implementation possibilities.

Another parallel with other media is the importance of the audience. Games are not the writers' story; they are the players' stories. Writers are producing something for the players to inhabit and call their own, which is sometimes difficult to implement. The temptation is always there to take the narrative by the horns and ride it in the direction the writer thinks it should go. Doing so, however, railroads the player and may seriously diminish the game experience—a problematic situation of which some players can be all too keenly aware. Even heavily scripted, linear games such as *Call of Duty* (Infinity Ward, 2003) place the player experience front and center, using writing to reinforce the notion that the player is the protagonist in the unfolding story and not a spectator.

The expectation in game writing is that the player will firstly be the center of the experience and secondly have a good time. Creating a brilliant narrative wherein the NPCs fight all the big battles and the player watches from the sidelines might defeat this purpose. It makes players simultaneously into audience and voyeur when they signed up for the starring role. Or to put it another way, do you want to play Sly Cooper or his turtle buddy Bentley, sitting back home and watching the action onscreen?

The same holds true for the flip side of the equation. Making the player the center of a miserable narrative is the sort of attention most people would rather do without. There's a reason nobody's lining up to do a game based upon the book of Job, and it has a lot to do with the fact that Job's not a fun person to be. The narrative must support the desired fantasy of the game, or else it risks defeating itself.

However, having said that the player is expected to be the center of the *experience* does not automatically equate to the player being at the center of the *plot* in the beginning. For instance, a game may be set at the fringes of a major event in the game world, but the story focuses on events that at first seem trivial and perfunctory. Usually, however, this is a ruse to misdirect the player, and the trivialities will eventually coincide with the larger events, thrusting the player into the center of events. This happens, for instance, in *The Legend of Zelda: The Wind Waker* (Nintendo, 2002). The player's initial motivation for action is rescuing Link's sister. Only later does it transpire that Link is a more significant player in world events than at first it seems.

With all these points in mind—the similarities and differences from other media, the unique requirements of a narrative that is both flexible and constrained, and the central role of the player—the pragmatics of game writing are that it often involves writing many consecutive variations on the same theme. Almost every writer working in videogames has had to deal with a task such as writing hundreds of variations of a line like "Arrgh! He shot me!" (This sort of task is so common, that short interjections such as this have even picked up their own term: *barks.*) This micro-scale scripting is neither glamorous work, nor rewarding, but it is a necessary task writers must tackle to fully implement a game narrative.

WHAT ARE THE BASICS OF GAME WRITING?

Having looked at how game writing is both similar to and distinct from writing in other media, we are ready to look at some of the central tenets of game writing. Chiefly, the basics of writing for a game involves:

- Ensuring that the writing relates to the gameplay
- Properly using the narrative tools the game provides

Keeping Gameplay in the Writing

When writing for games, it's absolutely essential that the gameplay and the writing remain closely tied to one another. Some core elements of traditional writing—lengthy exposition, internal monologue, switching character perspectives—can be utterly deadly to gameplay if not handled carefully. The players wants to play, they (generally) want to keep playing continuously, and they don't want to be given the impression that they are merely escorting the main character through a predefined set of actions.

Consider the *Splinter Cell* series of games. One of the techniques used to remind the player of his next objective is, in fact, internal monologue. Sam Fisher often gets short reminders to himself that he needs to disarm a bomb, take out a particular enemy, and the like. What he does not get are lengthy ruminations on the nature of his relationship with his formerly estranged daughter, X-rated musings about his sexy *krav maga* instructor, or a detailed economic assessment of the geopolitical situation in which he finds himself. The narrative technique (internal monologue) is used to support the gameplay (going off and achieving objectives) and not derailing it (subjecting the player to the writer's deathless prose).

What is important, then, is continually asking: "how does this support the game?" Does it reward the player, advance the action, provide depth without slowing the pace or otherwise move the player forward? If the answer is yes, then the gameplay has been kept in the writing. If the answer is no, if the reason something is in the script is to show off how incredibly cool it is, then the gameplay has been lost, and the writing is extraneous. No matter how wonderful a writer's exposition of dwarven tiddlywinks rituals might be (unless there's a key element of gameplay that hinges on a dwarf literally losing his marbles), it should generally be saved for the promotional materials, tie-in novels, or projects that are personal to the writer. Many players won't want to hear it.

As with every rule, there are exceptions. Certain adventure games, for example, have escaped criticism for their verbosity. Because the classic adventure is in many ways closely tied to the novel in terms of the narrative form employed, it is perhaps more acceptable for these games to indulge in additional exposition—especially if it can be organized so that the players can explore it at their leisure. Being able to find a book in the library on dwarven tiddlywinks is a different proposition from forcing the player to listen to a character drone on about the subject. This is especially true when adapting a game from a license, which is, in itself, relatively verbose. The same issues can apply to a cRPG, especially when the details of the setting must be conveyed to the player by some means—player knowledge and character knowledge is often mismatched, an issue that must be addressed. (Only so many games can use amnesia to sidestep this problem.)

Using the Tools the Game Provides

Different game types support different techniques for advancing the narrative. The cRPG *Neverwinter Nights*, for example, uses many approaches: dialogue with NPCs, in-game artifact texts, character advancement, and cut scenes, just to name a few. Horror-shooter *Cold Fear* (Darkworks, 2005), on the other hand, sticks primarily to cut scenes and in-game artifacts to inform the player. This choice should be made deliberately based upon the goals of the game. *Neverwinter Nights* is an open, exploration-based experience wherein the player is encouraged to go everywhere and do everything, and where the player is rewarded for exploring. If the player does not go into the cave, they do not meet the friendly dragon that can provide assistance. If the player doesn't read the in-game artifact book, they do not learn an interesting fact about the face of ancient lizard-beings that are trying to take over the world.

Cold Fear, on the other hand, is a claustrophobic, tightly controlled experience punctuated by sudden violence. In-game artifacts are kept short and sweet to reinforce the feeling that the player could be ambushed at any moment, and are done in a format that reinforces the decaying, monster-ridden setting. Conversations are limited to cut scenes to prevent slowing of the pace or the possibility of interruption by enemies.

In both cases, the narrative interacts with the central thrust of the game, taking its shape from and reinforcing the game. Trying to shove a lengthy conversation tree into a horror-shooter would be frustrating for the player who feels taken out of the action, whereas removing long conversations from a cRPG could be equally annoying to a player who wants to explore the world and its background.

WHAT ARE THE TASKS INVOLVED?

There is no single thing that can be described as game writing. A videogame, after all, is a wildly complex combination of code, art, sound, and myriad other elements, all of which combine to make a game. As such, writing is used in plenty of ways to help produce the game, in tasks ranging from the big-picture creative to detailed and technical.

Story

The most glamorous part of game writing is creating the story. Coming up with what happens is what many people view as the core of the writers' art and task, and in many cases, story gets inextricably intertwined with core design.

Dialogue

Dialogue is what's said in the game. Superficially similar to a film script, dialogue lists the lines that are played in-game. These are generally created in conjunction with the game designer, who outlines what dialogue is needed, and the sound engineer, who establishes the technical constraints.

Dialogue is not written in a vacuum. For financial and technical reasons, word and line counts are carefully controlled. Because it's not a script that will be filmed, dialogue also needs to be written with context. The entire cast won't be in the recording studio trading lines back and forth. Usually, one actor at a time records his or her lines, which means every line needs to be established in terms of tone, mood, location in the game, and purpose. (As ever, there are exceptions, and dual recording sessions are not uncommon.) Writing dialogue is, in the end, a much more complicated process than just composing the dialogue.

Supporting Texts

The game writer's task can extend outside of the game itself. World bibles, character descriptions, teaser fiction, and other similar texts are all potentially important. They're useful as reference to the team—for example, the character artists need to know ahead of time if the dwarves in the game are derived from Celtic culture, Norse, or something entirely different to avoid embarrassing and expensive mix-ups. This material can also be used for marketing, put up on the game Web site to promote interest, and otherwise promote the game even if it never makes it into the game itself.

Cut Scenes and Scripted Events

The scripts for cut scenes and scripted events need to be created by writers in conjunction with the rest of the team. Contrary to popular belief, there are limits to what can be created with CGI, and those limits are frequently found in the schedule and the budget. The cut scenes need to balance the needs of the narrative on one end and the availability of resources on the other. As such, cut scene writing is often iterative, with the phrase "we can't do that" scribbled in the margins by someone else on the team.

Other Tasks

Numerous other tasks are involved in generating the writing for a game narrative. In-game artifacts need to be generated with an eye toward the game's central idioms—there are no emails in *World of Warcraft* (Blizzard, 2004), for example, and no elvish ballads in *Doom 3* (id, 2004). Game manuals often support the narrative, with expository or in-character sections serving to help create the world for the player.

CREATING STORY

The act of story creation is the most important creative task game writers face, as the story simultaneously makes up the bulk of the narrative and arranges all the game elements. The story describes what happens, when it happens, what order it happens in, and what results. As such, the game story needs to be crafted in careful collaboration with the rest of the team and the game designers in particular. It must be built in conjunction with the aims of the design and the vision, in awareness of the limitations of the engine and assets, and with the understanding that it is a game story, not a novel or a movie.

In many ways, creating a game story is about creating opportunities and effects. The opportunities are for gameplay, moments in the story where the player takes heroic control and succeeds in action. The effects are chiefly those experienced by the player: moments of emotional intensity. The story, then, must be created with more than its artistic component in mind. It also needs to serve as a framework for gameplay to be hung upon, and a road map to reward and catharsis. No game writer can afford to lose sight of this.

Story Arc

The *story arc* is essentially the curve described by the intensity of the action. In story terms, the action rises, growing more and more intense, until the climax, at which point it starts to drop off and the reader gets rewarded with the denouement. In gaming, the challenges, fights, and puzzles get more and more intense until the climax, which is often rendered as a boss fight. After this, the player is rewarded with denouement and, possibly, power ups. Crafting the story arc maps the narrative to the design and the level of challenge to the player contained within.

Pacing

Pacing in a narrative is as much a function of asset as it is of story. A story comprised solely of endless melee quickly grows dull, as does a game built from nothing but endless waves of enemies. Pacing is the art of spreading out the action to appropriate moments, saving it for when the player is ready, and pulling back when the player is likely to have had enough.

In story terms, this means introducing enemies or obstacles when the player is ready for them and not before, and providing revelations and rewards sufficient to keep the player encouraged.

Climax

The climax is the big showdown. Because of their length, videogame stories often have a series of multiple, rising climaxes that culminate in the game's ultimate challenge. In general terms, everything in the game story needs to lead to this moment, when the player must use everything he has learned through the course of the game in order to triumph.

The onus falls on writers to make climactic scenes worthwhile. The villain (if the narrative calls for such a character) needs to be sufficiently threatening, evil, and villainous that it does indeed feel like the ultimate challenge. The threat must be sufficiently intense in its potential emotional impact to leave little doubt that this is the culmination of the story. In other words, the stakes need to be high enough that the players will feel they have accomplished something by winning—something other than just making it to the end of the game. And, of course, all the narrative threads, and all the clues and hints and revelations must lead naturally to the final encounter.

Often, a game story climax offers few opportunities for actual writing. The player is too busy playing. The trick can be letting the player make the final leap to what must happen, sliding effortlessly into the desired outcome and borne forward on the story's momentum. The climax should feel like the character has been working relentlessly toward this moment, just as the player has been. Conversely, a game climax that is detached from the story, bringing in a new enemy with no connection to the previous story, can weaken or destroy a game's effect entirely.

CREATING CHARACTERS

Character in conjunction with events moves the narrative forward. This means that the characters need to be created with the needs of the narrative in mind. On one level, that means making a protagonist whom the player is willing to inhabit throughout the story—someone who presents an appealing fantasy and an interesting persona. On another, the characters need to be designed with their role in the narrative in mind. A love interest, for example, needs to be lovable, and worth rescuing when he or she inevitably gets into trouble. This is how character moves the plot, by helping to create context and motivation for the player action. Creating strong characters allows the narrative to drive forward naturally.

A game character's needs are dependent on said character's role. Minor characters need very few things—a look, a tone, a place in the world, and sometimes, a bit of information to pass on. Returning to *Far Cry*, the guards have a look (guys with guns), a tone (dumb and sadistic, but talkative), a place in the world (they're working for the bad guy as muscle, and therefore will shoot you), and occasionally, some info they can deliver.

More important characters have bigger roles and thus need more information. The longer they're going to be on stage, the more the player will see of them, and thus the more substance they need to have. This necessitates building those characters from the ground up, often putting together vast amounts of detail that the player will never see to make the stuff that the player does see logical and consistent. Jack Carver (the protagonist in *Far Cry*) never has his backstory appear onscreen— the player never finds out where he came from, why he's captaining a boat in the middle of nowhere, or where he got his god-awful Hawaiian shirt. But the writer and the team need to know. They need to know where he's from, so his dialogue can have appropriate phrasing and colloquialism, and so that translators can export this into other languages. They need to know his age and build, so they can construct appropriate models and motion sets. They need to know what he's done, so appropriate tidbits and references can be dropped into his dialogue. And all of these things show up onscreen for the player, enabling the character to perform his role.

Finally, characters need the traits that make them appealing to the player so that they can serve their roles in the narrative. Much of the action in *Far Cry* consists of the player trying to rescue, catch up with, or otherwise help out the character of Val. The player feels no resentment at doing this because he wants to rescue Val. Her character traits—attractive, funny, appreciative, brave—(in principle) encourage the player to want to move forward with the action when the narrative says, "Save Val."

Character is vital in creating the framework of the narrative. The world is not worth saving if there's nobody in it you want to save. Character can intensify the sense of immersion—you're working to save people (or elves, or talking animals), not collections of polygons and voice cues. Perhaps most importantly, character drives interaction—in other words, "who" sets the framework for "how," and in many cases, "why." Garrett (the protagonist in *Thief*) is a rogue, a character trait that simultaneously helps define his actions and goals and provides a justification for why it would be unsuitable for the player to rush into a situation prematurely. Miku in *Fatal Frame* (Tecmo, 2001) has no reason to be in the abandoned mansion except for character. She's searching for her brother, and that characterization is enough to drive her—and the player—forward.

Whereas new videogames have a freedom to create new characters, for many games, this is not a luxury that can be afforded. Many of the titles produced by the games industry each year are either derived from outside properties—such as the *Star Wars* films—or exist as sequels in an existing series—such as *Resident Evil 4* (Capcom, 2004), *Ultima V: Warriors of Destiny* (Origin, 1988), or *King's Quest VI: Heir Today, Gone Tomorrow* (Sierra, 1992). Whether the franchise originates inside or outside of games, the issues facing a game in a licensed or franchise context are quite specific.

Because franchise characters have already been established, either in previous iterations of the franchise or in the outside medium that spawned them, there are limits on what can be done to those characters. Particularly in a character-driven franchise such as *Batman*, the character *is* the franchise. Any damage or alteration to the character alters everything hinging on the character—comic books, movies, toys, action figures, and more.

Even if the subject is a game character without an outside existence, there are still concerns; for example, if you shatter Mario's femur in one game, he's going to have a heck of a time jumping in the next one. As such, the writer is a caretaker of the franchise, understanding the parameters of the work and ensuring that the character if handed off to the next game in good shape.

The flip side is that franchise characters come with expectations—catchphrases and identifiers, history, and backstory that the fans know and expect to see again. Duke Nukem can't suddenly become a pipe-smoking scholar of the later works of Jane Austen; the franchise demands that he be a square-jawed, rootin'-tootin' killing machine who spouts the phrase, "Suck it down" at every opportunity. Writers who ignore or bypass essentials such as these aren't doing their job. Part of the writing role is respecting and understanding what has gone before, because if what had gone before didn't work, there wouldn't be a title for the writer to work on.

Whether a game features original characters or characters from a franchise, the role of the characters remains the same: they are the vehicle for the narrative, the means by which it progresses and the focus of the story. Without characters, there can be no story. This is as true in games as it is in any other media.

IMMERSION

Immersion is arguably the ultimate goal of videogames. Immersion is making players forget that they're sitting on their couch twiddling joysticks with their thumbs, and instead making them believe they're mowing down Nazis, leaping from platform to platform over boiling space sludge, or exploring a mansion full of masticating mutants. Good writing can be a vital support for this hoped-for experience.

This means that game writing needs to support the core experience in idiom, word, and phrase. It needs to avoid seams that provide a jagged end to suspension of disbelief, and remain consistent in usage and tone. It also needs to focus on the fact that the game is, after all, a game, and bend all its efforts toward supporting, not overwhelming, the game experience.

The core unique factor of game writing is the role of the audience. The player lives the game much more intensely than most readers "live" the book. The player's actions have direct and immediately visible consequence, with reward or punishment as a result.

Game writing, then, needs to focus on maximizing the player's experience and supporting the player's role as protagonist in the narrative. The best writing in the world is worthless if the player never encounters it. It's worse than no good if the writing calls attention to itself, instead of the player, or it jerks the player out of the game's fantasy by disrupting the narrative flow.

Because the audience for the game is actively participating in the narrative flow, the narrative has to be built around the concept of audience buy-in. Players need to be fully committed to the game fantasy, whether that is to win World War II or tackle the ravening orcish hordes with sword in hand. They must also have enough information to make rewarding and appropriate choices in the context of the game world and to use those choices to drive forward through the narrative. In other words, the narrative needs to be constructed with the notion that the player will do, not observe; will act, not listen.

UNIQUE CHALLENGES AND PITFALLS

Because game writing is not quite like any other kind of writing, writers working in this field face unique problems that other writers may never experience. First, some time-honored dramatic and rhetorical techniques have no place in games. These techniques are not inherently bad, but the demands of the gaming experience don't leave room for them. Stichomythia (single lines are spoken by alternate speakers) might work fabulously in Shakespearean plays, but outside of the *Monkey Island* series (LucasArts, 1990) there's precious little use for it in games. As such, the writer must always be asking: "How will this play?" Just because something works in a novel doesn't mean that it's appropriate for a player-driven experience. A lengthy, tense conversation fraught with emotional violence is superb in a Harold Pinter drama, but what does the player potentially do during that time? Sit and watch? Press buttons to skip the voice-over and just read the text? Let the whole thing play out and go get a drink? Whatever the players decide to do, they are not *playing*, and that can be deadly to a game.

Each technique, therefore, needs to be reevaluated in terms of what it does for the player and what the player does with it. Just as not every play adapts to a film, not every writing technique is suitable to every media.

A specific example of this with particular relevance to games is *forced failure*. This classic reverse in prose writing refers to the sudden circumstance whereby the hero is betrayed or walks into a trap, is subdued, and has all of his possessions taken from him. The hero then proceeds to get free somehow and, using only found objects and his native cunning, finds a way to defeat the villain.

For a film or novel character, this can work well. But think about what it means for a game player. In a very real sense, what this structure does is stop the player's advance, penalize the player for reaching a certain point in the game, punish the player for succeeding, and most likely frustrate the player, who having previously taken joy in all of their achievements has now found that these have suddenly been stripped away. How would you feel, after all, if it were your hard-earned magic sword that someone removed from your inventory during a cut scene?

This is an example of a forced failure. Forced failures are a technique for channeling the narrative down a certain path regardless, and sometimes in spite of, player action. This type of outcome can be handled much more gracefully in prose than in games. The novelist can describe the escape of the villain, for example, as happening amidst a hail of bullets, but videogame players instead see multiple rounds bouncing off a suddenly invincible target that will doubtless reemerge later to torment them.

Forced failures are perfect examples of instances when narrative trumps gameplay, diminishing the player experience. As such, it's generally best to construct a narrative free from such cases, to prevent the player from growing frustrated. The best narrative twist will fall flat in a game if it causes the players to throw down their controllers in disgust.

Furthermore, gameplay generally includes its own cycle of failure and success as the players make their own mistakes and pay the attached price—losing "lives" or having to start again back at a checkpoint or previously saved position in the game. Writers should not forget this aspect of the success/failure experience for the players of many games and should avoid compounding any frustrations inherent to the gameplay with frustrations that originate in the narrative.

Conversely, the writer's arsenal contains numerous weapons for assisting the player within the bounds of the narrative. Consider the opening sequence of *Halo: Combat Evolved* (Bungee, 2001). Within the fiction that the ship's crew is testing out the Master Chief's reactions and kit, the game cleverly instructs the player in how to perform all the basic game functions and thus, advance through the story-line. More heavy-handed examples can include everything from having an NPC shout out an enemy weakness to subtle suggestions from teammates that, just maybe, left is the way to go in this instance. As the narrative is directed toward the player experience, it only makes sense that elements within the narrative guide the player toward the optimum experience as well.

THE WRITER AND THE DEVELOPMENT TEAM

Writers do not create videogames. At best, they help shape the vision, provide important elements in game creation, and help to create the assets that make up the game itself. They generally do not program, create levels or character models, wrangle animations, or tag map locations with sound files. Rather, the writer is just one part of the development team—an important part, and one whose contribution should not be undervalued, but a part nonetheless.

In games development, the writer's role is not to lead the team any more than the writers take the lead in film or TV production. Writers work within the team, using words to craft and support their vision and labors. Writers who put together a story and then expect the rest of the team to implement their grand epic with verve and style are in for a disappointment. Writers who work with the team, crafting a story that takes advantage of the feature set and art assets and shows them off to good effect, are a lot more likely to be pleased with the end result.

Ultimately, writers fulfill multiple roles on game development teams, depending on the demands of the project. Everything from crafting the story to coaching the voice actors during recording sessions can land on a writer's plate, with the expectation that this role within the team will be picked up and carried forward to meet the project's needs. The trick, therefore, is to recognize that the writer's place is as part of the team, not something outside, beside, and certainly neither above nor below it.

Writer and Producer

The producer on a game project is the person in charge of the development process. They are sometimes like a film director, in that they are also the vision-keeper for the project, but more commonly they are facilitators whose task is to ensure that the game is delivered on time and to a professional standard.

The producer is often the writer's key point of contact, especially if the writer is working externally and therefore not in the same building as the development team. Clear, complete, and frequent communication is absolutely vital. If the producer doesn't know the writer's concerns, issues, and potential problems, then these issues can't be resolved, and the game as a whole can potentially be put at risk.

Writer and Designer

A common misconception is that game writing and game design are the same discipline. Much of this results from the difficulty in expressing the role of the game designer to people outside of the games industry. Whereas the game writer's role is chiefly to guide, develop, and script the *narrative* of the game, the game designer's role is to guide, develop, and document the *gameplay*—a task that generally requires a diverse set of skills that can range from conceiving or expanding broad concepts at the highest level of abstraction, to wrangling mathematics or applying psychology at the most pragmatic end of a game's design.

Many games have been written and designed by the same individual; the author of this chapter fulfilled the role of writer-designer for *Anne McCaffrey's Freedom: First Resistance* (Red Storm, 2000), and many of the other authors in this volume have similarly served in this unique dual role. The reason for this comparatively common confluence between the role of game writer and that of game designer is in part due to the fact that both roles require one to be a competent wordsmith. Additionally, the vision of the game and of its narrative can be so intertwined that it made sense to have both jobs done by one team member. As projects have grown ever more complex, however, the demands on both design and writing have grown immensely, and it is now generally considered preferable to separate the tasks, not to mention extremely common to employ multiple designers and writers on a single game.

The writer and the designer, then, need to coexist and recognize their respective roles. The designer needs to communicate the vision and proposed design of the game to the writer and offer feedback on the writers' efforts to make sure they're congruent with the needs of the game as a whole. The writer needs to contribute to the vision and understand that writing is an aspect of the development process, not necessarily the engine that drives the design.

Writer and Programmer

The writer has no choice but to work within the constraints of the game's capabilities. Anyone who writes scenes that cannot be supported in the game's engine will rapidly find themselves in conflict with the programming team. Writers who have a good relationship with the programming team (or teams) can discuss the story's needs versus the rigors of the technology, communicating what the needs of the narrative might be and, in return, gaining useful and practical knowledge of the boundaries within which the story must be developed.

Additionally, the writer needs to produce work in a form that is easy for the programmers to deal with. This means writing text blocks that fit within their on-screen fields, producing deliverables on time for localization, making sure dialogue can be produced within a logical file naming system, and more. It is the programmers' technology that ultimately presents the writer's work to the world. As such, programmers must communicate how the writers' content is to be presented while the writer must understand how to present his work and do so accordingly.

Writer and Artist

Writing and visual art have relatively sparse interaction, intersecting most frequently in specific instances such as character design, in-game artifact manufacture, and cut scenes. Both are creative disciplines, and the key to the writer's interaction with artists is communication. The better the communication of the needs of the story, scene, or character to the artists, the more likely the end result will match what was originally envisioned (and also what is required by the needs of the gameplay or narrative). At the same time, the writer needs to remain open to the artists' creativity, and incorporate worthwhile new elements that the artists generate into the story, character design, and other written aspects of the game.

There is much to be said for allowing the writer to adjust the game script *after* the artist has rendered the scenes. Not every game schedule affords such luxury—sometimes the dialogue must be recorded early for reasons as varied as synchronization with cut scenes to limited availability of specific voice actors (often an issue in games licensed from TV or film).

THE PRAGMATICS OF GAME WRITING

The writer, encouraged by the design, can put literally anything on the page—armadas of cloud galleons, katana-wielding robot ninjas with 16 arms apiece, cute little kids that don't immediately send hard-core gamers screaming into the night. All of these are possible in the imagination and with the written word. When these ideas meet the practical limitations of the game's physics engine, however, they can become problematic.

For example, the animation system used for *Tom Clancy's Rainbow Six* (Red Storm, 1998) was predicated entirely on character skeletons with two arms, two legs, and an upright stance. That meant, among other things, no dogs. No policemen on horses. The only characters available were people. This automatically created certain restrictions on the writing for the game, and had repercussions that echoed down multiple levels of decision making. So it goes for literally everything a game engine can or cannot do—it empowers or restricts the writing, and the writer must learn what the boundaries are, help establish them if possible, and ultimately learn to work within them.

This leads to the obvious and recurring game development question: "Can it be done?" This can mean many different things. Can the engine support it? Are there enough models to produce the crowd scene? Do we have enough time to render it out properly? Do we have enough money to afford the production time on all the assets this will require? All these questions and more need to be taken into account by the writer. The first draft can sometimes shoot for the moon, but subsequent drafts need to be trimmed and adjusted based on what the game, the team, and the budget can do.

Often this means scaling back to achievable aims and getting a good estimate of what can and cannot be done before the first word gets written. A producer who allows a writer to script completely undoable cut scenes is doing no one any favors. The writers' time is wasted and so is the money paid them for the useless draft. The artists creating the assets need to wait longer to receive the materials they'll be working from, crunching their deadlines. The engineers are forced to go through the script, hacking out bits that are suddenly revealed as unattainable, potentially creating hard feelings. Scaling the writing to the capabilities of the team from the get-go makes more sense and allows the writer to focus more tightly on the task at hand. All the resource limitations—time, money, and technical—need to be explored and laid out as soon as possible to provide the greatest benefit to the entire team.

As a game project progresses, adaptation and revision are unavoidable. Precisely because a game is a team endeavor, writers cannot become too emotionally invested in their work. After all, someone else's work might force it to change. Writers should be prepared to modify as needed. If a level space simply isn't working and must be excised from the game, the writer is tasked with providing the narrative glue to close the gap seamlessly. If a feature is unworkable, any dialogue or story hinging on it needs to come out and, if necessary, be replaced. As such, writers needs to be flexible and, at times, staunchly practical, prepared for the parameters that have been established to shift around them. Game development is still an inexact science, and the game will necessarily change throughout its development cycle. Writers need to be prepared to meet these changes and revise their work as a result.

As well as covering for necessary changes caused by the innate friction of the development process, writers need to be prepared to adapt their work for the team. After all, it's the team that puts the writer's work onscreen. To do so well, it helps to have the team firmly behind the writer's content and contributions. This is sometimes termed as getting buy-in from the team and is arguably essential if a project is going to excel rather than achieve adequate results. If the team is excited over the writing, if they think it's cool or shows off the team's work to great advantage, they'll be more excited about what it means for their own work. Conversely, if the team is not buying it, then the end result is often endless argument, resentment, and potentially even less-than-optimal implementation.

To get the team's buy-in is to invite the team into the process. Canvassing ideas from the team, letting the team members see the work in progress, and showing off the cool parts of the writing all go a long way toward getting the team on board. Genuine discussion of team suggestions or concerns also helps tremendously, as the team members are quick to recognize when they're being humored or ignored. Writers should know that it's always better to have the team on your side, than against you. Give them reasons to be on your side and continue to provide reasons for them to stay there, and the result can only be an improvement in the final outcome of the development process.

CONCLUSION

Game narrative is infinitely more complicated than it might seem at first, both in its generation and in its execution. Unique in its demands and needs, it requires a combination of collaboration and artistic vision, storytelling technique, and technical awareness. Many of the traditional writing techniques will work for games, but just as many do not, or require significant modification to adapt to a scenario where the player, not the protagonist, is the star of the game.

Game writing is also the place where new ground is being broken in the field of narrative. Whether the fractured narration of *Indigo Prophecy* (Quantic Dream, 2005), the unreliable narrator—and narration device—of *Eternal Darkness: Sanity's Requiem* (Silicon Knights, 2002), or the experimental narrative seen in games such as *Façade* (Procedural Arts, 2005), the opportunities for creativity in game narrative are as breathtaking as the limitations are daunting.

2 The Basics of Narrative
Stephen Jacobs

"There are 8 million stories in the naked city…" and this chapter examines some of the underpinnings.

Long before written language emerged, the storyteller had a privileged place in early societies. The stories we've come to think of as unchanged from time immemorial likely shifted from telling to telling. We've learned that bards and poets such as Homer likely played with their stories almost like jazz musicians. They would tie them more tightly to a given audience's location and/or current events making them partially dynamic in nature. Eventually, these early stories were immortalized as our first written texts.

Later "new" narrative forms emerged, such as the novel (roughly a thousand years old, depending on which literary historians you ask) and eventually those new kids on the block, radio, cinema, television. Each of them borrowed from the previous and eventually found their own strengths and media-specific methods for storytelling. Games are in the process of doing the same.

Almost as old as written storytelling is the analysis of how stories "work," a process that continues today. What follows is therefore a quick overview of the components of narrative that writers can spend a lifetime grappling with and a brief introduction to the history and analysis of narrative.

ARISTOTLE'S *POETICS*

Roughly 2,300 years ago, Aristotle wrote the seminal analysis of literary criticism, the *Poetics,* which has been a cornerstone of Western literary theory ever since. Far from being old, dead history, the *Poetics* have been applied to almost every dramatized (and even undramatized) media form since antiquity. Brenda Laurel, theorist, virtual reality artist, and game developer, extended the *Poetics* to interactive drama in her 1986 PhD thesis, and subsequently to computer interfaces in general in her seminal 1991 book *Computers as Theater*. Later Laurel would run her own game company, Purple Moon, Inc., which produced games with an emphasis on story. Laurel is currently a Professor at the Art Center College of Design.

Academic, theorist, and game developer Michael Mateas, currently a professor at the Georgia Institute of Technology, applied the six components to games in his 1995 article "A Preliminary Poetics for Interactive Drama and Games."[1] His experimental game, *Façade* (Procedural Arts, 2005), pushes the current limits of interactive narrative and won the Slamdance Grand Jury Prize in January of 2006.

Within the *Poetics*, Aristotle established the following six components of tragedy: Plot, Character, Thought, Diction, Pattern, and Spectacle.

PLOT

Plot was defined by Aristotle as "the arrangement of incidents," that is, the events that make up a story. Many writers use the words story and plot interchangeably when discussing narrative. Aristotle said that plot unfolds as a result of an internal or external conflict experienced by the main character of the story. For Aristotle, plot plays out with a beginning, middle, and end that progress in a specific manner. The first part, *diesis*, is a beginning that builds slowly to a crisis point. Aristotle called the crisis point the *peripeteia*, which was followed by *lusis*, a resolution of the story. In film, the *lusis* is also referred to as the *denouement*, a term from the French word for "an unraveling."

As mentioned in the previous chapter, the flow of a specific story's plot, its rise and fall of events, is often called a *story arc*. This term is used both for stories that are complete unto themselves and, more recently, to describe the flow of a continuous story through multiple episodes. Multiple episodes might be the books of a multivolume series, such as the Harry Potter books, or a five-year bible of a network television series, or even the multiple levels and events of 40 to 80 hours of gameplay.

German Theater critic Gustav Freytag developed a visualization of Aristotle's view of plot in the 1860s called *Freytag's Triangle*, or *Freytag's Pyramid* (see Figure 2.1). Both Aristotle's components and Freytag's triangle will be discussed further as this chapter develops.

Some analysts keep the "Pyramid" a truly equilateral one, equal on both sides of the rise and fall of the story's emotional build. Others shift the position of the peak of the triangle and length of the sides to indicate a slower or faster rise or fall, relative to a story's emotional build over time. This will also be explored later in this chapter.

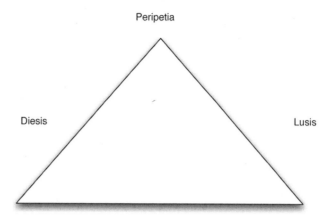

FIGURE 2.1 Aristotle's terms on a Freytag Pyramid.

Joseph Campbell's Hero's Journey Model

A self-taught scholar of the myths and legends of the world, Joseph Campbell released a book in 1949 called *The Hero with a Thousand Faces* [Campbell49]. In this book, Campbell analyzed stories from around the globe to identify a common pattern or theme that was intrinsic in many cultures and religious traditions, even though they had no contact with each other throughout their histories. Campbell then applied this pattern to our own psychic and emotional development.

Campbell had also studied the works of Carl Jung, the psychologist and one-time disciple of Freud, who had done something similar when he conceived of the concept of "a collective unconsciousness." Jung's collective unconsciousness is a collection of symbols, myths, sounds, images, and even chunks of what we would call pop culture. Jung suggested that we all unknowingly draw from this collective unconsciousness to create meaning into our lives. Campbell narrowed and deepened Jung's vision with his template for "The Hero's Journey."

Every 20 years or so, Campbell's work seems to come back into vogue to influence a new generation of thinkers and writers. In the late 1960s and early 1970s, during the explosion of pop culture in that era, Campbell's book enjoyed a spike in popularity. In the late 1980s Chris Vogler wrote a seven-page memo to Disney execs summarizing Campbell that generated a lot of buzz at the time. Vogler later evolved the memo into a book for screenwriters published in 1992 called *The Writer's Journey*, which attempts to make Campbell more accessible and directly applicable to the film industry [Vogler92].

Adventure games, cRPGs (Complete Role Playing Game), MMORPGs (Massive Multiplayer Online Role-Playing Games), and many other game genres often rely on variations of the Hero's Journey. Whether the Hero is Link from the numerous *Legend of Zelda* games (Nintendo, 1986 onwards), Manny Calvera from *Grim Fandango* (LucasArts, 1998), or Lara Croft from the *Tomb Raider* games (Core et al., 1996 onwards), the pattern of the Hero's Journey can be found at the core of many successful games.

According to Campbell, the "Journey" consists of three main phases: Departure, Initiation, and Return, each with their own subcomponents. Campbell's model can be looked at as a type of plot, but it also mentions aspects of character, which will be examined more closely later. The individual steps presented here make up one of several variations of Campbell's original version and differ slightly from those he laid out in his original analysis.

Departure

In the departure portion of the Hero's Journey, we are introduced to the Hero in his *Ordinary World*. Often he's either underappreciated or an underachiever at home, even though he may have a heroic or divine lineage, as with the Minotaur slayer Theseus. The Hero is often missing one or more parents (either dead or inexplicably missing). He may have one or more talents that help make him special, although sometimes these talents can be linked to character flaws. (The hero may also be a heroine; the pattern is in no way gender dependent.)

At a certain point, the Hero receives a *Call to Adventure*, which can come about from anything as simple as a generic call for help all the way up to a direct summons from the gods. In many cases, there may be a *Refusal of the Call*; for some reason the hero resists. Family, friends, indecision, or even what we call today "low self-esteem" keep him from moving ahead, just as the Old Testament's Jonah's self-doubt had him run literally in the opposite direction God wanted him to go.

Soon after the refusal, another event spurs the reluctant Hero down the "road to glory" after all. Often that motivating event is bad news for the Hero or some supporting characters in the story. Campbell suggests that when bad news is the cause of the Hero taking action, it is a direct consequence of the Hero's decision to refuse the *Call to Adventure*, although this can be seen as moral causality, rather than proceeding from a literal chain of events.

Sometimes the Hero receives *Supernatural Aid* in the form of gifts, talismans, and/or meeting a Mentor. The Mentor might appear before the beginning of the Hero's journey; other times the Mentor appears only after the journey's begun. In some myths and legends, the Hero's search for a Mentor is sufficient impetus to take the Journey in the first place.

The first step in the Journey, which can have both physical and/or metaphysical components, is often undertaken by crossing *The First Threshold* and/or meeting and beating the *Threshold Demon* (*Threshold Guardian* in the original terminology). This is not the "Main Boss" at the end of the game, but the first thing that keeps the Hero from leaving the ordinary world and following the call.

It's not necessarily an actual demon or even a physical entity. For instance, Jonah's self-doubt was his threshold demon.

Initiation

In the Initiation phase, the Hero's mettle is tested by a journey down *The Road of Trials*, a series of tests through which the Hero achieves inner growth and/or additional skill sets. In many respects, this part of the Hero's Journey typifies the main body of most cRPGs. It is, in effect, where the game heroes spend their time "leveling up" in the story. The Hero also acquires *Allies and Enemies* along the way. Finally, he *Approaches His Inmost Cave*, which is the place and time where he will face his greatest challenge.

Return

In the return portion of the Journey, the Hero succeeds in facing his *Supreme Ordeal*. He takes *The Road Back*, achieves a *Resurrection*—especially in those cases where he may have renounced his heritage as part of the First Threshold—and *Returns with the Elixir*, which can simply be his gaining the ultimate resolution. The return in the Hero's journey doesn't necessarily bring him back home. Sometimes it leads him to a new home.

Hero's Journey as Plot Model

The general structure of the Hero's Journey is summarized in Figure 2.2; it is part narrative/plot structure and part character description/arc in that it assumes some common character traits and changes, as well as the kind of events the character must experience in a given order. Not all stories are Hero's Journeys, and not all Hero's Journeys have all the components listed here. Campbell was quick to observe that individual stories may be comprised of just a part of the complete cycle

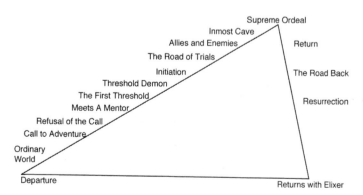

FIGURE 2.2   The Hero's Journey model.

or multiple cycles joined together. Relating the stages of the journey to particular characters and events in novels, movies, or games is generally not difficult. This may reflect the ubiquity of quest stories in our culture.

Despite the extensive manner in which Campbell's work has been applied to writing fiction, the original work was intended solely for the analysis and interpretation of mythology, never as a "how to" for story construction. Yet, this role is one that has largely emerged first as a consequence of George Lucas' well-publicized interest in his, and then later, Vogler's memo and book. *Hero with a Thousand Faces* was the first book Campbell published on the subject of mythology, and it represents only a small portion of Campbell's academic work on the subject, which arguably culminates with the four-volume magnum opus *The Masks of God*. However, the accessible simplicity of the model of the Hero's Journey has allowed the model to acquire a life of its own outside of the context of Campbell's original work.

Campbell and the Hero's Journey are not universally adored, any more than they're universally applied. For example, one of Campbell's best known critics, author Kurt Vonnegut, famously reduced the Hero's Journey to, "Hero gets into trouble, Hero gets out of trouble."

Syd Field's Screenplay Model

Syd Field is a Hollywood screenwriter, and a teacher of other Hollywood screenwriters, who takes a certain, formulaic approach to the writing of screenplays. Field is both celebrated and reviled for his formula; however, the formula seems to be employed often. Field's approach is offered here as just one example of how narrative is implemented in the motion picture industry. According to Field's paradigm, a Hollywood movie has three acts that break down according to the following formula [Field99]. In reading the following, assume that one page of screenplay corresponds to one minute of screen time:

> **Act One:** Sets up the story, mood, and tone from pages 1–30. In the first 10 pages, we should meet the main character and get a good feel for where we're going, with a plot point on pages 25–27. Field defines a *plot point* as "an incident, episode or event that 'hooks' into the action and spins it around into another direction." Plot points are also referred to by other writers (in and out of Hollywood) as *reversals*.

> **Act Two:** 60 pages long, deals with confrontation and moves from plot point one to plot point two. This doesn't mean that there won't be major and minor obstacles and hurdles between plot points one and two, but that the plot points are the lynchpins for the film. Plot point two occurs around pages 85–87. There should be a mid-point around page 60 where there's a definite change in the story and something intensifies.

Act Three: Everything comes together, or falls apart, as appropriate.

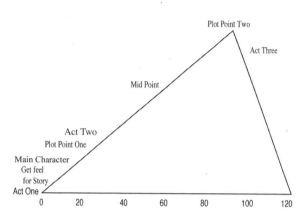

FIGURE 2.3   Field's Screenplay model.

Although this *Three Act Structure* is perhaps the most widely known of Hollywood formulas, the theme has many variations and no shortage of writers peddling their own version of this paradigm.

Bending and Breaking Models

These three models give you tools for understanding how narrative functions. They also, by virtue of laying down an established pattern, provide the opportunities for certain narratives to stand out by going against the orthodox expectations.

Akira Kurasawa's classic film *Rashomon* tells the story of an apparent robbery, rape, and murder multiple times with multiple narrators, each seeing and defining the events in a different way, sidestepping all assumptions of a central protagonist or narrative progression. Kurasawa's *The Hidden Fortress* also plays with expectations by centering the narrative upon two innocuous and largely incompetent farmers who are little more than observers in dramatic events—a trick Lucas borrowed for *Star Wars*, placing the two droids in the equivalent position to the two farmers. Kurasawa's most personal film, *Akira Kurasawa's Dreams*, dispenses with notions of conventional narrative entirely and represents the director's own dreams as beautiful and sometimes disturbing vignettes.

Events need not be organized in chronological sequence. Quentin Tarantino's *Pulp Fiction* begins in the chronological middle of a series of related stories with overlapping characters comprised of primarily anti-heroes, criminal enforcers, and thugs, attempting to regenerate the mythology of pulp paperback novels with a modern spin. *Memento* is told is a strange kind of forward flashback. It's character is incapaable of making new memories and must refer back to notes to know what's happening. Similarly, Michael Moorcock's award-winning novel *Mother London* works backwards in time to the center point of the story, the bombing of London during the Blitz, before working forwards in time towards the story's resolution. Moorcock's acclaimed Jerry Cornelius novels also explored radically different structures, including a narrative in which the central character spends the entire story dead in a coffin (*The English Assassin*), and another in which it is difficult, if not impossible, to establish what is the beginning, middle, or end of the story (*A Cure for Cancer*)[2].

The movies *Run, Lola, Run* and *Groundhog Day* allow their characters to "replay" their stories and "try again," in a manner not unlike the structure of many games, which require the player to repeat a challenge over and over until success is finally achieved. This trans-temporal structure even makes its way back into games: Eiji Aonuma's first game as director of the *Legend of Zelda* franchise, *Majora's Mask* (Nintendo, 2000), is structured around a repeating loop of three days, within which the player struggles to understand the problem they are facing, and ultimately divine its solution, before culminating in one of the most surreal narrative sequences in videogame history as the player encounters two children at the foot of a monstrous tree—a metaphorical manifestation of the crisis at the heart of the story.

Models for narrative should therefore be recognized only as tools for understanding the conventional structure of a story, not as eternal laws that cannot be varied.

Examining *Star Wars*

When looking for a narrative common denominator succinct enough to be used in this chapter, one film comes immediately to mind. The motion picture *Star Wars* (later renamed as *Star Wars Episode IV: A New Hope*) is sufficiently ubiquitous to be used as an example with the confidence that most readers will be familiar with it.

George Lucas has often acknowledged Campbell's influence on him, and in the 1980s, Lucas worked with Bill Moyers to produce a series of video programs on Campbell's work called *Joseph Campbell and the Power of Myth*. In the 1990s, the Smithsonian Air and Space Museum mounted an exhibit and published a book, *Star Wars: The Magic of Myth*, which carried out a deep analysis of the initial *Star Wars* trilogy and its links to the Hero's Journey across the story arc of all three films [Henderson97].

This section considers how Aristotle, Campbell, Field, and Lucas relate in the context of *Star Wars*.

The Beginning of the Film

We are 17 minutes into *Star Wars* before Lucas introduces our Hero. However, in the first 10 minutes (defined by Field as critical to establishing plot setting and character), we do get a good idea of where the story is set and what's happening. Lucas has given us a solid tone, a central problem, and plot device. We've read the famous titles that place us in galactic political history; been treated to a spectacular battle; met the droids (around whom the entire narrative is structured), the Princess, and our villain; heard of some plans; and seen the wheels of the story get into motion before we've met Luke.

All stories have some need for exposition: the who, what, where, when, how, and why we often need to establish a story. Exposition is often a burden for a writer and a reader/audience/player unless it's handled skillfully and embedded into the story in a way that seems natural. Science fiction and fantasy stories often require more exposition than other genres because they are taking us out of the everyday world. Therefore, it's not surprising that the initial part of *Star Wars* doesn't introduce our lead character until some time later than Field's model suggests.

Luke's Departure

At last, we meet Luke in his Ordinary World, an orphaned farm boy itching to get out to the "Space Academy." Four minutes later, the Call to Adventure begins as Luke discovers the holographic video that R2D2 is carrying of Princess Leia asking Obi-Wan Kenobi for help. Field's complexities arise soon after as R2 escapes, and Luke and C3PO head out to find him. On their way, the three are attacked by the Sand People, and soon-to-be Mentor Obi-Wan appears right at Field's plot point one. Meanwhile, the search for the robots and their copy of the Death Star plans heats up. Things get more complicated when Luke learns of his father's life as a Jedi. Obi-Wan issues the official Call to Adventure by suggesting that Luke join him on the "road" to Alderaan.

Things have been happening a bit too fast for young Luke, and he refuses Obi Wan's call/invitation as he feels he must be the dutiful nephew. He "owes too much" to his aunt and uncle to take off and leave them; even though he was bitterly complaining about having to delay his Space Academy entrance for another year just minutes before. As mentioned before, in a Hero's Journey, fate—or at least the author—often deals cruelly with those who support or are responsible for the Hero's refusal of the call. Minutes after his refusal, Luke learns that his aunt, uncle (his Threshold Guardians), and their farm are no more. At 43 minutes into the film, Luke steps over his First Threshold and begins to grow his character by requesting to be trained in the ways of the Force, and committing to join his Mentor on the trip to Tatooine and from there to Alderaan.

Luke's Initiation

In the Cantina, Luke acquires his first Enemies (some of whom Obi-Wan dispatches, others live to inform the Storm Troopers) and Allies (in the form of Han and Chewbacca). His trials are about to begin, as is his growth as a character and his training in the force. Sixty minutes into the film is the mid-point defined by Field as a place the writer should "bump it up another notch," and Lucas does. Especially for Han and Chewbacca, who realize that the "nice easy charter" they had picked up was neither as nice nor as easy as they thought. They flee attacking Imperial ships into hyperspace and end up in the asteroid field that used to be Alderaan.

Luke (and his companions) are tested and tried by the infiltration of the ship, the acquisition of the Princess, the passage through the garbage compactor and monster at the bottom of the Death Star, and the climb back up to Han's ship. In a game, these would be the challenges that allowed a player to acquire experience or "level up."

Luke's lowest spiritual point comes in at about 90 minutes into the film when he sees Obi-Wan cut down before his eyes by Darth Vader, just a few minutes late relative to Field's definition of "plot point two."[3] The ship's "escape" from the Death Star comes seconds later.

Luke's Return

Luke joins the rebels, which has been his dream from the onset. It's all coming together for him. Luke's defining moment, his Supreme Ordeal, is his letting go of his technological support system in the cockpit and using the force to guide his torpedo shot into the "Achilles Exhaust Vent" of the Death Star. He has begun to achieve mastery of the Force and returns home a hero (see Figure 2.4), at least until *The Empire Strikes Back*.

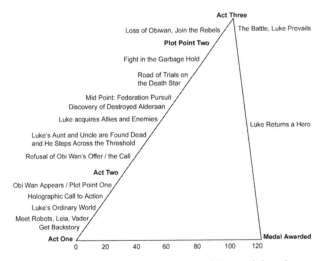

FIGURE 2.4 Star Wars mapped to Field's model and Campbell's model.

CHARACTER

"No character, no story," says Aristotle. A story must have at least one character that the audience can care about (either positively or negatively) for the audience to be engaged by the story. In games, the character must often be a role the player cares to adopt or become.

For tragedy, the lead character in the drama needs to be likeable and multidimensional so that his fall from grace inspires empathy from the audience. From Aristotle's perspective, the actions of the protagonist have to make sense within the context of the story, yet they must also have a nobility about them.

Beyond this, Aristotle broke down character into those who were greater, lesser, or equal to the common person in the audience. This was mainly determined by how they acted when everything "fell apart" for them in a tragedy. Take the old metaphor of the captain on the sinking ship or a male passenger on the Titanic for that matter. A greater than average character would "manfully" go down with the ship with his chin raised high. A lesser than average character would hurl women and orphans into the frigid seas to get his own seat in a lifeboat.

For a story to reach us, we look for a change in the major character that shows the events of the plot have evolved him, for better or worse. Such a change needn't occur *only* in the main character but can happen to the better-defined supporting characters as well. So, between *Star Wars* and *Return of the Jedi*, Han Solo changes from a mercenary (occupying either Aristotle's lesser or equal category) to one more noble. He becomes capable of taking risks and making sacrifices for his comrades-in-arms and the woman he loves. Yet he remains a truly independent spirit at the same time.

Having a character undergo change, while staying true to their essence, represents a basic challenge of writing narrative. Consider Tom Hanks' character in *Big*, the boy who got his wish only to learn that adulthood wasn't what he wanted after all.

An even greater challenge is the character that cannot or does not change. Director Barry Levinson has spoken about the challenges and evolution of the film *Rain Man*, a film about the relationship between an older autistic brother and his younger hotshot salesman brother. The script was originally written as a standard buddy flick. However, Dustin Hoffman's research into his character and autism showed that a significant change in the story would be required. Even though the autistic brother Raymond (Rain Man) was the heart of the film, it would have to be his brother Charlie who changed. Raymond, by the definition of his affliction, could not.

Generally, we expect less from supporting characters within narrative; not every one of them can be fully realized and multidimensional. Often they are present in the story solely to support crucial pieces of action or to provide information to move the story along. Take a classic example, the red shirted *Star Trek* security personnel who die in the first five minutes in seemingly every episode of the show. The writer needs to demonstrate that the captain and crew are in deadly peril but can't kill off (or at least, can do so very rarely) a major or significant supporting character. Inevitably, the man or woman in the red security shirt must die to convince us of the gravity of the situation.

Archetypes

Both Jung and Campbell identified *archetypes*. These are the various kinds of characters that are common across most cultures. Heroes and Mentors are two such archetypes, and the sections that follow provide some additional samples of archetypal characters. As mentioned previously, these are characters that often have jobs to do in the story itself. Some of them are actual steps in a Hero's Journey. Others provide the necessary tension to be a basis for the struggles the protagonist must endure.

The challenge to writing archetypical characters is to keep them fresh. In some ways, we want the reader/audience/player to be able to recognize them quickly. The very presence of one of these archetypes can be like a signpost in the landscape or a rhythmic undertone in a piece of music. They can tell an audience where they are in the story or pick up the pace of a narrative just by "walking in the door."

What we don't want is for our archetypes to become stereotypes, a theme discussed further in later chapters. As writers, we want to layer our archetypes, make them different, more interesting, challenging, and real than our average red-shirted Ensign Cannon Fodder. We often can't spend the time or detail on them that we would our protagonist, antagonist, or main supporting characters. In some ways, this is the true mark of a skilled writer, to make the simplest archetypical and/or simply supporting cast members as memorable as possible.

One of my favorite examples of this in games comes from *Grim Fandango*. Along the way, our protagonist encounters an animal balloon twister at a Day of the Dead Festival. The character's role is simply to provide Manny Calavera with some animal balloons (both sculpted and uninflated) that will prove vital to the solution to problems/puzzles Manny must solve. Instead of simply providing a one-dimensional character, Tim Schaffer gave the character a Jack Nicholson impersonating voice and a snappy collection of attitude rich lines that's still memorable even though the game was released in 1998.

The Threshold Guardian

The Threshold Guardian is the character that must be defeated or bypassed in a Hero's Journey, so that the Hero can enter into the other world and begin down the Road of Trials. This need not be an overt guardian, such as the riddling Sphinx or a level boss with a big weapon that says, "You're gonna have to get through me first." A Threshold Guardian can be the lover who forces the hero into a "You'll have to choose between your quest and me" or the boss who gets told to "take their job and shove it" as in the movie *Hitch*. This character can easily be a sympathetic one, with all the best intentions in the world for our protagonist and still serve the role required within the story.

The Trickster

In mythology, the *Trickster* character is often a god or demi-god who could be on the side of good or evil, but is most often working for his own benefit. The Native American Coyote and Anansi the Spider/Old Man from African and Island folk tales are tricksters. Shakespeare's Puck delights in the chaos he causes, with little re-gard for the results. Warner Bros' Bugs Bunny, Matt Groening's Bart Simpson and Bender are all card-carrying members of the Trickster's International Club and often end up the worse for their own machinations. In today's live-action Holly-wood films, confidence men and hustlers are most often the Tricksters, such as Al-ison Lohman's "daughter" character in *Matchstick Men*. Although they sometimes win the day (usually only when their motivation is pure), these characters can be written in on either side of the story, and sometimes both; can keep us guessing throughout the piece; can change sides like a skin changer; or make it clear that they've always been on the one side that matters, their own. Tricksters often end up worse off at the end of the story than they were when they began.

In Neil Gaiman's excellently crafted *American Gods*, the Trickster Loki and his blood brother Odin foster a war between the old and new gods as part of a plan to seize power over both, but the plan is foiled and leads to their end, at least in the in-carnations we come to know through the book.

The Herald

The *Herald* is the messenger that (according to the adage) we're not supposed to kill. The news may be good or bad, but whatever the Herald brings often sets the Hero down the road, or introduces a reversal or a plot point. The Herald may do their bit and then leave, as with Apollo/Mercury in many Greek and Roman myths, Western Union in all too many Westerns, and the "you've got mail" email an-nouncement in recent movies. Alternatively, a Herald can "join the party" and be-come a member of the team, as with certain of the heroes in *Jason and the Argonauts* and C3PO and R2-D2 in *Star Wars*. In *The Hobbit*, Gandalf first functions as a Her-ald for Bilbo; later he's the wizard (Mentor) in both *The Hobbit* and again in *The Lord of the Rings*.

The Shapeshifter

The *Shapeshifter* is the character who "went over to their side" or "came over to ours," the Undercover Agent and the Betrayer/Traitor. They build tension into the story as we, the audience, are never sure what role they really play until the denouement of the story, film, or game. In *Alien*, the android Ash not only misleads the crew of the Nostromo on their mission, but covers up his own physical nature as well. Shakespeare's characters in his comedies often shifted gender to provide the identity questions at the heart of the plays. The title character in *Schindler's List* seems more like a Trickster than a Hero, as he's exploiting the war and his oppressed Jewish employees for his own ends and profits. But as the war his own situation and that of "his Jews" worsens, he becomes something more, a true savior, though a complicated one.

The Shadow

The *Shadow* in this context is not Lamont Cranston (who clouded men's minds on the radio, in pulp fiction, and on the silver screen), but The Bad Guy. Jadis the Ice Queen of Narnia is just bad to the bone, without any real depth to the character beyond that of evil, power hungry antagonist. Darth Vader is more complex, a Shadow, yes, but due to tragic character flaws, and he is redeemed with his last act and breath.

Hannibal Lecter, Thomas Harris' wonderfully rich character wears many hats in the books that featured him. In *Red Dragon,* he is what Sherlock Holmes and Arthur Conan Doyle warned us against, a medical man gone bad. He is mostly Shadow in this book; as Shapeshifter and a Shadow, he helps Will Graham while he simultaneously attempts to double deal and assassinate him by proxy from his cell.

In *Silence of the Lambs*, Lecter's facets multiply, still Shadow and Shapeshifter, Lecter also becomes Mentor, of a sort, to Clarice Starling. In the last book to feature him, *Hannibal,* he becomes even more of a Mentor to Clarice, saving her life and awakening her own shadow side within her, making her his soul mate.

Other Archetypes

There are many others archetypes, including the wise child (Tommy from *Rugrats*), the child-like innocent adult (Will Ferrell in *Elf*), the sidekick/buddy, the maiden, mother, father, and so on.

Christopher Booker, in his book *The Seven Basic Plots*, explores Jungian archetypes and their relationship to various stories in considerable depth. His treatise is that all storytelling is, in some sense, a manifestation of an archetypal family drama—the Hero's Journey is, in effect, a surrogate for the child's journey to adulthood. By following this vein of thinking, Booker suggests that most of the archetypal roles can be resolved as "dark" or "light" manifestations of the four roles in a hypothetical family: father, mother, friend/rival (which are extensions of the protagonist), and finally other half/temptress (who, in the light manifestation is the ultimate life partner of the protagonist) [Booker05]. The only archetypes he excludes from this scheme are the child, the animal helper, and the trickster. Although Booker's work has not been enormously well received, it nonetheless follows both logically and methodically from Jung's work, and provides a noteworthy alternative view of the notion of archetypes.

From the preceding discussions, it's clear that archetypical characters can serve different archetypical roles at different times within the same story, and the most memorable ones have added color, depth, or even blurred the lines their roles first seem defined by.

REMAINING ARISTOTELIAN CONCEPTS

Having looked at the key elements of plot and character, we still have four elements of Aristotle's *Poetics* to examine briefly.

Theme

Aristotle's characteristic of "thought" has been interpreted as being the equivalent of what we now tend to term *theme*, but also includes the motivations and cogitations of the characters in the play. In novels and plays, we often get inside the character's head. We get to read what they're thinking or hear their soliloquies—"To be, or not to be? That is the question."

We get somewhat less of this interior view in film than in literature. Sometimes it's in a character's voice-over in film noir detective films, or from a dead character, as in *American Beauty*. Sometimes there are speeches to rooms of others such as the Senate in *Mr. Smith Goes to Washington*; a courtroom, such as in the film *Philadelphia*; or in a living room at the end of a detective film such as *The Thin Man*. But often we leave it to the actors to communicate the character's thoughts with the inflection on a delivery of a line, a gesture, a look, or body language.

Diction and Pattern

Diction and pattern refers to how lines are spoken, including the language chosen and the manner in which they are spoken and sung—which Aristotle called the *medium*. Modern world culture gives us a wide spectrum of languages to speak in. Not so much French versus English, but more in the coloring of accents from Brooklyn to Texas to the United Kingdom, each of which carry a variety of cultural implications along with them. Word choice, from Oxford to Compton, and word choice's close cousin, regional slang, both have implications for characterization and for setting. In the film *Serenity*, the writer purposefully chose to have some of the heroic characters use archaic vocabulary and sentence structure taken from the American frontier period to underscore the nature of the part of space they come from (a wild frontier).

Spectacle

Lastly, Aristotle's characteristic of *spectacle* is comprised of setting, sets, and special effects. It is perfectly possible to render the same story in a different setting. The plot of Akira Kurasawa's masterful *Seven Samurai* was rendered in a cowboy context for John Sturges' *The Magnificent Seven*, in a space opera setting for Roger Corman's *Battle Beyond the Stars*, and in the context of animated insects for Pixar's *A Bug's Life*. Similarly, we have seen Shakespeare plays set and rewritten into every era and in every medium.

Joseph Papp's New York City renditions alone, from Broadway to Central Park, used a wide range of settings in time and place. Regardless of when and where the story is set, Shakespeare usually remains recognizable as Shakespeare: *Ten Things I Hate About You* is set in a modern high school, not renaissance Italy, but it is still recognizable as a rendition of *The Taming of the Shrew*.

More recently, some modern productions have changed the diction and pattern of Shakespeare's plays. If a modern theatre company decides to slice, dice, and reformat Shakespeare's language to today's vernacular (with or without hip-hop and/or rap songs added), have Shakespeare's comedies and tragedies remained his? Aristotle might say yes as the object, the core plot, characters, and thoughts remain the same, although scholars of Elizabethan drama may beg to differ.

What happens when even the object changes? Is *West Side Story* still *Romeo and Juliet*? Not quite. Like Shakespeare's play, *West Side Story* is a tragedy of star-crossed young lovers from different family backgrounds (that is, Anglo and Chicano street gangs), with street-fighting duels and death by the blade, it's true. But in this musical tragedy, only the thought remains the same, as the plot, character, language, and spectacle are all different in some ways. Even the ending of the story differs: no double suicide in an Abbey in *West Side Story*. Instead, Tony dies in a fight and Maria threatens to kill herself as part of her plea that the fighting must end. Not that the changes made for a bad play (and later film); they just weren't Shakespeare.

Spectacle adapts to the needs of the audience of its day: Shakespeare wrote about what he believed an Elizabethan audience wanted to see on stage. Modern filmmakers make movies with settings suitable to their audience. The spectacle, the setting for a narrative, is merely the trappings of the story. Its essence remains the same regardless of how it is rendered.

CONCLUSION

To understand narrative, it's best to begin at looking what the term means outside of the context of games. Through the models of Aristotle, Campbell, and (to a lesser extent) Field, we have examined the importance and structure of plot; through Jung, Campbell, and Booker, we have looked at the archetypes that (arguably) underlie the use of characters. Finally, we have examined the other elements of Aristotle's *Poetics,* which complete the narrative picture.

For the most part, we have examined films, plays, and novels, because the narrative implications of these forms are easier to examine, being essentially fixed and static (at least in terms of plot and character). As we move into examining how narrative applies to games, suddenly everything enters a state of flux. We cannot trust conventional models of plot or character because in an interactive media the lines may become immeasurably blurred. This is why interactive narrative is becoming increasingly interesting as the new frontier of storytelling. No one truly knows what this brave new world will herald for future scholars of narrative.

ENDNOTES

[1] The article is available at *http://www.lcc.gatech.edu/~mateas/publications.html.* The innovative storytelling game *Façade,* which Michael Mateas was intimately involved in developing, can be downloaded from *http://www.interactivestory.net.*

[2] The novel is prefaced with a disclaimer reading "This book has an unconventional structure."

[3] It can be argued that since Obi Wan meets Vader a few minutes earlier, this happens "right on time" for Field's model.

3 Writing for Games
Richard Boon

In terms of delivering narrative material, every medium provides its own challenges. Videogames, being relatively new, are still developing their storytelling capacity. This is complicated by the fact that videogames are not solely a narrative medium—a videogame may justify itself through play, without any aspect of story whatsoever. Clearly videogames may deliver stories with play, many players enjoy experiencing story via the medium, and videogame developers usually consider story to be a necessary element of the experience they provide to their customers. As such, capable storytellers are required to develop the narrative language of the medium with the goal of expressing meaningful, entertaining stories.

Interactivity is the primary difference between narrative delivery in videogames when compared to other established narrative media. For a game narrative to be satisfying to a player, it must consider the needs of the player *as* a player, rather than a passive observer. Within noninteractive fiction, the audience reacts to the fiction, whereas with a videogame, the audience reacts to the fiction that in turn may react back.

The primary concern of the game writer, then, is that almost every narrative element in the game is triggered by an action on the part of the player. The job of a game writer is to understand, predict, and enable the role that the player takes within the narrative and game-spaces presented.

GAME NARRATIVE

Although the terms *narrative* and *story* are often used interchangeably as umbrella terms, it is useful to distinguish between them. *Narrative* is here defined as the methods by which the story materials are communicated to the audience. *Story*, meanwhile, can be taken to refer to all story details and primarily to a set of events as driven by characters within a fictional space. A given story may be re-imagined through different narratives—as we have already seen in movies with the classic story of *The Seven Samurai* being retold as *The Magnificent Seven, Battle Beyond the Stars,* or *A Bug's Life.*

By this reading, movie techniques such as the flashback or dream sequence are considered to be narrative techniques. Using symbols to deepen the emotional resonance of a scene is also a narrative technique—the writer has a choice regarding their use of symbols to create different emotional responses in the audience. Changes of event, however (such as a given archetypal character dying in one telling of a story and not in another), must be seen as changes to the story itself, not to the narrative.

This is important to videogame writing because the fundamental interactivity of videogames means that control of narrative elements are often ceded to the player. At a basic level, players are routinely given control of the game camera and therefore choose what to see. Though most games still enforce certain camera views for specific events (by removing the player's camera control—usually in cut scenes), some games such as *Half-Life* (Valve, 1998) go to great lengths to preserve player control. The player often has a simplistic narrative choice of whether to look or whether not to look, for instance.

This may be extended to other narrative concepts, such as choice of location, choice of NPC interaction, or choice of the tool with which to interact with the game world (usually, at this stage of the development of the videogame medium, a weapon). So-called *side-quests* (minor narrative threads that may be pursued by players for game advantage, but which have no impact on the main story) may also be considered to present a narrative choice to the player—typically, whether the spinal story will be told directly, or whether it will be interspersed with unrelated events (which may nevertheless offer some level of thematic resonance with the spinal story).

Compare this to allowing players control of the story. Allowing a player a degree of control over *how* a story is communicated between player and game differs greatly from allowing players control of *the story* itself. In the latter, players may be able to halt the tragedy, or choose a different lover, or play their hero as a villain. In the former, the player's hero is always heroic, the lover is defined, and the tragedy is irrevocable. The player merely controls the "how," not the "what."

Due to this potential for narrative interactivity, a game writer must understand the requirements of their project. Just because deeply interactive storytelling is theoretically possible, doesn't mean that it's a suitable goal for every game project. Sometimes more modest goals are appropriate.

Videogame storytelling may be broadly divided into four basic forms:

- Implicit narrative
- Formal narrative
- Interactive narrative
- Interactive story

Implicit Narrative

Implicit narrative, often called *emergent narrative*, involves the interaction of elements within the game system to develop events that may be interpreted by the player as story—narrative results that are implicit to the game system. Games are, at root, systems constructed from interrelating elements—consider a sport such as baseball, in which game "elements" such as pitching, catching, running, and hitting combine to create drama when expressed within a definite ruleset.

This system of interacting elements may be called the *game-space*, and applies both to apparently physical interactions seen by the player and to purely mechanical interactions behind the scenes.

In a baseball game, the actual events—a strikeout, a home run—may be completely unrelated to one another. However, in the minds of the audience, stories are developed by creating connections. A given hitter has never scored a home run off a given pitcher—but does so in the ninth inning of a crucial game. This event appears to be motivated by fate, as the drama works better if the events are considered to be causally related.

Similarly, in a videogame, story may emerge from the interaction of game elements, with no formal narrative design having taken place. Let's say that the player is exploring an underground fantasy dungeon. Crawling along a small ledge above a torrent of rushing water, the player reaches an opening in the wall, a crack just large enough for the player's virtual form to squeeze through. But as the player attempts this, a horde of bats explodes from the crack, causing the shocked player to instinctively move backward—falling from the ledge into the river beneath and swept away to further adventure.

Here, the elements are predetermined, but no element is formally scripted. The ledge, the crack, the bats, the river—all are open to interpretation by the player through their play. The player may not even notice that the sequence wasn't scripted, unless they play again and witness a different occurrence at the same point in the game's physical landscape.

Many videogame developers and theorists support implicit narrative as a mode of narrative available to games but unavailable to movies or novels, and so worthy of further development. The downside resides in the uncertainty of development for such games—the designers do not know whether their balance of game elements is suitable for the generation of interesting events until near the end of the project.

Although a game writer is not required for the development of implicit narrative, some understanding of games as systems—and the possibilities this presents for narrative development—is recommended for game writers. While playing a game, consider which events are prescripted and which are due to system interactions. As previously noted, the majority of the narrative material presented in videogames is presented in response to player action—learning what type of system interaction works well with which type of narrative reaction is an important step in writing for games.

Formal Narrative

Formal narrative simply involves storytelling that is delivered via prescribed methods. Whereas implicit narrative is generated through player interpretation of game system interactions and is therefore unplanned by the game creators, formal narrative involves planned story elements.

Story events may be communicated to the player via different formal narrative techniques. For instance, dialogue is often used to inform players of story material via NPCs. Alternatively, the player may be presented with animated scenes, text files triggered from within the game, or even text materials displayed during loading between game sections.

Additionally, part of the game writer's job is to recognize storytelling opportunities that arise naturally within the game-space. Formal narrative elements (such as dialogue) may be triggered from game system interactions, as long as the game writer has predicted that specific interaction. The writer creates dialogue for circumstances that *may* arise, effectively combining implicit and formal narrative styles. This is a technique that may be used to generate interactive narrative.

Interactive Narrative

Interactive narrative combines implicit and formal narrative to relate interacting game elements to formal narrative, allowing the player's actions to affect the delivery of narrative.

In a game story, the majority of narrative elements will be presented to the player in response to the player's actions. Interactive narrative attempts to broaden this factor as far as possible, to create a game in which the player's game actions are echoed by the game in narrative form at every step of the way. An obvious form of interactive narrative is to prescript a set of responses to player success, in, for example, a race. If the player does well (places first), a line plays saying, "Wow, that was awesome, dude! You totally burned rubber!" If they don't do as well, a second line suggests, "Whoa, dude, nice going! With a bit of practice you could be a totally gnarly racer!" Other finishing positions elicit similarly appropriate responses. Here we see a predictable set of natural gameplay outcomes (implicit narrative) being reinforced by scripted content (formal narrative) to create an increased sense of relationship between game and player.

Naturally, creating enough formal narrative material to cover all situations is an impossible task, and so the game's development team (which includes the game writer) must pick which elements of feedback to concentrate on to deliver a specific play and/or narrative experience.

Interactive Story

A broader reading of interactive narrative results in an *interactive story*—a story in which the player actions have direct consequences for the story as a whole. Here, events may be changed by player choice, which is to say that player choice revolves not around narrative elements alone (which merely deliver the story to the player) but in terms of structure as well. The current high-water mark of the form is perhaps *Deus Ex* (Ion Storm, 2000), which allows the player to make choices regarding which of a set of prescripted formal narrative events is played at specific points within the game structure, giving the player a degree of control of the plot of the story.

Some commentators consider it impossible to create a satisfying story while still providing such a degree of agency to the player due to the lack of authorial control—if events may be changed, for instance, there is no inevitability, which makes certain potent story forms, such as the tragedy, impossible to create.

Perhaps more pertinently, interactive stories cannot realistically be created by diligent use of formal materials in a traditional manner. Games such as *Deus Ex,* which do currently offer player choice in plot development, do so by providing different prescripted scenes that may then play at specific points in response to a player-controlled trigger. To allow any true depth of choice to a player using this technique would overload the developer's ability to create and structure enough scenes. A more distributed system is required, treating the game narrative in a systematic manner, in line with the structuring of play elements. Untested models for structuring this style of game do already exist, but lie beyond the scope of this chapter.

THE GAME WRITER

As noted, the primary concern of the game writer is that almost every narrative element in the game is triggered by an action on the part of the player. Most simplistically, this may mean that the completion of a game challenge triggers a between-levels cut scene (a short, noninteractive game "movie"). It may mean that a button press directly initiates a particular line of dialogue, played live, in-game. It may mean that the choice of the player to talk to character A instead of character B (for instance) may effect the long-term development of the story.

The first job of the game writer, then, is to understand possible interactions between player and game and determine how these actions may be used to enhance the narrative experience. In short, the writer must attempt to understand the game-space, the system of interactions that generates gameplay between player and game. This is no easy task, especially because scripts are required long before the game is playable. It seems obvious, therefore, that game writers should afford themselves a broad experience of different game genres, initially noting the play aspects rather than the narrative techniques apparent therein.

The primary concern for player agency leads to the second consideration of game writing: *pacing*. Although older videogames often forced pace upon the player, this technique is currently unfashionable; the current trends in videogames favor free-range exploration on the part of the player. The player therefore dictates the pace of the game, and the writer must understand this.

To pace effectively, the writer must understand the nature of the medium. Videogames almost always incorporate a *progress structure*—a connection between player and game that limits the proportion of the game-space that the player is allowed to explore at any given time. Effectively, gameplay is paced by the game designer imposing limits in the form of barriers, coupled with the means to bypass those barriers (keys). Barriers may be literal barriers in-game (such as a wall of flame that must be doused with water to pass) or may be less tangible aspects of the game-space (such as a secondary play mode, accessed from a menu when certain challenges within the primary game mode have been completed). As soon as players are given access to the relevant key, they may access the corresponding barriers. Narrative pacing may use this—for example, if the player acquires a water bucket and may douse burning walls, dialogue may be played to provide appropriate notification. Or, from a more story-oriented point of view, this juncture may be used to deliver necessary narrative information completely unrelated to the bucket. By tying narrative triggers to a key, it is ensured that the player will encounter them.

Different games structure their progress in different ways, but, in terms of narrative-oriented games, progress structure usually dictates narrative structure. Without an understanding of the design of a game, the writer will not be able to effectively draw their audience into the story.

After pacing has been considered, writers turn to narrative delivery—their third task. A number of different narrative techniques are currently used in videogames. These range from Full Motion Video (FMV)—scenes played as videos from the game disc—to written text, including options of varying levels of cost in between. Here, knowledge of the technical aspects of the medium is essential in terms of budget. As in movies, not everything writers can imagine is transferable to the audience, as some things are more expensive to show than others. Videogames are made on a wide range of budgets, and writers who understand this are better positioned to use suitable narrative methods to deliver their stories.

In summary, the game writer has three basic concerns:

- Narrative delivery
- Pacing and structure
- Player agency

Narrative Delivery

A number of basic methods of narrative delivery exist, as currently seen in modern videogames. Each may be used in different ways (and in combination with other methods), and each has its own related advantages and disadvantages, one of which will inevitably relate to financial cost.

Text

This is the simplest and cheapest method of narrative delivery—the player must read story developments onscreen. In terms of videogame history, text adventures such as *Zork* (Infocom, 1980) relied entirely upon text for both input and output. Due to input issues (commands often had to be guessed) and the obvious resistance of a mass market to text-only games, these games exist only within a hardcore underground, and have been renamed *interactive fiction* (IF). Nevertheless, good work is being done in this area, which, due to the low overheads (excellent IF scripting packages are available, meaning that the writer can concentrate upon writing and structuring, rather than coding the game) is far more experimental (and intellectual) in tone than mainstream videogames.

In mainstream games, text is seen in three primary areas (outside of subtitling recorded dialogue). The first is in large games of relatively low budget, in which recording is either unfeasible due to the sheer volume of dialogue or because the project budget is insufficient for such dialogue to be recorded. PC-format cRPGs often use this technique, and it is still accepted by that genre's audience that reading will be necessary to gameplay. This may change, but it seems likely that there will always be a core audience that is willing to accept full text dialogue in suitable game formats.

The second use of text is seen most commonly in console-style action adventure games, such as *Resident Evil* (Capcom, 1996), which provide in-game artifacts as text files in the form of diaries, letters, computer files, and so forth. In older games, it was acceptable for these text files to be compulsory reading—reading being enforced by such game techniques as embedding door key codes in the texts themselves, so that the player could not physically progress without at least scanning the files. In modern games, it is generally unacceptable to force players to read these files, and they are used primarily for game color, and for background information. Some players enjoy exploring the narrative space of a game by tracking down all the files, whereas others don't. Nevertheless, this is an inexpensive method of adding depth to a story or game world.

Text files may actually aid in the pacing of a game. The majority of successful survival horror games rely upon keen pacing, alternating between tension and safety, action and exploration. If writers want to slow a player down during a given section, a few text files will likely do that; such a play section will feel to the player like a lull in the action, which, depending upon the game, may be desirable. One danger, however, is that players will only read the files once at most, and so if they fail a game challenge and are repositioned at a previous point in the game, they will not experience the lull again. As such, writers often place a checkpoint after such a pacing section to ensure that it need only be passed once (depending upon the save game scheme used in the design, of course).

The final use of text is seen primarily in Japanese console games. Here, sound effects are used to present character vocalization, with any relevant text being presented onscreen. This technique has an advantage in that it requires a single sound file for all territories, lowering the cost of localization (the process of adapting the game into other languages or cultures). It also preserves a certain almost naïve tone, which only Japanese developers seem to be able to achieve. *The Legend of Zelda* series (Nintendo, 1986 onwards) is an excellent example. Whether this technique is preserved for aesthetic reasons or is simply a hangover from days of cartridge game storage is difficult to say. Nevertheless, this is a valid technique that shouldn't be discounted.

The production cycle of a game often leads to its tutorial being written, or at least amended, very late in the day. As such, tutorial information is often presented as written text only, as all other dialogue has been recorded months earlier. Text should always be considered as a solution to last minute panics, as long as consistency can be achieved.

When using text dialogue, writers must understand that the player is likely to stop playing to read the text. In most cRPGs, this halt is made mandatory, although bugs or bad design sometimes creep through, resulting in players being butchered while reading. This is obviously of greater concern in action games, where constant pauses for reading can seriously damage game flow. If tutorial information threatens to upset flow in this manner, it may be useful to place all help text on a separate screen in the pause menu, and merely tell players where to find it if they get stuck. Whatever the fix, text dialogue must suit the game style—it must engage, not irritate the player, and text length and frequency are the key factors in this.

Recorded Dialogue

Recorded dialogue is much more flexible than text-only dialogue, although this comes at greater cost. Its many advantages include the ability of the player to listen and play simultaneously (an easier task than reading and playing, thus allowing for more fluid play) and the increased immersion (and authorial control) gained by the use of voice actors to realize characters, set tone and rhythm of dialogue, and so forth.

A good game writer uses the ability to play dialogue at any point in the game. Key information should be reserved for times when the player is focused upon listening—if the information is absolutely vital to game progress, it should either be delivered in cut scenes or be somehow replayable (as NPC dialogue, for instance). Nonessential dialogue may be played at any time, however.

Even in this case, there are good times and bad times to play recorded dialogue. The player of a fast-action melee combat game is unlikely to be able to concentrate fully upon dialogue in the midst of an intense battle, for instance. On the other end of the spectrum, a long ladder climb or elevator ride may benefit from some incidental dialogue, to keep the player engaged. The game writer can estimate the majority of these crunch and drag moments by assessing the level design documentation and then plan accordingly.

Another reason to accurately assess level design is when considering dialogue triggering. It's all very well to spot potential dialogue points, but for most game engines, only one line of dialogue may be played at once—if a second line is triggered before the first is finished, a clash occurs. Dialogue clashes are usually resolved by prioritizing either the initial or subsequent line—either play out the first line and ignore the second, or play the second by cutting the first dead at the second's trigger. Neither is fully satisfying (although the latter is less disrupting than it might seem and is probably preferable). Technical developments may eventually remove this problem, but for the current games industry, it remains largely inescapable.

Considering dialogue triggered by location (that is, when a player enters a room, dialogue is triggered), a solid estimate of both dialogue line length and the speed of player travel in-game helps avoid dialogue clashes. The most significant difficulty here is estimating player speed from design documents. In general, player movement will always be faster than you think—and dialogue will always take longer to play (within reason, disallowing improvisation by talented voice actors on the grounds of line length is improper). At least, it's safest to assume this.

Even more so than text dialogue, writers must judge the length of recorded dialogue. It's easy in both cut scenes and in-game settings to overwrite dialogue. Writers do not like to shut their characters up or compromise a character detail or joke, but videogame dialogue is, in general, better when kept short and sweet. As such, each line is likely to be required to serve multiple purposes. Here we stray into traditional writing territory, which is beyond the scope of the chapter, but it's sensible to note that on top of exposition requirements, character detail, entertainment value, and setting reinforcement, game dialogue may also be called upon to provide gameplay information or advice. Beyond suggesting that game information should never be obscured by the writer's desire to provide vocal color and entertainment, the only other caveat is to avoid character traits such as stuttering or slow speech. These provide unnecessary complications and are difficult to render in a satisfying fashion.

One possibly unexpected downside to recorded dialogue occurs through repetition. A person will never read the same text in exactly the same way twice, but recorded dialogue always sounds the same when replayed—and so quickly becomes tiresome. If a line is to be used multiple times, record multiple lines. Line content can be provided in a few variant forms in the script, with instructions to record a certain number of versions of each line. A good voice actor can say "Ow!" in 30 different ways, but even the best writer will struggle to rewrite "Ow!" more than a few times without the dialogue becoming contrived.

Another good reason for recording multiple lines is in replay. If a game is designed around strict fail-repeat rules (that is, if the player fails, they have to repeat the failed gameplay section), it is wise to record as many line variants as is reasonable (one per expected play is a good rule of thumb, with cycling being acceptable after four to six distinct lines, dependent upon the rate of replay). This is especially true if the game design expects the player to repeat numerous times.

A final reason for recording multiple lines is to have some "spares" for emergency situations. If, for example, you aren't sure whether a certain word can be used, record multiple lines (especially with swear words, which can be ambiguous in terms of what will be allowed into the game by the publisher, licensor, or platform-license holder). If a certain game detail can't be locked in quickly enough, or if there is any doubt at all, record multiple lines.

The word "damn" is actually very difficult to employ in games, as are any other religious references. These words are often best steered away from period, unless the game's producer is very certain they can be used.

When writing dialect, remember that the dialogue is to be recorded. Rather than write in dialect, which can be difficult to read and may threaten to slow down voice recording, write in clear language, allowing the voice actor to add the dialect as they see fit for their character. Traditional dramatic scripts and screenplays often contain directions/suggestion for the ways in which actors should approach readings, and game scripts should as well.

Static Images

Videogames are an audio-visual medium, and visuals can be effective narrative devices. The cheapest form of visual to use is a static image—a drawing, painting, or CG still. Older videogames, which were limited in their narratives by the memory size of the media upon which they were recorded (floppy disks, game cartridges), often used static images, or very basic animations created by moving one static image upon another, to aid their narrative development. Some games still use this technique. *Katamari Damacy* (Namco, 2004) and its sequel have used simply animated storyboards as a cost-effective narrative technique, although it should be noted that this game's unconventional nature allows it a certain latitude perhaps not available to a more conventional game title.

Static images can also be used in games involving long periods of loading, giving the player something to watch during these periods of downtime. Loading screens can be considered for narrative delivery, especially during very linear games in which the player position is known. Even if player position is not so obvious, the use of game art can increase the player's attachment to the game world. Loading screens are also a useful method of delivering gameplay tutorials, but make sure to keep any text used for this purpose as short as possible, to allow players to read it.

Certain genres of game also use static images for cut scene narrative delivery. For instance, cRPGs, which by their nature involve a great amount of narrative material, often use static images for storytelling. Usually, images in such sequences are composited in a dynamic manner—pans, zooms, fades, and so forth distract from the fundamentally static nature of the images. A narrator vocal is also usually used to deliver exposition over such scenes, but more inventive solutions may be found.

A second, less common, form of static image is the comic strip. *Max Payne* (Remedy, 1998) uses a comic strip during its cut scenes, and such a technique is dynamic while remaining cheap to produce. Naturally, creating comic strips is the domain of the writer. Knowledge of comic aesthetics can be useful here—a superhero game naturally suggests comic book styling, but a horror adventure might also be improved at low cost by using a comic book style evocative of classic horror comics of the 1950s and 1960s. Scott Adams' guide *Understanding Comics* provides a good stepping point for game writers looking to bring a comic book sensibility and visual vocabulary to their work.

Camera Cases

The term *camera case* is used to describe any scene that may be created through camera movements within the game world, possibly also using stock (rather than purposely created) animations for character movement. The most common type of camera case in games is the flyby, in which the camera moves through the world as a heads-up for the player. A second form of flyby is commonly used to highlight specific game objectives—here we see the camera move from the player's position to the objective goal, displaying the path from the former to the latter. Both these forms are primarily player aids rather than expositional in nature, and so are not the remit of the writer, but similar techniques may be adapted for storytelling purposes.

This type of camera case usually takes the form of a static camera showing game characters within the game world. Here stock animations (precreated for such situations and reused throughout the game to reduce costs) are used to keep the characters dynamic while recorded dialogue plays, creating a cheap cut scene. The writer usually need not worry about lip-synching—the majority of modern games allow lip synching to text, rather than forcing lip-synching to be hand-animated, and so any dialogue may be matched procedurally to character lip movements. Check with the project producer or technical manager to be sure.

Beyond knowledge of the available animations and considering the pacing of the game (removal of player control should be kept to a minimum and used primarily for delivery of essential information), the only other concern of the game writer is data. A camera case requires the game environment it shows to be loaded in its entirety into RAM, and so the writer must be careful not to request a camera case cutaway to a level not loaded, as loading levels for narrative purpose alone should be avoided (it increases player downtime without in-game justification).

The primary advantage of the camera case is its low cost, although the writer should be aware that all camera cases require implementation by hand, and so should still be considered in terms of the overall development pipeline. Check with the game designers regarding the amount of camera case material they feel is appropriate for the game. Otherwise, players do not dislike this narrative technique, but neither will it impress anyone or convince anyone that the project hits above its cost weight. It therefore remains a functional technique, available for limited use in basic exposition and character color.

Cut Scenes (In-Engine)

As already noted, a cut scene is a short movie presented to the player at specific points in the game and should only be used to advance the story in some significant way because it removes control from the player. In general, cut scenes should be seen as a reward to the player—they should play after a significant success on the player's part. Thus the player is granted a small rest after some intense play. This aspect of pacing, in which game and story support each other in rewarding the player, is key to game writing.

More does not necessarily equate to better, in terms of cut scene-as-reward— in general, no cut scene should be longer than two minutes except when opening or closing the game, or when delivering specific information at a crux point in the story (though this depends upon the pacing of play—slow games may support longer cut scenes). One of the game writer's key tasks when plotting videogame stories is to ensure that exposition doesn't "crunch" at any point; that is, there is never so much vital story information to deliver to the player that a cut scene needs to be extended beyond a player's attention span.

When writing cut scenes, the writer is in complete control of the content, as player control is suspended while the cut scene plays. In this regard, writing a cut scene is very similar to writing a scene for TV or cinema, and a similar format of script may be adopted. The game writer will be supported by the developer during cut scene production—a storyboard artist will be assigned to the task—and so it is usually up to the writer as to the depth of material they create. Some game writers prefer to draft the whole scene in terms of cuts, camera angles, and so forth, whereas others write only the sparsest of essential direction, and concentrate on dialogue. As with all aspects of videogame production, teamwork is the key, and the writer should talk to the developer regarding such matters to ascertain the preferable method of work.

An in-engine cut scene is created using the game engine to produce the visuals, as opposed to an FMV cut scene, in which the scene is played as video, and therefore may be prerendered or filmed with a camera. As videogame technology increases in power, graphics improve to the point that in-engine cut scenes are often preferable to FMV, as they preserve continuity in the visuals. The primary difference between an in-engine cut scene and live exposition during play is that cut scenes may use custom animations, which is where the cost lies.

As the scene is rendered in-engine, any feature or character must also be created for use in-engine. Cost is kept to a minimum if no custom features are requested for the scene—all features and characters should already exist in-game to avoid having the developer generate new assets for narrative purposes only. If your scene requires a feature not seen in-game, talk to the developers and allow them to assess its value with relation to cost. Static features are moderately cheap to produce, but animated features may be prohibitively expensive. Should you lack a feature, consider using camera angles and cutaways to suggest its presence, and reinforce this with dialogue.

Because cut scenes are by necessity custom animated, it is sensible to make them very dynamic and include a lot of character action. Camera cases are better employed for talking head sequences, as stock animations may be used. It is also wise to use a variety of camera angles—because most games are played from one specific camera angle, cut scenes can distinguish themselves by providing visual variety in this way.

The cut scene script for a game is often required long before any in-game dialogue. There are several reasons for this, including the use of external animation companies to compose cut scenes, and the need to have any voice recording completed before the construction of the animation begins. This means that the game writer will generally be creating the material in two batches—one cut scene script and one in-game script (usually, two recording sessions are used, one for each type of script, because cut scene dialogue must be recorded early in the development cycle). Preparation is therefore of paramount importance if the scenes and in-game materials are to appear seamless to the player. The writer must decide what aspects of the story are to be communicated by which method, and then commit to cut scene material with the knowledge that any mistakes cannot be retracted.

Scripted Events

Related to in-engine cut scenes are scripted events, which are in effect "live" cut scenes (although the term is clearly oxymoronic). *Half-Life* first used the technique of playing precreated, purpose animations within the game environment without removing control from the player, and the technique can be very effective. Naturally, the player has the choice of whether to watch or not, and so the positioning of the action is very important—play an animation in a place where players are not guaranteed to be looking, and they may well miss it. Careful level design is the key here, using enclosed pathways to funnel players toward animations, but this task is not usually within the remit of the game writer.

Such scenes are also required to be short, and are difficult to effectively support with large amounts of dialogue. Because control remains live, the point of the technique is lost if the player is required to sit still and wait for the dialogue to play out. Also, the player must not be allowed to interfere with the animation. The technique should therefore be used in short bursts rather than extended scenes—and only when sanctioned by the developer, as it is expensive.

Cut Scenes (FMV)

With the advent of CD-ROMs in the early 1990s, suddenly there was plenty of storage space to fill with expensive prerendered animations and live action videos. After a short burst of high-cost, low-play-value content, the use of FMV has settled down to an accepted set of uses, and is generally reserved for high-profile titles, due to their high cost.

Although developers have experimented with live action video, perhaps most notably in *Wing Commander 3* (Origin, 1994), the clash of visual tone between game graphics and video is such that the majority of players dislike the technique. It is now seen as rather passé to attempt such things. As such, in this section FMV refers to prerendered computer graphics imagery (CGI), although the term FMV properly applies to any prerecorded visual used in this manner.

The most obvious use for FMV is in a game intro. A glossy FMV intro reassures a player that the game purchase decision has been a wise one, because it suggests quality. An important point is that FMV can display pretty much anything the writer wishes, with generally little difference in cost. This is another good reason to employ it in story set-up. FMV also suggests that it does what the game engine can't—usually highly dynamic action sequences, or sequences with many moving features. It is a crime to waste an FMV budget on slow, rigid talky sequences.

Key sequences may also be rendered in FMV, as this sends an immediate message of importance to the player. Again, it is a waste of an FMV to present story content that would be as possible to deliver via engine cut scene or camera case, so the writer should choose the material carefully. The majority of developers will budget for a specific total length of FMV; it may be wise to use this budget on one or two lengthy, strong scenes than divide it between multiple scenes of lesser importance.

As with engine cut scenes, most developers employ external companies to generate their FMV, and similarly all dialogue must be recorded beforehand. The writer must therefore prepare very carefully for FMV sequences, as the material must be finalized very early in the development process, and later changes will not be possible.

Game Structure

Structure is important to any story—the audience must be given pertinent material when they need it. Basic story information (exposition such as the protagonist's identity, her job, her social situation) is usually required from the very start of the story. Some other types of material—the identity of the murderer, for instance—mustn't be given away too soon. So structuring lies in the art of presenting the correct material at the correct time to benefit the audience's understanding of the story.

This is difficult enough in traditional media—organizing material to create the optimum flow of exposition, character expression, plot development, and visceral excitement is the business of practiced, professional Hollywood screenwriters. In a videogame, the task is further complicated by the structural needs of the game at the level of the game mechanics.

In videogame terms, structure concerns the ordering and pacing of the delivered play materials. All play materials, including bonuses, cheats, and other sundries, may be considered aspects of the game-space. How and when these materials are delivered determines the game structure. For instance, *Tom Clancy's Splinter Cell* (Ubisoft, 2002) presents a series of linearly delivered missions to the player, within which all game elements are also delivered linearly (that is, in a completely fixed order).

The Legend of Zelda: Ocarina of Time (Nintendo, 1998), on the other hand, divides its play environments into two broad types: overworld and dungeon. Dungeons are delivered linearly and involve a linear sequence of play situations. The overworld, however, is designed so that the player may explore it almost at will. The two areas are linked by a series of tools (which act as keys) to be collected in the dungeons, which allow progress beyond certain barriers in the overworld. Thus the player has a degree of freedom in the overworld, but must progress through the dungeons to facilitate further overworld exploration.

Progress Structure

From a narrative perspective, the most important aspect of videogame structure is the progress structure, which determines when, and in response to what, progress within the game-space is allowed.

Such progress structures are not inevitable. Games that give players access to all material from the outset could be created. However, gameplay-oriented reasons for including progress structures exist. The most important of these are training, pacing, and reward. The player must be trained in the rules of the game, so game elements are added incrementally to avoid overwhelming the player with possibilities. The game must also be effectively paced—small events usually build up to a series of crescendos, both in terms of gameplay and narrative delivery. The player must be rewarded for playing, and discovery is a potent reward.

In the *Legend of Zelda: Ocarina of Time*, narrative delivery occurs at specific, predetermined points in the game—upon the defeat of a major boss (for which the acquisition of a game tool is a prerequisite), by talking to characters at specific points in the game (and progress of time in the game isn't, from the narrative perspective, determined in a continuous manner, but rather by game goals achieved), or by entering new areas for the first time.

Each of these moments is completely determined by the progress structure of the game. It is impossible for the player to miss aspects of the story because they are all delivered in an utterly predictable manner. Only the time taken by particular players to achieve that position within the game may change—not the players' circumstances when they get there.

Four basic progress structures occur in narrative-oriented games (although the specifics may differ radically, especially with regard to delivery of bonus material):

- Linear
- Continuous
- Domain
- Contiguous

Linear Structures

The most basic progress structure involves the player's advancement through a linear series of game levels. The challenge in each level is to find the way to its exit point, achieving any game challenges the designer requires the player to achieve to progress. The exit point may be physical (a door) or may be triggered from some other event (completion of a puzzle, defeat of a boss).

Typical narrative delivery within this structure occurs between levels, in the form of cut scenes, mission briefings, story texts, or the like. Because level order is fixed, event order is also fixed, and story materials may be planned exactly.

This is the simplest and cheapest of the common game structures. Although it offers little in the way of challenge for the writer (beyond the ever-present challenge of creating pertinent story materials of high quality), the structure is very suitable for certain players. Consider the linear level structure to be akin to the narrative development in a kung-fu movie—static chunks of narrative that efficiently move the story forward, positioned between the real draw of the product (fighting and stunts in kung-fu movies, gameplay in the case of the game).

When the core gameplay of a game is adrenaline fuelled, and based more upon spectacle than texture, a linear structure may be the most suitable choice for narrative delivery.

Continuous Structures

Similar to the linear structure, in that game progress is linear in nature, the continuous structure allows no conceptual break between game areas. This is to say that the player is not removed from the game-world when a new area is required to be loaded and then repositioned within the new circumstances—rather, the player's progress from area to area is presented as a single journey.

The most tangible difference between the linear and continuous structures is that reverse movement may be allowed in the latter. If the designer doesn't specifically block the players' retreat, they may wander back through the game to the start point. (A game should create certainties in the mind of the player, especially when backtracking is possible. Dialogue may aid in this goal, by telling players that they are backtracking unnecessarily.) More importantly, from the point of view of the game writer, there is a less explicit structure for narrative delivery because natural between-level break points no longer exist.

Half-Life is an example of a game in which a continuous structure is used to good effect. Valve took the decision to center the players in their character in such a way as to deny any external shots of that character—the entire game is seen from Gordon Freeman's point of view. To cement this connection between player and avatar, cut scenes have been eliminated. All narrative material is presented live, occurring in a prescribed form but allowing the player to retain control (and, potentially, giving the player the choice to turn away and miss the narrative segment).

This is an expensive (although successful) technique of dealing with the problems of the continuous structure. Other games simply define certain trigger points, which, when tripped by the player, initiate conventional cut scenes, lines of dialogue, text files, and so forth.

Domain Structures

Domain structures operate by presenting the player with a central hub, from which all other play areas may be accessed (usually in response to a progression mechanic, such as collecting a number of objects or completing a number of tasks to open a new domain). Crucially, each domain is only accessible from the hub—there is no route directly from domain to domain.

Super Mario 64 (Nintendo, 1996) uses a domain structure. A cartoon castle represents the hub, and Mario may explore this to find paintings hung upon the walls. Certain paintings provide transport to other worlds, in which stars may be collected. In turn, collecting set numbers of stars acts as the key, activating new paintings and allowing further progress.

The key difference between the domain structure and the linear structure, which also uses hermetic environments, is that within the domain structure, the player is allowed to return at will to any previously accessed domain. This means that narrative material, if used in-domain, must be positioned in such a way that the players *must* encounter it, to avoid them chancing upon redundant material later in the game. If regular repeat visits to a domain are expected, the writer should supply multiple versions of incidental dialogue, and even specific lines (triggered in part by a player's specific number of visits to the domain, for instance), to avoid repetition and dead time.

The usual solution for spinal narrative material within a domain-structured game is to present the majority of story material within the hub. Each time the player succeeds at a challenge, that success is recorded, and the number of challenges, or the completion of specific challenges, may be used as narrative triggers.

Contiguous Structures

A contiguous structure attempts to create the illusion of a complete, explorable world. Unlike the domain structure, which allows access to game environments exclusively from a central hub, contiguous structures connect game environments in a realistic fashion, each leading to the next. The player can walk from one end of the world to the other. The *Grand Theft Auto* series (DMA Design et al, 1997 onwards) are perhaps the most famous examples of this approach.

The difference between the continuous and contiguous structures is one of convenience only; the former are linear in nature and may or may not allow backtracking, whereas the latter must be designed to allow the player freedom of movement in all directions.

Note also that domains may be accessed from a contiguous overworld (as seen in *The Legend of Zelda: Ocarina of Time*, for instance), combining the domain and contiguous approaches.

Because of the freedom of movement allowed within the game world, location-based triggers are less suitable for narrative use, except where planned for in the level design. Rather, game-state triggers are required, which in turn requires the game writer to understand the specific progress structure to be incorporated. Specifically, how is exploration of the contiguous world to be regulated? If specific game tasks must be completed before a certain key allows progress beyond a specific type of barrier, the game writer may relate pertinent narrative triggers to that acquisition of that key.

Distributed narrative techniques are also possible. Basically, these techniques involve the creation of modular story materials, which are unconnected to other aspects of the story progression and so may be triggered at any (suitable) time. For instance, the protagonist of a game may be able to kill a specific number of a specific foe, at which point an NPC may be programmed to deliver a certain line of dialogue ("Wow, you sure hate Orcs, don't you?").

However, the key story events still must be paced in line with the progress structure, as certain events will not be able to occur until previous events have passed. In this way, a core set of events usually exists; here, each event must exist with a certain relationship to the other events of the set. This set of key events constitutes the *game spine* and is inevitably directly related to the progress structure of the game. The game spine may be intertwined with the central story, although it is not the only way a game can be arranged.

Structuring the Story

Upon receipt of the design documentation, the writer must determine the structure to be used in the game. At the time of this writing, no universal language of videogame design exists, and so the writer may find discussing the structural details of the story to be difficult. However, all game design documents contain a section and usually a flowchart or other diagram indicating the intended game flow, level arrangement, or structure. Print this out and nail it to the nearest wall.

One of the key differences between noninteractive and videogame writing is that, in the latter, changes of location are (currently at least) mandatory and usually rapid. Players have come to expect a significant variety of location within which to play, and so games tend to place their players in a series of disparate environments in a relatively short period of (narrative) time. Similarly, game environments are usually designed with a specific challenge or series of challenges in mind, which do not bear revisiting.

A typical noninteractive story may take its audience on a travelogue, keeping the scenery varied, but then again it may not. A movie may be set entirely in a single room (most courtroom drama spends a great proportion of time in a single location, for instance), and a novel could be written in which the protagonist never leaves his airplane seat (or, as in Stephen King's *Misery*, barely leaves his bed). In a videogame, writers usually must create stories that justify more variety and less repetition of location.

Location is obviously pertinent to the game's progress structure. Most likely, the game developer has planned a series of locations to develop before a writer is even hired (as the majority of developers do not employ full time writers). The creation of game environments is time-intensive and must proceed as soon as possible if the development pipeline is to be maintained further into the project. This obviously poses challenges to a game writer being brought into a project already in progress, however, who must take an extant series of locations and build a logically progressive story from that series.

The writer must check, at the earliest possible opportunity (usually after delivery of game documentation has been taken and analyzed), whether there is any freedom in terms of location sequencing. Often the structure of a game may be altered if the project is young enough. Also check to see whether the developer may be willing to allow the player to revisit already-seen locations for narrative purposes (the writer will often want a character to revisit a particular place at a given point in the story—and would not have to think twice before doing so while writing a novel). Even if the writer ends up not taking advantage of these possibilities, it is important to know how much plotting flexibility is available.

In a linearly structured game with a straightforward story, it's usually advantageous for the writer to keep the narrative simple and justify the progress of location as simply as possible. Remember, as long as the narrative doesn't damage a player's experience, it doesn't need to make sense of every aspect of the game. More damage is done by trying to make narrative sense of every game feature than is done by ignoring the occasional peculiarity forced upon the story by the game.

With the structure established, the writer may begin to consider the expositional necessities. These fall broadly into two categories—things the player must know to play the game (gameplay information), and things the player must know to understand the story (story information). The writer must then consider which information they intend to deliver to the player at which point in the game. If cut scenes are to be used, now is the time to design and write them. After deciding what exposition to deliver by cut scenes, determining what requires in-game delivery becomes easier.

Player Agency

Agency refers to the capacity for a player to effect meaningful changes in a game world, or at least the illusion that the player has this capacity. As suggested at the start of this chapter, the key aspect of game writing is that the majority of narrative material in games is delivered in response to player action. The player has agency in terms of the narrative, and the game writer must consider the player's role in the game and deliver narrative that takes this role into account.

The primary method of doing this is, as much as possible, to respond to the player's actions within the game-space. To do this, the writer must know what actions are possible of the player.

As suggested, all games are systems of interactions bounded by rulesets. The rules of a game determine the possibilities for player agency; in totality, these rules create the game-space within which the player can act. The player cannot generally take any action that is not allowed by the rules (although some outcomes may emerge organically from the rules and be difficult to anticipate in advance). This applies both on the physical level of the game—the player character cannot walk through walls—and to the abstract level of the game—players cannot upgrade their characters' skills except via the mechanism provided. Similarly, if an action can be taken, there must be a way for the player to take that action, facilitated by the game interface.

By understanding what actions are possible and how those actions are taken in terms of the game interface, the game writer can both understand the aesthetic of the game (and thus better serve it with narrative material) and also predict the level of player interaction with the game-space. This latter is particularly important, as the writer wants to support and acknowledge those interactions as much as possible, in service to the story.

Narrative Triggering and Narrative Engines

The key element to in-game narrative is to recognize which form of trigger is the most useful to the storyteller. A trigger is an event within the game-space that creates a tangible effect on the game program. For instance, if the player unlocks a door, a flag is set to indicate that this door is now open. This event may also be used to trigger dialogue or other narrative material.

There are various possibilities for narrative triggers. The most basic is a location-based method in which the player enters a specific area of the game environment, and this triggers narrative material. An event-based method involves the player completing a given challenge, which triggers the narrative material. Note that in both cases, although it's usual to deliver material relevant to the location, event, or game situation, it isn't necessary. Triggers may be used to deliver material for color (that is to say, to enrich the feeling of authenticity) or to advance a sub-plot or character relations.

Other triggers may also be used. Within a specific area, time-based triggers can be useful to deliver gameplay tips; if a player hasn't solved a certain puzzle or reached a certain stage of the challenge in a given time, help dialogue can be provided. Color dialogue may also be time-activated, if the writer wants to ensure a constantly paced stream of color. Time-activated dialogue runs the risk of clashing with other dialogue, however, so location-triggered methods are preferable because they allow for greater control. Look for any periods of play downtime within a level, and use these to deliver inessential color.

An obvious trigger is that of NPCs. A given game design will have specific rules for NPC dialogue; sometimes the player must approach the NPC and trigger dialogue via a control, and sometimes NPCs will talk when triggered by player proximity.

Another form of player-solicited dialogue involves a talk control. Here, a player control activates speech, either from the player character or via some other device such as a sidekick. This may relate to location, to allow the player to gain information, or may be general in nature, and be limited to color. This latter requires a large amount of alternative lines to be generated, to ensure that the player doesn't hear the same line again and again should they press their talk button repeatedly. Different dialogue should be written for each discrete portion of the game.

One last form of triggering involves multiple game events, such as collecting a number of like objects or completing a number of challenges. A player's relationship with a game may be deepened if the game actively comments upon their successes. For instance, an NPC in a platform adventure is intended to provide game tutorial information; after this role is complete, the NPC may be used as a form of statistical database, possibly commenting upon the number of successes the player has had in relation to the activity the NPC taught. A character who trains the player in combat may be written as having a dislike of trolls, for instance, and may count and comment upon how many trolls the player has defeated. Lines of dialogue may be written for every 10 trolls slain. This style of writing encourages the player to return and talk to NPCs, which in turn deepens the feeling of the game world being a real place in which to spend time and enhances the player's relationship with the game.

The determination of narrative triggers is a vital part of dialogue engine design. Dialogue engines are game systems devoted to the delivery of narrative material, such as speech and cut scenes. Although the dialogue engine is usually created by the designer, the game writer may and perhaps should be at least involved in the task. Chapter 14 devotes itself to dialogue engine design in detail.

The game writer should be encouraged to be creative when considering the use of their narrative materials. Specifically, any technique that aids the illusion that the game understands the player's actions is of tremendous benefit.

Assisting the Player

A key aspect of game writing is in aiding the player. To begin with, information must be written for the game to be able to teach its own play via game tutorials. Also, certain game puzzles or challenges may require optional or time-based aid to the player to avoid play bottlenecks. Finally, players must always be aware of their goals and must have a method of checking those goals should they forget.

One of the key decisions that must be made by the development team as a whole is how to approach nongame-reality material, specifically within game tutorials. For instance, an NPC is teaching the player how to use the game's combat system. Does the character use the terms "A button," "B button," and so on? Do they refer to the controls in terms of their uses ("press the attack button!")? Do they avoid all reference to game controls in an attempt to preserve game reality ("Attack me!" rather than "Press A to attack me!").

Different teams prefer different solutions. Japanese developers seem to have no issue with characters talking about buttons and controls, whereas Western developers seem to dislike it. A common solution, which may be used as standard, is to have the game characters talk about actions entirely in terms suitable to game reality, while informing players of control information via unspoken text subtitle dialogue or visual display of the required buttons. Other, better solutions may be developed in the future.

In-game hints are tricky to get right. Some players may need help, but others may resent being helped when aid isn't necessary. One excellent, but expensive, solution is to use a talk button to allow the player to solicit help. This requires that a set of color dialogue should also be prepared for circumstances in which player help is unavailable, as a button should never fail to respond if it has any function at all. A second solution is to trigger help from a clock within a given game area. If the player hasn't progressed in a given time, drop a hint. This technique, however, can be dangerous, especially in games rich with exploration and collection. Players who are taking their time and searching every nook and cranny may be annoyed if the game constantly demands that they progress and repeatedly provides tips on how to do it.

In a free-roaming, exploration-oriented game, players may get lost in terms of what the story wants them to do next. This is undesirable for the majority of players, who want the story to advance at regular, paced intervals. A technique known as funneling may be used here. *Funneling* involves creating dialogue for one or more NPCs that are designed to lead the player back to the main game spine (discussed in detail in Chapter 5).

The usual technique is to use a single character, defined at an early point in the games as the go-to character should the player become stuck. Multiple lines of dialogue are written for this character, which are triggered at different points in the game. The specific points are determined by the progress structure, but they are likely to be successes in game challenges—bosses defeated, objects collected, puzzles solved. At each of these points, the writer should know where the player should go next if they want to continue with the spinal story. The funneling NPC may therefore point the player in the right direction.

The game writer must remember that the player's goal is to have fun. Different players achieve fun in different ways, but very few enjoy being stuck or lost in their game. All plot progression should be definitive, and all aid should be given to allow players to advance the plot should they lose sight of their current objectives.

Inessential Story Material

One concept that aids player involvement in a game is to allow them a certain amount of exploration of the story by seeding the game world with optional narrative triggers. For instance, text file in-game artifacts may deepen the player's understanding of the game world, and may be presented in the form of books in a library, files on a computer, recordings on a tape, and so forth. This information should be kept inessential to game progress, because not every player will want to seek out every last scrap of information.

Sensitivity to play pacing is important when incorporating these little details. Such inessential information should not interfere with fast-paced or tense sections of gameplay. Do not, for instance, position a text file just before a boss fight. After a boss fight is far more suitable, because at this point the player will be happy to take a short break from play. Better still, make the materials player-solicited by, for instance, having them for sale at an in-game shop.

Dialogue may also deliver inessential material, although its placement may be tricky. Naturally, NPC conversations will often involve information unrelated or tangential to the game spine. But comments from the player character themselves or a sidekick may be used to add color or deepen their personalities if triggered in the correct locations. These techniques can also be used to avoid large spaces of dialogue dead time. In general, such dialogue should occur at a roughly constant rate—although lines may be minutes apart, they should play regularly. Try to avoid following minutes of constant babble with minutes of silence. Dead time can be avoided by using a timer—if a few minutes go by without comment, trigger one from a set of color lines designed for that purpose.

CONCLUSION: A SUGGESTED WRITING PROCESS

This section presents a suggested writing process as a means of summarization. The art of game writing is in its infancy, and the game writer should feel free to experiment with process and technique to find better ways of strengthening the videogame experience with story materials. This suggested process provides a useful starting point for new game writers.

Property Analysis

The game writer must be fully aware of the intentions of the game development project. The first step is for the game writer to become familiar with game content (in terms of game system and intended play experience), any license or IP involved in the project, and the game's intended audience. At this stage, a broad understanding is sufficient. If the writer is not working in-house, a face-to-face meeting with key development staff is likely necessary.

If the game is based upon existing IP, research is required, and the writer will find it useful to compile a set of notes, including reference dialogue for key characters, to help set the IP tone. Most TV shows have a *bible*—a document that summarizes the key information about the show's characters and format. Always ask if there is a bible to accompany the IP, as it is a vital tool, and most licenses will have one that can be acquired by the developer from the licensor.

Story Overview/Story Design

If the game writer is to provide story design, this occurs immediately. In many cases, however, a story design will already have been created by development staff, so the writer must become familiar with it.

A basic narrative design overview document may be submitted that contains a breakdown of the required story exposition and any relevant dialogue engine details.

Narrative Design

When the story design is complete, the writer should begin determining expositional needs. Cut scene and in-game scripting likely will occur as two separate phases, and they should be treated as such. At this stage, the writer should determine which expositional material will occur in cut scene, which will be handled in-game, which is pertinent to the game's spine, and which is nonessential to the player.

If a complex dialogue engine is required, design should occur at this stage, either by the game designer or by the game designer in conjunction with the game writer. All possible narrative triggers should be reviewed, and narrative techniques should be assessed in line with the game budget. The dialogue engine should be documented and submitted to relevant parties. This document may also contain a detailed breakdown of cut scene materials.

Cut Scene Creation

Having ascertained the level of scripting detail required by the developer (from full direction to dialogue only), the writer prepares an initial draft of the cut scene script. This draft is assessed by the relevant development staff and is likely to proceed through a number of iterations. An external producer or similar representative of the publisher is likely to be involved on one pass, and, if relevant, any licensor representative will also be involved.

The final document will take the form of a series of scenes formatted in a similar manner to that of a TV or movie screenplay. Some developers prefer dialogue to be presented via spreadsheet, but nontechnical readers (such as external producers) and voice actors prefer traditional scripts, and such scripts are recommended for cut scene materials.

Full Design/Level Analysis

At this point, usually while other parties review cut scene materials, writers should immerse themselves in the game design documents. Ideally, level design documents will be available, but sometimes the development pipeline requires certain environments to be developed at a later stage, meaning that the writer must proceed when they can. Key issues at this stage involve the writer visualizing the player experience, considering how best to approach the narrative engine, and considering the necessary pacing issues.

No documentation is required at this stage, although the writer may find it useful to compile personal notes.

In-Game Narrative Materials

The writer now generates the in-game narrative materials, which is most likely dialogue. This is usually the largest portion of the work, and the writer should bear in mind that changes may be made to the game design at any point, which may necessitate changes to the scripting. Generate multiple lines of dialogue in cases of uncertainty.

For large, distributed scripts, a spreadsheet may be the most functional writing tool. For smaller scripts, a word processor document is common, in a similar format to that of the cut scene script. Never replicate material internal to a script, as this may lead to it being recorded twice.

Initial Testing and Checking

In games with a complex narrative engine, the script is usually checked in situ via subtitles, although test dialogue is sometimes recorded using development staff. Look for clashes in dialogue, as well as obvious mistakes such as dialogue that is triggered in the wrong place or lines that fail to make sense in the context in which they appear (something that often happens when a single set of dialogue lines is used for multiple circumstances in the game).

Dialogue Recording

Voice actors are key to defining the personality of characters. Before recording begins, no matter how little time is available, take the time to fully explore the voice actors' range, and ask them to provide a few different voice concepts for their characters. Record a few key lines in the chosen style to use in confirming the chosen voice should it begin to slip during long recording sessions.

Allow voice actors to improvise, but don't hesitate to ask them to read a line several times. Be prepared to rewrite lines on the spot, should the lines prove to be unwieldy, inauthentic, or if the voice actors feels that they are out of character. This is especially useful when writing for voice actors from the same native country as their character; for instance, a UK writer, no matter how accomplished, is not as likely to nail various US dialects as well as a professional American voice actor.

Writers should take a spare copy of the script to the recording session, and change any lines that become altered during recording on that script. It may then act as a template for subtitle material with all the necessary changes compiled in one place.

Voice actors are discussed in more detail in Chapter 12.

Final Testing and Checking

A second round of checking occurs, with the recorded dialogue *in situ* (in place). The game writer is unlikely to be involved at this stage, however. After the work is completed, all that is left is to wait nine months for your contributor's copy of the game and assess how you can improve next time.

4 Nonlinear Game Narrative

Mary DeMarle

Awriter walks into a design meeting at We Make Fantasy Games, Inc., an independent game developer. She's ready. She's prepared. She's thought about the "Hero's Journey" and knows exactly how events in the game must transpire to bring about the story's maximum emotional impact. The design team is going to love it!

She starts her pitch. She's barely five minutes into her description of how the hero stumbles upon a nondescript cabin in the woods and goes inside, only to encounter the old woman who's been concealing the "Rubric of Time" beneath a glazed yellow flower pot for months, when the lead game designer interrupts her.

"Hold on. What if the player doesn't go in the cabin?"

"Sorry?"

"I asked, what if the player doesn't go in the cabin?"

"He has to go in the cabin."

"Well, what if he doesn't? What if he decides to check out the next town first? Or what if he decides to blow the cabin up? I mean, he's just discovered the Rod of Cataclysmic Infernos hidden in a stump in the woods. What if he aims it at the cabin and fires?"

"Why would he do that?"

"Because he can."

These three words can prove the bane of a game writer's existence. No matter how skilled writers become, how much time they spend studying fiction, how much experience they have acquired writing novels, plays, or screenplays, nothing adequately prepares them for the consequences resulting from the player's actions. In effect, game writers are co-writing stories with people they never meet: the players. The player has more control over how the action unfolds than the writer and, in some cases, will take a perverse delight in trying to break the mechanisms put in place to ensure the orderly unfolding of the narrative.

71

Writing a story for a nonlinear game is vastly different from writing a book or a movie. Elements of the process may be the same—the need to create characters, dialogues, settings, and conflicts, for instance—but the manner in which game writers must approach them is significantly different. The recipient of a nonlinear game story isn't passive to the process—he or she is an active participant in the way the plot unfolds. No matter how game writers define their protagonists' motivations, the behavior of the *player* determines how they will act in the final game. And often, the player won't want to do what the writer's storyline requires.

This is the challenge that underlies writing nonlinear games. Game writers who want to create nonlinear stories must first understand the problems presented by this unique form, and then learn techniques to make the process manageable. This chapter examines the process of creating nonlinear game narratives, and the problems and pitfalls therein.

STORY VERSUS GAME

Stories in games have a job to do. They need to *motivate* (keep the player engaged) and *entertain* (by supporting the gameplay and pacing of core aspects of the game). The value of a game's story is that it can detach the players from familiar surroundings for awhile, allowing them to become wholly immersed in the game experience. The caveat is that once drawn into the game, players expect that engrossment to be complete. Any inconsistency or implausibility in the story raises doubts. Too many doubts and the player may abandon the game altogether or at least have their enjoyment of the experience marred.

Writing an effective nonlinear game story is a challenge because *story* and *game* are essentially incompatible. Their end goal is similar—each seeks to create an unpredictable, yet highly satisfying entertainment experience—but to achieve it, they rely on opposite constraints. The power of a story comes from its *structure*. The power of a game comes from its *freedom*.

When designing a story, a writer comes up with a sequence of scenes and dialogues that unfolds consecutively in front of the audience. As each new piece is revealed, it adds to the audience's understanding and shapes how they think and feel about what's going to come next. Traditionally, the structure of a story resembles what is depicted in Figure 4.1.

The ordering of each scene is important because of the information it contains. Because the goal is to build to a dramatic climax, certain elements must be revealed before others. Likewise, all the characters involved in the story must be made ready, physically and psychologically, so that by the time the climax comes, characters' actions makes sense. If not, the audience will have grave questions, such as "Wait a minute. How did he know that gun wasn't loaded?" or "When did the hero learn to speak Vietnamese?"

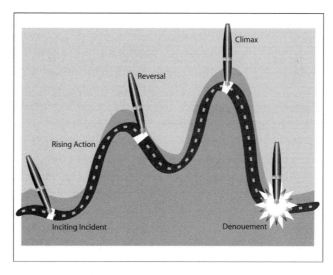

FIGURE 4.1   The narrative structure of a story.

In books, television, and movies, this presents a challenge, but it's one the writer has total control over. Characters must go where the writer sends them. Once there, they'll discover exactly what the writer needs them to know. Thus, when the time comes for the dramatic climax to take place, the hero will have found every clue and every weapon because the writer has very carefully made sure of it.

The same is not true in a nonlinear game. In a nonlinear game, there's always a character who is out of the writer's control: the player character (or avatar). As enacted by the player, the avatar is doing whatever it wants, experimenting with different paths, and constantly bypassing the writer's ever-so-carefully planned structure.

The avatar is empowered to do so because the game's designers have provided a whole toolbox of elements from which the player can choose: abilities, weapons, power-ups, obstacles, even game levels. And while these tools might all be governed by fixed rules and constraints, the player's decision to use them—let alone take the path that will lead to uncovering them—is not.

This leads to an inevitable problem: how can game writers ensure that when the dramatic moment in the game's story is reached, the player will have definitely seen all the major story points and acquired every tool, weapon, or clue needed to fully appreciate it? Game designers and writers have struggled with this issue for some time. This next section examines some of the techniques that writers can use to help overcome this problem.

MERGING STORY AND GAME

Story and game can be combined in many different ways. In the previous chapter, these were characterized as implicit narrative (where the story is largely in the mind of the player), formal narrative (where the story is chiefly linear), interactive narrative (where the exposition of the story relates to player action), and interactive story (where the plot itself may alter as a result of player action).

In the context of a formal narrative, the usual option for merging a linear story with a nonlinear game is by defining the game and the story as two separate entities being delivered in the same product. Interactivity is constrained to being part of the game, whereas the story remains linear and static. As has already been discussed in earlier chapters, this is acceptable but has limitations. Cut scenes are expensive and only work in a game context when delivered at suitable junctures: if the bulk of the player's time with a game is spent with cut scenes that must be watched instead of game material that can be played, why make a game in the first place?

In the context of implicit narrative, it is possible to provide a high degree of interactivity but for it all to be effectively meaningless at the story level; the game essentially deceives the player as to the degree of influence they wield. For instance, in a game such as *Grand Theft Auto: San Andreas* (Rockstar North, 2004), the player can do just about anything to people they meet on the street; can be chased by the police; can earn money from any one of a vast variety of activities, including robbery and vigilantism; and can even purchase houses and clothing. In terms of the implicit narrative that emerges from the player's interaction with the game world, this is highly satisfactory. However, nothing that the player does will in any way affect any cut scene that occurs because these are prescripted. If the player has $2 million in the bank, it won't stop C.J. (the protagonist in *San Andreas*) from commenting in a cut scene that he needs money even if this makes no sense in terms of the implicit narrative the player has been enjoying.

In the context of interactive narrative, there are more advanced ways of merging a linear story with nonlinear gameplay. One such approach is to view the game as a series of challenges that players can undertake in any order. The game writer can just assume that the player will be able to get through each challenge *somehow*, and then map the story's linear progression over the progression of completed game challenges (as shown in Figure 4.2).

This technique, which has been called *gating the story*, is relatively effective, and is used in many games as a simple solution to the problems of nonlinearity. In a gated story, the plot unfolds as a series of linear checkpoints that players unlock in sequence after having explored groupings of game sections in any order they choose. This has the advantage of being easy to both conceive and implement and can be found in a large number of commercial games.

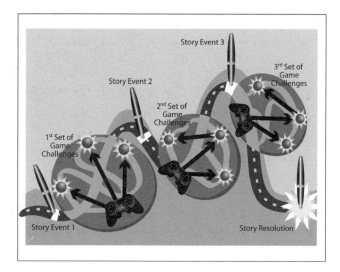

FIGURE 4.2   One method of mapping a linear story to a nonlinear game.

However, as the game literacy of players has risen, there has been an increasing capability among players to recognize when they are granted some agency and when it is denied to them. Because stories require a willing suspension of disbelief before emotional involvement can take hold, we are in problematic territory when we present a story that is self evidently rigged. Players may still manage to enjoy the game, but they may struggle to enjoy the story when it is so separated from their actions. (The exception to this lies in games whose core experience is so focused on adrenalin-pounding action that the story elements exist primarily as relief and reward, such that player agency in the narrative elements is inessential.)

In the context of interactive story, we have the option of allowing one or more aspects of the story to change in response to the player's actions. NPCs may reveal different pieces of information depending on how the player chooses to interact with them. Or, plot events that occur within the story may unfold in different ways depending on which environments the player investigates first and what he chooses to do when he gets there. To achieve this kind of player-driven story, you have to set up branch points in your plot, and then determine every single outcome to which they lead. A branching story structure ends up looking like the one depicted in Figure 4.3.

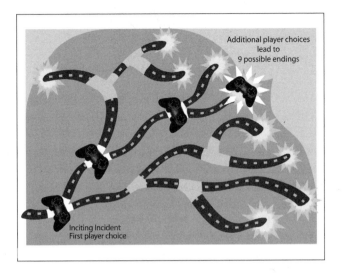

FIGURE 4.3 Example of a branching story structure.

The problem with this structure is that it creates a combinatorial explosion of unused resources—3D environments, character animations, dialog recordings, and so on—that players never experience, but which the game's production team has to create nonetheless. Because every resource created requires time and money to build, your producer is more than likely to squash this approach the minute you present it. You may be able to successfully argue that a branching storyline increases the game's replay value, but most players will only play a story-based game once before moving on to something new.

You can limit the combinatorial explosion by recombining paths at certain key story points. Players are then required to pass through every reconnected point in a specific order, but they have some freedom in deciding how they're going to get there, as shown in Figure 4.4.

This method, which has been called *parallel paths*, balances linear and branching structures. It is the essence of the manner by which *Deus Ex* (Ion Storm, 2000) achieved its nonlinear story content. This approach can greatly increase the player's involvement in the game's story because it grants the player some agency in the development of the story. However, the parallel path system is still, at heart, a branching story structure. To implement such a model, more resources must be built for the game than players will see. Plus, to be successful, each branch must provide an experience that is significantly different from any other; otherwise, the players' choices become meaningless. *Deus Ex* may have been praised for its nonlinear narrative content, but it came at a very literal price: the additional development costs this method engendered meant the game required a larger audience to make back its development costs. No game yet has definitively turned interactive story into a profitable endeavor.

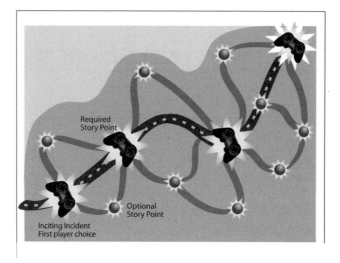

FIGURE 4.4   A branching story structure in which branches recombine.

It seems that however a linear story is merged with a nonlinear game (or for that matter, a nonlinear story with a nonlinear game), there are problems that are at the very least awkward and in the worst case, insurmountable. However, we have already seen that there is a tremendous difference between the narrative and the story of a game. It is easier to render an interactive narrative than an interactive story because in interactive narrative, the story can remain essentially linear even though the player's experience of that story occurs nonlinearly. If the only problem with "gating the story" is that the players may uncover their lack of agency, can we not take steps to create a satisfying illusion of agency?

LEVERAGING PLAYER EXPERIENCE

For any given game, the term story can be applied at essentially two levels. In the first case, there is the story that the writer sets out to tell. This includes all the major plot events, any and all character development, and whatever plot devices the writer introduces to create a powerful experience. This can be considered the *high-level* story. It's the story you hear summarized in game magazine reviews; the story with which game writers are traditionally most occupied. The player uncovers this high-level story through the narrative experience of the game.

The other level at which story exists in a game is less often recognized, but is inherent to all games, even those with no overt narrative. This is the story that the player *experiences* when playing the game. It's completely personal and different every time because it's the story of that particular player's experience with this particular game. This can be considered the *immediate-level* story. This is created by what the player thinks and feels while playing, by the strategies employed to figure out how to win, and even through the irrelevant distractions the player chooses for entertainment within the game. It's the internal narrative players create that recaps their gameplay experience.

For example:

> "My brother and I were playing *Stratego* last night. He'd beaten me three times already and I really didn't want to lose again. I thought about placing my flag in the corner and surrounding it completely with bombs, but he always goes straight for the corners. So then I thought why not place the bombs there anyway, but instead of putting the flag behind them, I'd place the Marshal there, as kind of a ruse. Meanwhile, the real flag would be closer to the center of the board, with the Admiral and maybe the Spy close by. It was a risk, but I thought it might work. Sure enough, he went straight for the corner. When that first bomb blew up, and then the Marshal attacked, man was he annoyed!"

Obviously, there's a very powerful story going on here. Just as obviously, it was certainly never written into the original game of *Stratego* when Milton Bradley created it in 1960. But stories like this are being created and experienced by players every day, every time they play a game. When gamers talk about playing *Halo* (Bungie, 2003) or *Half Life 2* (Valve, 2004), they do not talk about what the Master Chief or Gordon Freeman accomplished, they talk about what *they* did or felt when facing a specific moment in the game. They tell their own immediate-level story.

Because immediate-level stories are so personal, they can be more powerful than any high-level story a writer creates. By leveraging the player's experience, game writers can use the immediate-level stories that naturally occur as opportunities to get players more emotionally invested in the story of the game.

Consider this example: Someone is playing a third-person mystery game. In the course of the hero's investigation, the trail leads into a three-story apartment complex at night. The player decides it's the perfect opportunity to find out exactly how much of the game environment he can screw around with. He enters one of the bathrooms and starts turning on faucets. Then, just for fun, he flushes the toilet several times. The story doesn't require the player to do this; he does it because he wants to test the limits of the world. He also doesn't think anything will result from his actions. After all, why should it?

So what happens to the player's appreciation of the game if, in the very next apartment he visits, he overhears someone complaining about how water must be running somewhere because the water pressure keeps getting worse? What happens to his appreciation of the *story* if the very next morning he walks into a nearby café and hears the waitress complaining about getting burned while taking a shower the night before because, "Some idiot in the building kept flushing the toilet!"

This tiny, unexpected detail makes it clear to players that their actions are important. The player in the example did something on a whim and not only did the game recognize it, but the narrative reflected the consequences of this action. Naturally, the high-level story was unaffected, but the illusion of agency has been delivered to the player, and the player as a result has become more emotionally invested in the story.

Another example can be found in *Myst IV: Revelation* (Ubisoft Montreal Studios, 2004). In the early portion of the game, a limited branching path is provided to the player. While following a walkway outside a series of buildings, the player sees a young girl step into a doorway ahead and say, "Hey, come here! You've got to see this!" At this point, the player has a choice: go to the girl immediately or ignore her and check out a side path.

If the player heads straight to the girl, she'll show him the item she's found. But if he checks out the side path first, he'll enter a room that contains, among other things, a terrarium full of flying beetles. If the player plays with the terrarium, all of its beetles immediately escape. At which point, most players start thinking, "Uh-oh…!"

The player can now return to the main path and approach the girl. When he gets to her, she tells him he's too late to see the item she'd found and instead, tells him about the beetle project she's been working on. Knowing he just let all of her beetles escape, the player is thinking he's really in trouble at this point. Sure enough, later in the game the girl enters the beetle room while the player is there and berates him for ruining her experiment.

None of these actions affect the course of the high-level story. But they have a significant impact on players: from this point on, players are going to think twice about the actions they take in the game because the story seems to recognize what they do. Using the immediate-level story again to create similar experiences later on will only reinforce this feeling and keep players emotionally invested in your story.

The illusion of agency created by reflecting player action in dialogue is so powerful that it doesn't matter that players have little or no capability to alter the high-level story: their immediate-level stories has been enriched, and that means the players have almost certainly entered into a state of immersion with the game.

When attempting to construct stories for nonlinear games, the general goal is to *integrate* linear stories into nonlinear gameplay (accepting for the time being that nonlinear stories are expensive propositions, at least without further technical advances). That goal requires game writers to find ways to embed story into the player's gameplay experience.

TECHNIQUES FOR EMBEDDING STORY

Nonlinear game writers must by necessity think in different terms to writers in conventional media. Game writers cannot think exclusively about plot, rising action, and building to a climax, and instead must begin thinking about creating a *world* in which the line between narrative and gameplay is blurred. This doesn't mean that plot and dramatic climaxes aren't important: they remain essential to the high-level story and cannot be ignored. But as story becomes embedded with gameplay, players cease to be passively following a story and begin instead to explore their own story within the game-space. This section explores techniques that can be used to encourage this outcome.

Eliminate Internal Inconsistencies

Before anything else, it's essential to begin by plugging any holes in the story. Although this may seem obvious, it is vitally important that the story is internally consistent before anything more can be done. In a static media, inconsistencies can be hidden from the audience to a certain degree, but in a dynamic medium such as nonlinear games, the player has more time and capability to explore the narrative space—inconsistencies are not only at risk of being uncovered, they can begin to unravel the entire tapestry of the story.

Players will have a variety of different responses to inconsistencies—a few will devise their own mental models to eliminate them, but many will become confused or annoyed. Either way, the player's attention is diverted from play, which cannot be beneficial.

Internal consistency must apply to every character, every line of dialogue, and every branching story path the player encounters. This means game writers must be especially careful with recombinant branches, as the game state can become ambiguous, leading to dialogue that risks being inaccurate or in the worst cases wholly inappropriate.

Always strive to create new places and characters on a logical framework so that it will be possible later to pick and choose which elements best support the story and which are peripheral. The nature of a nonlinear game means that a game writer cannot communicate everything they perhaps would like, but players generally only need enough detail to convince them that they are within a consistent and believable world.

Provided the story is consistent, the risk of incongruent elements detracting from the player's immersion in the game world can be eliminated.

Identify Storytelling Vehicles

Books rely on words to create images and express conflict, and films use dialogue, close-ups, reaction shots, and music, among other techniques, but the narrative language of games is still being developed. Despite the apparent similarities between films and games, the opportunity exists in games to take storytelling further in part because the player has such increased access to a game-world relative to the world of a book or a movie. This situation means that game writers have access to a surprising variety of storytelling vehicles that can be co-opted to narrative purposes.

First, there are all the narrative delivery methods discussed in previous chapters—such as in-game artifacts, cut scenes, and dialogue. These are generally always available in one form or another, although the volume of cut scenes (camera cases, in-game, and FMV) varies from project to project and from budget to budget. Beyond these clearly defined areas, however, games present many additional options for contributing to the storytelling process.

Consider the environment a player passes through while trying to reach an important gameplay destination. For example, imagine a ramshackle city. The appearance of this location has no direct bearing on gameplay, but it can still be used as a vehicle for supporting storytelling. Are the buildings broken and falling to pieces the further inward the player goes? Perhaps it's because the city's inhabitants are too self-involved to repair them. Is there a layer of fog (a particle effect) that clings to the ground and grows thicker the closer you get to the city center? Maybe it means the corruption began with the city's rulers and is moving steadily outward to absorb everyone.

Similarly, in a game with an inventory, the appearance of objects can be used as a means to support the narrative. If inventory objects are to be modeled, visual clues can be used. For example, if a story surrounds a particular family, the family crest can be established visually in a certain location (perhaps via a camera case upon entry, so that the player will certainly see this emblem). Consequently, an object can be linked to the family solely by use of this crest. If handled carefully, this link need never be exposed in cumbersome dialogue; it can be a subtle detail for players to spot independently.

Although dialogue and cut scenes are the most direct storytelling vehicles and the chief areas that game writers wield influence, there is the potential for the story to affect *every* element of the game-world. It is simply a matter of effective communication between the game writer and the other members of the development team, and careful thought about which elements of the game-world can be used as storytelling vehicles.

Layer in the Details

Not every element of a story is essential to its resolution. Game writers should take the time to explore their options in this regard. Identify which details players absolutely *have* to encounter for the plot to be coherent and easily grasped, and note those that merely add depth to the tale—depth which may increase a player's appreciation for the story but that isn't critical to understand the plot.

Not every player will want to know every detail of any given story. Some just want to play through the game as fast as they can, enjoying the game mechanics or experience and ignoring the story entirely. Others will go down every path; read every signpost, diary entry, and scrap of paper lying around, before talking to every NPC they meet just to get the full scope of the story. Both approaches can be satisfied.

One approach is to determine a relevance rating for every detail you want to convey in the game. For example, consider a simple scale from one to six: details that are crucial for understanding the barest minimum of plot get a (1). Details that add to that understanding in decreasingly significant ways get a (2) or a (3) or a (4). Those that are merely icing on the cake are down in the (5) to (6) range.

Having examined the relevance of each detail, these can then be matched to the storytelling vehicles that have been identified. Some delivery methods are more effective at conveying important story details than others. For instance, visuals can be extremely effective at conveying mood and theme, and sometimes they can be used to express character. The bedroom of a king, for instance, might be populated with objects and decorated in a style that expresses his desire for power, love of wealth, and great antipathy toward people of a lower class. But not every player who sees the room will catch this, so if it's an important aspect of your plot, you need to use a storytelling vehicle that will express it more overtly, or reinforce the idea by expressing it in multiple ways.

Having determined which details are most crucial for players to learn, these can be assigned to the most effective storytelling vehicles available—be it a cinematic, an NPC interaction, or a voice-over dialogue that's delivered to the player at a specific story juncture. These vehicles must be placed within the game in areas where every player will, at some point, encounter them. Less important details can be relegated to vehicles that aren't as effective or placed in areas that players aren't required to visit.

Reinforce narrative details throughout the game as much as possible, especially the important ones! Most details can be expressed by more than one vehicle, which makes this easier to achieve. Layering details into the game in this way helps ensure that the story is embedded in the game and simultaneously helps ensure that the players will understand the story, no matter what order they encounter its details.

Think Modular

The key to designing stories for nonlinear games is to remember that, except when a game project relies upon programming tricks or carefully crafted linear level designs, players aren't going to encounter every detail in the order you want. They're going to go where *they* want to go and do the things they want to do first. For a story to make sense in a nonlinear context, you need to create story moments that allow players to travel from scene A to scene C and then back to scene B again and still get the same story—or at least the same value in the story—as if they had uncovered them in sequential order.

Fortunately, human nature can be trusted to apply most of the time, and it is human nature to attempt to predict outcomes. When people watch a movie or read a good book, it generally isn't an entirely passive experience. A part of their mind is actively at work, trying to predict where the story is going or at least trying to imagine the consequences of actions. Every new piece of information received, every consecutive scene or dialogue exchange witnessed, all adds to their comprehension, changing what they think about what's going to come. Give a person the slightest bit of information, and they will usually try to make sense of it. They'll wrap a story around its existence that explains where it came from and where it's most likely to lead. When the next piece of information arrives, they'll change their internal story to adapt to this new piece of knowledge, if necessary. And if it doesn't make perfect sense, chances are they'll wait a little while for another piece of information to get added that does.

When constructing a story for a nonlinear game, use this instinctive, internal thought process advantageously. Think in terms of modular narrative components: think of every individual story detail as a standalone piece from a puzzle that's yet to be assembled. As a mechanism for exploring this, writers can put the story details on index cards. These can then be shuffled and read through in a random sequence. This process can be repeated to see what effect a different sequence has on the outcome. If a coherent story lies underneath the modular components of the narrative, it should be possible to detect it each time the order is changed. If not, the story may need to be decomposed into more modular components.

By examining a story in this way, the underlying story might not be the same as was originally intended, but game writers should remain flexible when dealing with nonlinear narrative. If the essence of a story can be captured in isolated chunks that hint at possible directions—directions that become reshaped and clarified as a new piece of information is added at random—the story is already becoming a less linear, more emergent story.

CONCLUSION

Combining a formal narrative with a game through simple techniques (such as cut scenes between gameplay segments) represents a first step toward transforming a story into a game. Similarly, implicit narrative presents a first step in games transforming into stories—albeit mostly through the imagination of the player. In the middle ground—interactive narratives and interactive stories—the most creative and adventurous processes are at work, whether this is embedding an effectively linear story into a nonlinear game or the more ambitious work of rendering a nonlinear story in a nonlinear game. This can be achieved by gating the story via parallel paths or by more complicated methods (beyond the scope of this book).

Whatever approach is chosen, the illusion of player agency can be created and maintained through interactive narrative techniques and particularly by reflecting player actions in dialogue and set pieces. Such approaches leverage the player experience so that the players are sufficiently absorbed in the details of their immediate-level story that they will be less inclined to notice that they have little or no influence over the high-level story. By valuing each player's experience in this way, the quality of the story experience is heightened, and all players are likely to enjoy playing the game (and exploring the story) more than if their actions clearly have no tangible consequences.

The more nonlinear the game, the more the story must adapt to service it. This begins by eliminating all internal inconsistencies and proceeds through a process of arranging the narrative in modular sections that can be layered into the game-space via numerous different storytelling vehicles, both the classic game-writing tools and by more subtle methods requiring more intimate cooperation with the rest of the development team.

Ultimately, the purpose of attempting nonlinear narrative in games is to provide the player with an experience that is something more than just a conventionally delivered story and also something more than a typical gameplay experience. Nonlinear narrative allows people to play the story and (crucially) to play it how they choose. In the future, it may be possible to render true nonlinear interactive stories by procedural methods, but at the moment, such mechanisms are fanciful at best. Until then, game writers will continue to experiment with the narrative language of games and stretch the boundaries of interactive narrative by taking players on ever more inventive journeys.

5 Keeping the Player on Track

Chris Bateman

At the very core of the job of the game writer is communicating with the player. This may involve communicating elements of the narrative, passing on game information such as current goals, or tutoring the player in the game mechanics or other subtleties of the design. This communication is unlike any other in the modern world, as the player never gets to talk to the game writer. Instead, the writer must anticipate the issues the player will face, taking into account as broad a spectrum of problems as will encompass the likely difficulties faced by each and every member of the game's audience (a group of people of potentially infinite diversity).

Although the range of play experiences expressed within games is extremely large, in general terms, the game writer wants to deliver sufficient assistance to allow the player to enjoy the game and to do so using the least obtrusive mechanisms. Ideally, all the information is delivered through the metaphors and devices of the narrative, without recourse to meta-level references except when explicitly required (such as showing the player which control does what).

Each game has a very different feel in terms of how the player is to be instructed and led, as some game experiences are enhanced by subtle obfuscation, while others require a degree of explicit instruction that may border on the patronizing in the eyes of some players. No matter where the game is pitched in terms of its audience and the goals of its play, it will be necessary in some way to communicate to the player when they are doing what is expected of them or when they are behaving in a way contrary to what is required to progress. The path of the game should be clearly illuminated, even if the player is not expected or required to follow it.

FREEDOM VERSUS CLARITY

Game design and game writing are beset with issues of balance, often between two or more extremes. In terms of keeping the player on the path of the game, the essential tension is between the player's freedom and the need for clarity of instruction. On the one hand, we want the players to feel free to explore and to play within the game world, but on the other hand, we need players to know what they are supposed to be doing.

Every game needs to make a decision as to where to pitch itself between these two extremes—favoring either player freedom or clarity of instruction. Note that *clarity of instruction* refers to ongoing instructions the player is receiving about what to do *next*—not the initial instructions that the player receives in a tutorial or training level. Every game is assumed to have some degree of tutorial material, which should perhaps be considered by a separate standard to the main gameplay.

Why presuppose that clear instructions undermine player freedom and vice versa? It is a question of psychology. If players receive an instruction from the game, such as "go to the docks and buy a sandwich," they face an obvious choice: cooperate with the game and do as it asks or resist the game and attempt to do whatever they want to do instead. The more the game clarifies its goal by, for example, repeating the required action, the more the player is likely to feel constrained. Conversely, the more the game supports the player's ability to ignore the instructions it provides, the less clear the path of the game becomes.

For instance, if players do not immediately go to the docks and buy a sandwich, there are questions as to how the game reacts to this situation. Does it give the instruction again (favoring clarity) or wait for the players to comply (favoring freedom)? Does it automatically take players to the docks and force them to buy a sandwich (favoring clarity at the total expense of freedom) or adapt so that a player's choice not to follow this instruction is respected—perhaps by having an NPC purchase the sandwich independently.

In general, each game project must have its own policy as to the extent to which the player will be expected to follow a set path. In a game world, freedom can be seen as the capacity players possess to step away from the set path and define their own play and their own implicit story. At the furthest extreme of freedom, the player may be afforded so much autonomy that a conventional narrative can no longer be supported, and the role of the game writer ceases to be involved in story construction, but in a more complicated game design exercise beyond the scope of this chapter.

In any game with an explicit narrative, however, there must be one (or more) preset paths through the logical space of the game that constitute the story or stories of the game. Constructing this path—or the narrative materials associated with this path—is one of the more challenging tasks facing any game writer.

THE SPINE OF THE GAME AND THE GOLDEN PATH

In a book, film, play, or TV show, the story delivers itself automatically—from beginning, to middle, to end. In a game, however, the story is rarely delivered so automatically. Because the player is generally cast in the role of the central protagonist (although this need not be the case), the player is often obligated to travel to specific locations or complete certain tasks to complete the game. The sequence of journeys and tasks the player is expected to complete to follow the game story from the beginning to the end can be termed the *spine* of the game (or the *game spine*).

The spine of any game consists of events that are absolutely mandatory. If those events do not happen, the story will not progress. The game may feature any number of side-plots or optional activities that are not involved in completing the game or its story, and these cannot be (by definition) considered part of the game's spine. The spine therefore also specifies those elements of the story that the player is guaranteed to experience.

Most games have an entirely linear spine, or a spine that supports a small amount of flexibility in terms of the sequence of events but no variation in which events are involved in completing the game and its story. Often, those games that prominently feature a story prefer to have *all* the narrative material in the game spine, which is to say that these games do not afford the player any capacity to stray away from the path of the story. This, however, is by no means guaranteed.

Many games—in particular cRPGs and other games that place a premium on the players' ability to explore the game world at their own pace—allow the player some capacity to stray from the game's spine. Often such variations involve self-contained subquests (equivalent to subplots in conventional storytelling) that effectively branch from the spine at various points. As a general rule, the more expensive the cost of delivering narrative material, the less freedom the player is granted. For instance, if the story is delivered almost entirely in cut scenes, there will usually be very few cut scenes that are not part of the game spine. The developer invested considerable cost in making the cut scenes, so they want to ensure that all the players will get to see them. This is part of the reason that cRPGs conduct a large proportion of their narrative content in text, or in recorded voices, only. It would be too expensive to render all such interactions in cut scenes. If the actual dialogue is going to vary to any degree, even prerecorded voice isn't an option (at least until text-to-speech systems improve).

The *golden path* of a game can be taken to mean the optimal route through the game. It differs from the concept of a game spine only in that the golden path is assumed to be the route of least resistance and maximum reward. In many games, the golden path and the spine are essentially the same; however, some game designers prefer to obscure the golden path slightly. The player must venture away from the path that corresponds to the spine of the game to some degree to find the golden path.

Therefore, we have two paths to consider: the path the player must walk to complete the game (the spine) and the path the player is attempting to find (the golden path), upon which the player will experience the most game rewards. It follows that the golden path *must* include the spine of the game—else the golden path would not allow the player to complete the game.

Example: Game Spines

Let's consider the following hypothetical example:

> In a short game (or game segment) based upon the legend of Theseus and the Minotaur, the player is given the role of Theseus. The story begins with the player being dropped into the labyrinth where the fearsome half-man, half-bull creature, the minotaur, lurks. The player knows there is no escape if he does not kill the beast. The game ends when the player slays the minotaur and escapes the maze. In keeping with the legend, the player can (optionally) escape the labyrinth by laying a trail of golden thread. This thread is acquired from Ariadne, who can be found near the start of the maze.

The spine of this game includes two key events: finding and slaying the minotaur, and escaping the labyrinth. These are the requirements: the game will not allow the player to leave the labyrinth unless the minotaur is slain. (Perhaps because a particular character will let the player out of the maze only if the beast is killed.)

The golden path of this game, however, includes three events: finding Ariadne (and acquiring the golden thread), finding and slaying the minotaur, and escaping the labyrinth (by following the thread back to Ariadne).

Obviously, we would like the players to find Ariadne, but we need not guarantee it. The players' task is harder if they do not, but there is no especial reason that we should *obligate* all players to find Ariadne. If we choose to place meeting Ariadne into the game spine, we probably need to create a *narrative* reason that this is a requirement and not merely an optional event, or place the meeting with Ariadne at a *choke point* (a physical location the player must pass through). If neither of these cases applies, the player is placed in the questionable situation of being told a goal (find and kill the minotaur) when in fact they are expected to complete an entirely different goal (find Ariadne).

Which Path to Signpost?

The game writer inherits much of the obligation to guide the player through the game. But should the writer guide the player along the spine or the golden path?

Although this decision rests entirely in the hands of the development team, it is strongly recommended to guide the player along the golden path and not just the spine of the game. The reason for this is that for purely pragmatic reasons, most players will not follow the guidance they are given perfectly (if at all). If you guide the player toward the golden path, it is still highly likely that the player will not find each and every item or benefit on this path. Because the golden path includes the spine, however, you can be relatively confident that guiding the player along the golden path will provide sufficient information to enable the player to find the spine of the game at the very least.

Alternatively, the game writer can guide the player along both paths—but with different degrees of explicitness. The spine should be laid out in clear and certain terms, to ensure that all players can find it and therefore complete the game, but the signs and clues for the golden path can be slightly more concealed to allow for a greater sense of achievement when it is found.

Some players prefer not to have the path laid out, but except for games with variable degrees of player support according to difficulty level (which is rare), non-commercial projects (which can do whatever they want), or games targeting an audience of players whose play needs are met by obscure puzzles (which is a niche market), the game writer should always clearly mark out the spine of the game to some degree. This does not mean that there can be no puzzles in the game spine—just that any puzzles included as part of the spine of the game are clearly signposted. Solving the puzzle should be the challenge—not working out what to do next.

The game writer often has considerable assistance from the game design team, and the level designers in particular, when it comes to structuring the game spine. For instance, there is no need to include dialogue to assist the player in reaching a particular point in the game world if the player is setting off from a point from which the destination must inevitably be on the route (for instance, in an entirely linear level)—although there may still be narrative reasons to do so. The game writer's responsibilities thus begin where the design team's obligations end.

For the remainder of this chapter, when we talk about keeping the player on the golden path note that for some games keeping the player on the path corresponding to the spine is more appropriate, and not strictly the golden path. For simplicity, however, we will assume that the task is guiding the player along the golden path.

BREADCRUMBING: FOLLOWING THE PATH

The process of *breadcrumbing* is the means by which a game writer can lead the player forward with a trail of clues, or the level designers can lead the player via more physical symbols. In any game with a narrative, this "trail of breadcrumbs" is essential—not only so that the player can remain on the golden path but also so the player has a narrative reason to be doing so.

Providing narrative reasons for player actions is the other aspect that makes breadcrumbing so essential. Telling the player to travel to the Cathedral is one thing; it's quite another to make it feel as if traveling to the Cathedral is the right thing to do in terms of advancing the story. In this regard, archetypal situations and characters can be of great help. Suppose a friend of the player character is kidnapped and taken to the Cathedral. In this situation, it is implicit that the player should go to the Cathedral and rescue the friend. Similarly, if the player wants to get into (say) the Castle and needs a key to do so, learning that the key is in the Cathedral is sufficient motivation for the trail of breadcrumbs to lead there.

In the absence of a narrative or physical trail of breadcrumbs, the player is left to flail around to find their own way forward. Very few commercial games can afford this lack of direction because for every player who enjoys figuring out what to do without any instructions, there are a dozen more who will become frustrated the moment no specific goal exists for them to pursue.

Physical Trails of Breadcrumbs

Games with a physical trail do not necessarily need a narrative trail of breadcrumbs to accompany them. However, if a game has a story as one of its key elements, the absence of a narrative trail of breadcrumbs can create any number of strange situations.

One of the first games to explicitly include a physical golden path was *Turok 2: Seeds of Evil* (Iguana, 1999). In this game, small yellow health power ups were placed in a literal trail, marking the path through the game levels. However, this trail of breadcrumbs was flawed for two particular reasons. Firstly, the spine of the game included a large number of small puzzles between the trail of collectibles, many of which were not clearly signposted. This resulted in many players becoming confused as to what to do next, especially because the collectibles that constituted the trail disappeared after being collected—the player brushed clear the trail as they went along it.

Secondly, there was never a narrative reason for following the trail. This meant not only that many players were unaware of the existence of the trail at all, but that if and when the player became lost or disoriented, there was no basis for regaining the trail—and indeed, it was possible to end up rejoining the trail going in the wrong direction with inevitably confusing results.

More recently, the popular PlayStation 2 games in the *Grand Theft Auto* series (Rockstar North, 2002 onwards) have used a literal representation to denote the game spine. The missions that the player must complete to progress along the game spine are marked clearly upon the map. The player must therefore travel to these locations (marked in the world with a shimmering effect) to advance within the game.

This system works fine in terms of the basic goal of ensuring that the trail of breadcrumbs is clear to the player. However, it can be relatively questionable in narrative terms. Often players are given no narrative reason to be at the places in question—and, in extreme cases, have a strong narrative reason *not* to go there (for instance, when they know they are walking into a trap, or they are going to meet with a character who means them harm). The player is bullied into going to each point in the trail because the game will not progress otherwise.

The approach is sufficient for the *Grand Theft Auto* games because player freedom—and in particular the freedom for the player to wreak havoc—is more important to these games than the narrative, which serves merely as a conduit for reassuringly expensive cut scenes and a drip feed for new game materials. In a game with more strongly expressed narrative intentions, and particularly in a game with less player freedom (which is to say, games on lower development budgets), the game writer in general faces more of an obligation to provide narrative justification to accompany the physical trail.

Breadcrumbs in Dialogue

The most common mechanism for expressing a trail of breadcrumbs is via dialogue. This dialogue may be with a specific, single character (and may be monologue, especially if the character is a narrator), or it may be with many different characters, depending upon the nature of the game and of the story.

In the best case, the trail of breadcrumbs corresponds to the path of the narrative—and therefore the game writer need only write the dialogue that is appropriate for the story with some awareness of the need to explicitly guide the player with that dialogue. However, often the trail of breadcrumbs will be incomplete or will involve steps that are not overtly involved in the progress of the narrative.

This situation is largely equivalent to the problem any writer faces when there is a hole in the plot. The writer can plug the gap with a convenient *deus ex machina* or plot device, for instance. The usual solution in games is to simply provide the player with an instruction and count on the player to complete the assigned task, simply because it has been assigned to the player.

For instance, consider this extract from the script to *Jak and Daxter: The Precursor Legacy* (Naughty Dog, 2001). The narrative requires players to proceed across a lava flow using a vehicle for which they have now collected a certain number of power cells. However, the game wants players to go and play another level first. The narrative explanation is that a certain character needs time to make the vehicle work. This character tells the player:

"Listen, if you need something to keep you busy, my father always talked about an ancient Precursor pipeline hidden deep underground. Some of the pipes end in vents from which Eco flows freely, and some have been capped off so that the Eco is sealed back. There must be a way to turn the capped vents on. I traced part of the pipeline back to the Forbidden Temple. Maybe you should look there for some type of switch."

This gives the player an instruction to carry out a task, although they actually have no plot reason to do so. Although sufficient, in that players will go and do what is asked of them eventually (provided there's no other option), it is a slightly clumsy solution.

Compare this situation from *The Legend of Zelda: The Wind Waker* (Nintendo, 2002). The player has, once again, completed a task (getting into a special green set of clothes for the player character's birthday), and the game needs to direct the player to another location. The character speaking is the grandmother of the player character:

"Isn't that nice, Link? They suit you perfectly! A perfect fit! Well, tonight I'm going to invite the whole town over for your birthday party, so I'd better start getting ready, shouldn't I? Your grandma is going to make your favorite soup for you tonight. Mmmmm! I just know you're looking forward to it. Now go get your sister, Aryll."

At first glance, there is not a great deal of distinction between these two examples. However, there is a key difference in the narrative content of the second example. Players are told by their in-game grandmother to go and fetch their sister, which is a logical request from this character given the relationship between them. The story does not rest upon ad hoc justifications such as "if you need something to keep yourself busy," it provides the instruction in a narrative context that does not *seem* as arbitrary—even though, in reality, the instruction given is just as arbitrary as the prior example.

Notice how the second example works solely because the character in question is the grandmother of the player character. Equally, the player would be obligated to some degree to respond to an instruction from an employer or superior—but in such a context, players might legitimately wonder why they are being asked to carry out the instruction, so any instruction given must seem to fit with what is implicit in the player's job.

In fact, it becomes considerably easier to provide a trail of breadcrumbs at any point that the player's framing goal becomes an overarching quest—which is practically an endemic situation in games. The more the narrative heightens the sense that the player must complete the goal of the quest, the easier it is to provide a trail of breadcrumbs.

For instance, Jak and Daxter have the goal of returning Daxter to normal after he falls into a pool of plot device at the start of the game. The trouble with this goal is that it is slightly too contrived to have any meaning to the player. The player knows nothing about the plot device in question, and therefore is left waiting for the game to tell them what to do next. Conversely, Link in *Wind Waker* soon acquires the (initial) goal of recovering his sister after she is kidnapped—a situation for which the resolution (finding and rescuing Link's sister) is immediately apparent. This is the reason why archetypal situations are so valuable to the process of breadcrumbing: they allow the players to deduce the actions expected of them.

A clear example can be found in *Resident Evil 4* (Capcom, 2005), in which the player is cast in the role of a tough but bland action hero charged with the assignment of rescuing the President's daughter (the modern equivalent of the classical Princess archetype). Not only is the player's initial goal clear from the narrative context—find the President's daughter—but subsequent goals are equally clear: protect her and escape. There is no room for ambiguity in the trail of breadcrumbs in this particular game because the archetypes of the narrative situation already dictate *what* must be done—it is only *where* which needs to be conveyed.

Options in Dialogue

In games with dialogue mechanics that allow the player to choose different topics or sentences when in conversation, the trail of breadcrumbs runs into a serious issue. Suppose a particular piece of dialogue is required to be "discovered" by the player for the game to progress; that is, suppose there is a section of dialogue on the spine of the game that appears optional to the player. How do we deal with this situation?

In general, when game-literate players encounter options in dialogue, they feel obligated to listen to everything that a particular character says because if not, they might miss an important part of the conversation. This in itself is a reason games targeting the mass market should perhaps not use such dialogue systems—as not every player will be so thorough. Such dialogue systems may only be appropriate for niche market products, such as adventure games and cRPGs, where the audience is tolerant of or actively enjoys such mechanisms.

In games where such a dialogue system is being used, it is generally unwise to place elements of the game spine in apparently optional topics of conversation because even though many players will feel obligated to hear all the dialogue, it is questionable that they should have to do so. Game spine dialogue can be triggered at the start or end of a conversation, where it's essentially guaranteed to be found. However, dialogue that forms part of the golden path but not the game spine might legitimately be "hidden" in conversation, as might subquests or other optional activities.

An alternative approach is to provide second chances; that is, allow the players to discover the dialogue themselves, but if they do not, trigger an event that compensates for their lack of information at an appropriate juncture. Because this approach requires creating optional material, it is best suited for a game that has cheap forms of delivering narrative information—in particular games that deliver a substantial part of their narrative in text with no audio.

Triggering Events

A related issue to the trail of breadcrumbs is that many game stories require certain events to happen, and therefore the trail needs to lead the player to where the event is to occur. Many games that use cut scenes for story delivery, for instance, use a trail of breadcrumbs solely to lead the player to the next cut scene. This can happen principally in two ways: when the player expects it, in which case the cut scene is usually a confrontation of some kind, and when the player doesn't expect it, in which case it is more of an ambush. The latter kind will be discussed later; for now, we will focus on triggering events that the player is expecting.

In general, players should not have to flounder around searching for the trigger to an event that is on the spine of the game: an event that is required for the player to proceed must be found. The easiest solution is to side step the requirement for the player to carry out the journey—when the narrative dictates the next event is required, cut to the location and have it happen automatically. This is how it would be handled in other media. However, in games, a premium is placed upon the player's freedom of action, so such abstracted journeys should be used sparingly, if at all.

The issue at work here is one of pacing. During a period of the plot when tension is high, it may be appropriate to cut to the next logical location because to do otherwise is to lose the acquired narrative tension as players meander on to where they are supposed to be. At other times, players should generally be left in control of their own destinies.

The trail of breadcrumbs can lead a player to an essential event in two ways: the trail can explicitly state the next destination in dialogue ("go meet the Mayor at the well"), or the next event can be placed in a choke point on the player's path. Any place in a game world where the player goes from a freedom to explore to having to pass through a single physical space (including any time that a room has two doors—one where the player comes in and one where they leave) can be considered a choke point. However, for the choke point to be useful for triggering an event, it must be on the golden path (or at least on the spine of the game), or else the player may never go there.

There is also a variant on a choke point that deserves some mention. The mechanics of a particular game may require the player to travel to a specific location (or class of locations) periodically. For instance, in a game with resources that are used up and can only be purchased at shops, the player must inevitably travel to a shop at some point. Although not a literal choke point, the shop in this example serves as a functional choke point in that the pragmatic nature of the gameplay will inevitably lead the player there. If there is only one shop, all shops are identical in-side, or the game delivers some narrative material solely in dialogue, this functional choke point can be used to trigger a game event.

In deciding where and how an event is to be triggered, the game writer should begin with the needs of the narrative and then adapt this to the needs of the game. If players are searching for their long lost half-sister, and they learn she is waiting at the Cliffs of Cliché, it is reasonable to tell the players that their half-sister is there and expect them to go. If, on the other hand, the narrative requires a new sinister figure to be revealed (perhaps for foreshadowing), a choke point of some kind will be needed, unless a bait and switch is used. For example, players travel to the Cliffs of Cliché but find the sinister figure instead of their half-sister.

Dead Ends

Every trail of breadcrumbs will, by accident or design, eventually run dry. Players may wander so far from the trail that they no longer remember where it was, or they may go off and take part in some optional activity and not remember what they were doing. Also, players sometimes come back to a game after a considerable pe-riod of absence—they may literally not remember what the game expects of them. In these situations, a mechanism is needed to lead the player back to the path.

FUNNELING: LEADING BACK TO THE PATH

When a game is built on a literally linear pattern, there is little risk of the player be-coming lost or forgetting what they are meant to be doing. However, narrative games are rarely so overtly linear—even when the underlying structure is linear, the level designers usually go to some lengths to obfuscate this fact so that players at least feel they have a choice of places to go and things to do. Whenever there is a chance that a player can stray from the golden path, some kind of funneling mech-anism is required.

Funneling describes any system for ensuring that the players stay on or can find their way back to the spine of the game. The funnel can be overt and explicit, such as a narrator who tells the players what they should be doing; subtle and implicit, such as characters who offer advice to the players; or even couched at a meta-level to the game itself, such as a set of instructions shown on a pause screen.

The simplest and generally worst funneling method is to employ kill zones so that if players stray from the path, they die. The result is a linear game in which rather than fooling the players into believing they have more choice than they do, the game punishes the players for lacking the necessary knowledge to traverse the game world. An example is *Heart of Darkness* (Amazing Studio, 1998), which happily constrains the player with a large number of kill zones, many of which could not be anticipated, and some of which are in fact puzzles to be overcome. For a certain narrow audience, such an approach was sufficient. However, many players are easily discouraged and do not appreciate such capricious execution.

The narrator approach is not uncommon: a character tells the players what they should be doing if they spend too long doing other things. Because funneling is concerned with ensuring that the player returns to the path, providing such guidance only once is insufficient. The guidance must be provided repeatedly, until the player does what is expected. Such a character may not be a literal narrator in the sense the term is used in storytelling but may be a companion character used for explicit funneling.

The most famous, and most famously annoying, instance of an explicit funneling companion is the fairy Navi in *The Legend of Zelda: The Ocarina of Time* (Nintendo, 1998). If the player is not on the spine of the game, Navi pipes up with her familiar cry of "Hey!" and invites the player to press a control to speak to her. This in turn causes Navi to relate such wisdom as:

"That cloud over Death Mountain…there is something strange about it."

Meaning: Go to Death Mountain; that's where you're supposed to be right now.

The problem with Navi is not that she provides funneling—this is presumably an important aid to many players—the problem is that she is persistent and unwavering. Every few minutes, Navi pops up and says "Hey!"—a phrase that leads many players to develop a deep and lasting hatred for the little fairy. This is particularly frustrating in the case of *Ocarina of Time* because the game is packed full of side-quests and optional activities the player can legitimately invest considerable time in. Many players did not appreciate Navi's constant intrusion into what they had consciously chosen to pursue.

By *Wind Waker*, Nintendo had improved the design of the funneling companion in the Zelda series considerably. The King of Red Lions, a talking boat that the hero uses to traverse the game world, can be spoken to electively for guidance and offers unsolicited funneling advice only rarely. Because it's impossible to travel around the game world without this boat, it also acts as a functional choke point—an ideal situation for providing funneling information to the player.

A funneling character can also be provided in a slightly more subtle form, as a character that the players can turn to for advice when they need to. The key to making this work is to train the player that the character is a source of such advice, either explicitly ("come and see me if you need help") or implicitly. The important element is that the players know they can turn to this character for help, or that when all else fails, it is sensible within the narrative context to talk with this character.

An example is the character of Mina Habuka in *Castlevania: Aria of Sorrows* (Konami, 2003). Established within the opening sequence as a friend to the protagonist, she is positioned at a space in the game world that is a functional choke point because it is the location (at the entrance to the castle where the entire game is set) where a traveling salesman sets up shop. Talking to Mina is an entirely elective process—it is never required, but she has a different comment for each chapter of the game, which serves as funneling advice. For example:

> "If you stand on the water and jump from that spot, you'll be able to go up there. Stand on the water; what does that mean? Maybe you have to act like a ninja?"

or

> "There is an area accessible by treading through water. Without scuba gear, it may be too tough for a human to handle."

Both these examples illustrate how Mina functions as a funneling character. The backstory explains that she is receiving this advice from another character (Genya Arikado), thus allowing her to deliver sometimes cryptic information without any ability to elaborate. Some of the help she provides is explicitly involved in guiding the player back to the spine of the game, and some is helpful for finding hidden areas and bonuses (many of which could be considered part of the golden path of the game).

Mina only works, however, because there are so few characters that the player can choose to talk to, and therefore every time the player is near her, there is a certain obligation to hear what she has to say. In a game with many dozens of characters that can be spoken to, it's necessary to more explicitly foreshadow the role as a source of funneling information.

A final form of funneling occurs when the game provides explicit instructions via a pause screen—often in terms of mission objectives. Crude and unsophisticated, it does have the vast benefit of being instantly understandable and is highly recommended for games targeting a wide audience. A more complex version of the same mechanism is a *diary*, which records what the player learns. This will not suit every game because many players lack the patience to examine the contents of the diary. The more mass market a game is intended to be, the more explicit funneling advice is generally needed. This is simply because the larger a game audience is expected, the greater the chance of players who will fall off the path and lack the game literacy to guide themselves back to it on their own.

The Edge of the World

A special case of funneling occurs when the player reaches the edge of the game world. Often, games manage to keep the player corralled by using physical barriers, such as the now ubiquitous mountain ranges, rivers, seas, or chasms. The more freedom of movement the player has, however, the harder it is for level designers to keep the player constrained. The game writer may inherit some of the responsibility of dealing with the player's interaction with the edge of the world, although there are nonnarrative solutions—such as in *San Andreas*, where the player is free to continue traveling further and further out to sea, but in fact is kept at a maximum distance from the land in all cases.

Generally speaking, when the player hits the limits of the game world, it is sufficient for a line of dialogue from an appropriate character to indicate that the player either cannot or should not continue. Because the game will not physically let the player travel any further, they have no choice but to accept this situation. Of course, if there is no companion character, it may be necessary for the player character to pass comment on the situation. However, some games avoid the player character speaking to further the player's sense of involvement, because hearing the player character talk in a voice that is not the player's voice may ruin the illusion of being there. In this case, there may be no choice but to employ a *deus ex machina* of some kind—such as a whirlwind that picks the player up and drops them back down in bounds—although obviously this should be considered an extreme measure.

The players might also reach the edge of the area they are expected to be within but not strictly be at the edge of the world. Although for many players it can be frustrating to be artificially constrained, the economics of game development dictate that it may be necessary to limit where the player has access to at certain points in the story. The same basic rule applies: a line of dialogue to mark the edge of the world is needed or, if all else fails, a *deus ex machina*.

The edge of the world situation is illustrated clearly in *Resident Evil 4*. At the start of the game, the player has arrived at the edge of a town somewhere in rural Europe. The player is facing toward a house, and the vast majority of players head forward. However, players can also head back, in which case they find the car they arrived in with two nameless Spanish policía, and a wooden bridge. If the player attempts to cross the bridge (which is the edge of the road), one of the policemen says "Not that way, cowboy."

The line is delivered in a short cut scene and is used to mark the edge of the world. Shortly afterwards, there is a car accident and the bridge collapses (all out of the player's sight, using just sound effects) thus providing a permanent and immediately understandable limit to the edge of the world.

Funneling by Area

In a very large game world, in which there are subplots and narrative threads in separate regions (as happens for instance in many open-world cRPGs), it may be necessary to construct funneling systems on a wider scale. For instance, it may be necessary to have a funneling character for each separate region in the world, especially if there is no companion character to rely upon.

In this situation, it's often beneficial to use characters in the same role. For instance, all shopkeepers may be a source of rumors for the area, and these rumors can be used to funnel toward the golden path. Bartenders, doctors, clergy, and law enforcers could all potentially fulfill the same role, depending upon the game. Again, the best option is often to use a functional choke point—something the player is going to be visiting anyway.

In general terms, the more expansive the game world is, the more expansive the funneling mechanism must become, although the writer always has the option to provide a physical trail of breadcrumbs, as in the *Grand Theft Auto* games, thus removing (or at least obviating) the need for employing explicit funneling methods.

THE PLAYER'S PEACE OF MIND

The main purpose for breadcrumb and funneling systems is to keep the players on track and make sure they do not lose track of what is expected from them to advance in the game. Another aspect to keeping the player on track, however, is maintaining the player's peace of mind. Although it's acceptable to shock the player within the context of the game, it's not desirable for the player to be shocked by something in the meta-level of the game, for instance, by discovering only too late that there is no way back to an earlier area.

Many elements of game design serve little purpose but to reassure the players that they are on track. Many games, including all the games previously mentioned in this chapter, use an audio fanfare to accompany the acquisition of something the player needs to progress along the game spine. These audio fanfares not only provide a small reward to the players, they reassure the players that they are on track.

Game writers should feel free to specify the need for an audio fanfare in a game script, wherever it is appropriate.

Warning Signs: Proceed with Caution

Most games that feature a narrative component contain some irreversible events or major junctures that curtail the options the player has available. An area may be cut off, for pragmatic or narrative reasons, or the player may temporarily be constrained to a smaller area for the purposes of the story or for gameplay reasons (such as forcing the player to engage a major opponent or boss).

It is a courtesy for the game to inform the players—or at least to strongly hint—that they are approaching an irreversible event. Although clumsy, it is generally acceptable for the game to be honest with the player, offering such meta-level advice as "once you pass through this door there will be no turning back—are you sure you want to continue?" Generally it is better, of course, if this can be couched in purely narrative terms. For example, a bridge leading to a new area can be established through dialogue as unstable, and the idea put in the player's head that if they cross the bridge it would fall down. This implicitly informs the player of a future irreversible event.

In essence, these situations are unusual cases of foreshadowing a game element instead of a narrative element.

Simple versus Cryptic Language

Another area where the player's peace of mind is a key issue is in how cryptic the language of the game is allowed to become. Again, this is an instance of the balance between freedom and clarity—simple language favors clarity, but giving clear instructions removes the player's freedom to experiment with a solution. Conversely, cryptic language allows the player the chance to see what can be done, but at the cost that some players will be confused as to what is expected of them.

Unless the game is intended to be played as a series of puzzles, simple language should always be preferred for the spine of the game, and cryptic language should be reserved for flagging optional elements (that may or may not be on the golden path of the game). The more games have moved toward a mass-market audience, the less room there has been for cryptic language; games with highly obscure puzzles are now the exclusive domain of certain niche markets, such as modern adventure games.

In the days of pure text adventures (or text adventures with static graphics) such as the classic Magnetic Scrolls games *The Pawn* (1986), *Guild of Thieves* (1987), and *Jinxter* (1987), games supported different degrees of detail in the descriptions—the player could choose between varying degrees of terseness or verbosity. In some respects, choosing the terse descriptions was choosing to increase clarity at the cost of the flavor and challenge of the game (because deciding what to do on the basis of the text presented was part of the play of these games).

Some more recent games also feature similar choices. *Silent Hill 2* (Konami, 2001) gave the player a choice at the start of different "Riddle Levels"—Easy (in which the solutions to puzzles are explicitly told to the player), Normal (in which some help is provided, but solutions are never given), Hard (in which no help is given, and in at least one case, the solution is largely random), and Extra (in which puzzles are insanely obtuse, and a great degree of patience and guesswork is required). This option was possible because some of the game material is delivered in text only, which is inexpensive enough to be allowed to vary.

However, puzzles of significant difficulty are becoming less and less important in the more expensive videogames and are increasingly marginalized to niche market games, especially adventure games. The game design documentation should make it readily apparent whether puzzles figure into part of the game, and game writers are usually provided with the details of the puzzles, rather than being expected to create them, although there are exceptions.

As a general guideline, if the game you are working on is intended to reach a wide, mass-market audience, you should avoid any cryptic language except for a few hidden extra elements of the game. Even simple language can be misread or misunderstood, so it's too risky to allow the player the possibility of getting unnecessarily confused.

CONCLUSION

The game writer faces the task of being an invisible guide to the player as they travel through the game world and the game story. There will be at least one path that corresponds to the spine of the game, and the player requires some support in either finding the next step on this path (breadcrumbing) or being led back to the path (funneling). How explicitly these support mechanisms are rendered depends on the nature of the game. The more the game values the freedom of the player, the less the need for explicit details; the more the game values clarity of instruction, the less freedom will result.

In addition to the spine, which the player must follow to complete the game, there may also be a golden path—the path of maximum benefit or minimum risk, which in turn must include the spine (or it would not be a route to completing the game). This route may also be marked with a trail of breadcrumbs, although this trail is likely to be more subtly rendered and can be considerably more cryptic in its representation. Although not essential, game writers should usually guide the player along the golden path, on the assumption that doing so will provide two separate tiers of clues to the path the player should be on (clues for the spine and clues for the golden path).

In an ideal game narrative, the trail of breadcrumbs matches the path of the game story, but usually some steps must be taken either in the construction of the plot or the writing of dialogue to ensure that the spine and the story fit together completely. With this in mind, game stories can make considerable use of archetypal situations and characters as the narrative consequences (and hence the play implications) of these common stereotypes convey information to the player with the minimal need for exposition. This does not mean that game stories should be tired and clichéd, however, —merely that the game writers should make the best use of all the tools at their disposal.

In terms of guiding the player, hiding necessary events in dialogue or in the world is generally not a good idea. The spine of the game should be readily apparent. To assist in this, explicit directions in dialogue or choke points can be employed to ensure the player proceeds along the expected path. The actual opportunities for using choke points will vary from game to game and may include functional choke points as well as literal bottlenecks in the environment.

When the world is complex enough that the player can stray significantly from the path, guiding mechanisms, such as a narrator, a helpful companion, or a stationary funneling character, can be used, although in the last of these cases, the role of the NPC should be established clearly in the player's mind. Explicit objectives can also be given via a pause screen, as a final protection against the players being uncertain about what is expected of them. The more a game intends to court the mass market, the more the game writer needs to make the funneling explicit.

Finally, games can give players peace of mind by using mechanisms such as audio fanfares to assure them that they are still on track and appropriate measures to demark the edge of the world. Players should also be informed of any irreversible effect with consequences for the play of the game; these warnings should be rendered in a narrative context whenever possible—a process related to foreshadowing in a conventional story.

The craft of creating game narratives is more complicated than any other writing role in the modern world, and those who want to excel in this work must learn many skills and disciplines. Understanding how to construct the spine of a game, how to link that spine to the narrative, and how to effortlessly guide the player back to the path should they stray too far are all skills that any game writer should strive to master.

6 Game Characters
Andrew S. Walsh

The packet is shiny. On the cover is an oiled, muscled, fighting machine of a man and his sidekick who is sleek, silky, sexy, and massively underdressed, particularly when bearing in mind the effect of gravity on her prodigious bosom. On the back of the box the blurb entices you to play the seven-level story-line, unlock extra thongs for the lead characters, and play the game from the perspective of either of the two leads. Eagerly loading the game, the player is instantly immersed in a fast-moving cascade of action. However, aside from a certain amount of anatomical jiggling, there's no difference in the gameplay regardless of which of the two characters you select. The distinct perspectives sold on the back of the box only stretch as far as two unique combat moves and the characters' contrasting abilities to strain leather.

This is the view of game characters that many nongamers hold: that they are shallow and that the only difference between creating characters for games and other media is the fact that gamers are incapable of empathizing with characters. However, this situation is rapidly changing, and game stories are now increasingly populated with realistic and engaging characters, and fewer over-endowed, anatomically questionable character models. Although still in its infancy, the narrative language of games is now being explored by game writers who are discovering the approaches that will carry the medium of videogame stories into a new age when, hopefully, people will remember characters' personalities and not their bust size.

CHARACTER VERSUS ICON

In the days of pixilated graphics, where the platform game was king, creating a game character was easy. A game company only needed to decide what a character looked like, and the game was ready to go. This is because what many games called and still call a character is really just an icon—a visual image that acts as an interface between the player and the game. These images could just as well be the car in a driving game or the falling blocks in *Tetris* (AcademySoft, 1986). Even when the icon looks human, it doesn't mean it is a character.

In *Doom* (id, 1993), the players' view of the person they play is a face at the bottom of the screen. Although human, this image could have been female, alien, or a robot and there would have been no alteration to the way the game played or how the player reacted to it. The face was not a character, but a simple visual aid to show how much damage had been incurred.

Characters arise when a games company decides it wants the icon to be more than just an anonymous face; the company wants its character to interact with the player as well as with the game. Now, the icon must do more than act as a mere interface, it must create the illusion that it is alive. The character must assume a breathing personality to reach beyond simple fast finger reactions and hormone-teasing skin-tight uniforms and tap into the player's emotions.

Although gameplay is generally the most important aspect of any given game, there are types of games for which the story is incredibly important, and any game can benefit enormously from strong characterization. The sales figures of modern games demonstrate that titles can benefit hugely when they pay close attention to narrative content as well as gameplay. *Tomb Raider 2* (Core, 1997), *Half-Life* (Valve, 1998), and the recent PS2 iterations of the *Grand Theft Auto* franchises (Rockstar North, 2001 onwards) all sold more than 8 million units and relied on characters instead of icons. Properly used characters can make the gaming experience deeper, more involving, and ultimately more satisfying for the gamer, and happy gamers mean more profitable games.

PURPOSE AND PERSONALITY

If many games characters have evolved to be more than mere icons, then what are they now? At first look, some observers are tempted to equate game characters with movie characters. This forgets one simple fact—that game characters are interactive and movie characters are not. Unlike icons, therefore, games characters have personality, and unlike movie characters, they have an interactive game purpose. A games character has both purpose and personality.

Purpose relates to the game world, referring to how the character facilitates gameplay and allows the player to interface with the game. *Personality* describes how the game interfaces with the player, referring to how characters evoke an emotional response, making themselves and the world they inhabit believable and engaging.

Used properly, the character's personality disguises its purpose allowing the player to experience the games world as if it were real, as if the character is acting out of personal choice and not because the game design needs the character to behave that way.

Purpose

To explore the roles that a character must fulfill in a game, we need to consider the differences between the *game purpose* and the *narrative purpose* of a game character.

Game Purpose

A character's game purpose is its role within the game as defined by how the character interacts with the gameplay. This interaction is, in turn, determined by the type of game the character inhabits. If the game is a fighting game such as *Dead or Alive* (Tecmo, 1998), then the writer must create characters that possess the skills needed for them to face each other in hand-to-hand combat. Third-person shooters such as *Max Payne* (3D Realms, Remedy Entertainment, 2001) demand characters with different skills purely because the gameplay is different. The type of game governs the obstacles that face the character and therefore governs the character's attributes.

A game's style also influences a character's design. Although both broadly fitting the genre of platform games, *Sonic the Hedgehog* (Sonic Team, 1991)—a game with a cartoon design—and *Prince of Persia: The Sands of Time* (Ubisoft, 2003)—a game with a more mythological flavor—require different characters because of their style.

After the type of game, the game style, and the gameplay objectives have been determined, a character's design is then influenced by the needs of specific levels. For instance, if the game requires someone to open a door on level seven rather than the player character needing to locate a key, then the writer must create a character to fulfill the developer's gameplay requirements.

A character's game purpose is therefore the same as that of an icon: it is designed solely by the technical and design demands of the game.

Narrative Purpose

A character's narrative purpose is what a character must do for the plot to function. This can be separate from the character's gameplay purpose (although still defined by it). Because narrative purpose is focused solely on story, writing techniques used in other media work here too, as long as they do not conflict with the character's gameplay purpose.

Narrative purpose in games can change according to whether the story being told is a *closed story* or an *open story*. Closed stories follow traditional story structure. They have a beginning, middle and an end. This is a Three Act structure that is best defined in character terms as the following:

1. The central character wants something.
2. The central character tries to get what it wants.
3. The central character succeeds, or fails, in getting what it wants.

In the Four Act Structure, this becomes the following:

1. The central character wants something.
2. The central character tries to get what it wants.
3. The central character realizes it wants something else and tries to achieve it.
4. The character succeeds, or fails in getting what it wants.

A closed story follows the central character on a journey of enlightenment that changes the character. As the character strives for what it wants, it discovers something about itself that irrevocably alters the character's world. All the other characters and the plot are, therefore, defined by what the central character wants. This desire in turn must be something attainable and playable within that character's game world. The more playable the character's story, the greater the entwining of the game and plot will be.

Many games with closed stories have a story-led character. The character the player will assume is designed by the writer and designer and unchangeable by the player. This does not mean that the player will not be able to customize them in superficial ways—appearance, percentage changes to skill parameters, and so on, but rather that the player cannot change the way the character behaves within the story. To succeed at the game, the player must achieve the character's objectives as determined by the game developer.

Open stories do not follow the thematic structure of closed stories. Instead, they are a loosely linked series of challenges that players can undertake in any order they want. Progression is not marked by time or narrative, but by a change in the character's skills and game purpose.

Many Massively Multi-player Online Role-Playing Games (MMORPGs) employ open-story characters. Here, player characters aren't defined by one event or a single theme. Instead, they must face a series of ongoing problems that could (in theory) go on forever. Such open-ended game characters do not travel a single thematic line. Instead, they are defined by a set of characteristics that informs the writer/player of how that character will behave. In multi-player games, these characters must fit with other characters that also have their own competing characteristics and desires. A closed-world character defines its story world, whereas an open-world character is described not only by itself but also by the other characters in that world.

Open-story characters have more scope to be player driven than their closed-story counterparts. The players determine the way their characters behave and so can alter the course of the story. In effect, the players are offered building blocks from which they can create their own stories and experiences. Each choice the players make about what the character does then feeds into the playing experience. NPCs react to the player character in light of what the player has done and not what the writer has determined must happen. A writer is far from redundant in this situation, however, as the writer must help craft the parameters for such characters, set out the reactions to them, and provide the story building blocks for the character to inhabit. Although the player has a greater degree of influence over the character, the writer and designer are still able to control the character through the way they craft the parameters within which a character's behavior is defined.

Relating Gameplay Purpose and Narrative Purpose

The decision to use an open or a closed story is made at an early stage in the game-development process. This decision is defined by what the game engine can do and the role the character will have within it. Narrative purpose is therefore generally governed by game purpose.

Many games now combine open and closed storytelling. They offer the player a chance to play a series of defined story missions alongside the chance to explore a world in whatever order the player wants. When presented in this context, the world's rules govern the character. Many of these games utilize a character within the story, but revert to icon for the open play.

In *Grand Theft Auto: San Andreas* (Rockstar North, 2004), the character is presented in two ways. Within the plot, the player takes the part of Carl Johnson (C.J.), but as soon as the plot finishes, or while the player is not specifically pursuing the plot-related missions on the game spine, the character assumes a more ambiguous narrative role, closer to that of the icon described earlier in this chapter. During the closed story, the character acts as a framework for the action to take place around and an emotional hook to pull the player into it. At other times, such trappings are no longer required, and the character has ceased to be important within those sections.

By providing the surrounding character-based sections, however, the game generates the player's interest in the secondary gameplay sections. Even though the player has reverted to something akin to icon-based play, this experience is informed by the character-based play elsewhere in the game and so carries forward much of the emotional bond the game has generated. Furthermore, simplistic, interactive storytelling elements are provided within the open story world, such as the character's girlfriends, which allow the player to partly define the character's role in the game world. These elements enhance the illusion that there is connectivity between the plot and the free roaming play.

The recent *Grand Theft Auto* games are solid examples of both the advantages of closed-story narrative and how this can influence even icon-based play by making the experience feel deeper as a whole.

Personality

Whereas purpose defines how a player interfaces with the gameplay, personality defines how the player interfaces with the story. Adding personality should generate an emotional response in the player that deepens the playing experience and encourages the player to engage with it.

The decision to add personality is not just made for artistic reasons. The stronger the emotional bond between the player and the character, the more likely the player will buy the game's sequel, as well as the mug, lunchbox, T-shirt, and poster. This is one reason for the increase in the number of games containing characters and story—they create a brand. Good characters have the potential to earn a lot of money. As many companies have found, however, creating good characters is a tricky process.

Basic Personalities

A character's personality doesn't have to be complex. At their most basic, personalities can be expressed through only a few lines of dialogue. As soon as an icon exhibits behavior beyond that of just purpose, it has a personality and is therefore a character (if only a rudimentary one).

The success of *Doom* allowed for other similar games to follow. *Duke Nukem* (3D Realms, 1996), although overtly similar to *Doom* in terms of gameplay, added a very basic character to the formula—Duke Nukem himself. Throughout the game, a small number of lines of dialogue inform the player of the character's thoughts, feelings, and style. Another person's psychology is projected onto the player. The personality is paper thin, but it deepens the playing experience. Whereas conversations about *Doom* revolved solely around gameplay, when *Duke Nukem* is mentioned, the scattered one-liners are repeated verbatim, and the game is discussed through the character.

Complex Personalities

There is no harm in a game using a basic personality for the central character, especially if the game's narrative content is similarly simplistic, but many games have narrative content that requires deeper characters. These more complex personalities are designed to do more than just add a gloss to the game; they have their own psychologies and histories, which affect the gameplay. *Fatal Frame* (Tecmo, 2001) sees the player being asked to take the role of Miku in order to unravel the sinister mystery of Himura mansion. During the character's journey, the player discovers a lot about Miku's personality as well as about the mansion.

As a supernatural thriller title, *Fatal Frame* needs to build a sense of tension in the player. Identifying and caring about the heroine is an important part of this, so if the player doesn't believe in the character, then sections of the gameplay fail because they rely upon the player feeling the same fear as the character. To achieve this empathy, the game designers opted for a character that appears vulneraable and has a complex personality. As the player learns Miku's inner strengths and her feelings, the experience feels more believable and consequently more frightening for the player.

Although it is possible to generate fear in a player through an icon, the effects of such fear are magnified if the player believes in the character. In *Fatal Frame*, a nonspeaking, cartoon, PVC-clad icon would not have worked as well because the player would not have believed in her as real, which would lessen the player's emotional involvement. Instead, the *Fatal Frame* character has a full background that influences the gameplay precisely because it is designed around provoking strong emotional responses from the player.

Using Personality to Conceal Purpose

Sometimes it is desirable to use personality to conceal the purpose of a character, specifically the game purpose. For instance, whenever a game uses a funneling character, it is highly desirable that this character displays some personality that the player may warm to in order to partially conceal the game purpose. Similarly, if a game uses a tired mechanic such as a boss fight, it may be desirable to mitigate the players' indifference by giving their opponent some personality.

Furthermore, a touch of personality can be used sometimes to avoid more clumsy methods of exposition. For example, in *God of War* (Sony, 2005), there is a moment where the player character Kratos needs to traverse a chasm. However, a man on the other side is holding the release mechanism for a mechanical bridge that crosses it. This man is too afraid of the monsters attacking the city to release the bridge—as this could potentially allow the monsters to reach him. With the chasm blocking his way, Kratos is stuck on the wrong side of the city. To further Kratos' quest, the player must complete another task on the side where he is trapped. This, in turn, gives Kratos the power to hurl lightning bolts. The player can then go back, kill this man, and cross the bridge. The man's game purpose is to obstruct the player's progress until the player has achieved a series of game objectives. The man is then removed to allow the player to progress. However, since all we learn of the character is that he is a coward, why is it advantageous to a game's design to use a character to fulfill this gameplay role and not simply employ a rope to hold back the release mechanism instead?

Firstly, on a design level, the character is able to hint that he is the obstacle the player must overcome; if the obstacle were a rope, the designer would have had to use something like a cutaway close-up of the rope to visually highlight it. Alternatively, the writer/designer could have had the player character say "let me across" and the man on the bridge say "I'm not untying that rope!" and then run away. The problem here would be if the player returned to the bridge and had forgotten this disappearing character, then the player would be stuck. The fact that the man's personality defines him as scared explains his actions and makes the character memorable while disguising the fact that, in gameplay terms, the character is, in effect, a talking rope.

A further reason for using a man instead of a rope is the fact that the incident informs the player about the personality of Kratos. They learn that the player character is someone who is prepared to kill an innocent man to achieve his goals. Thus the choice to use a man helps to define the player character as well as provide an obstacle in the game.

TYPES OF CHARACTER

Much of a character's purpose and personality are determined by the character's type. To properly populate a game, each character type needs to be carefully assessed in terms of its role and the particular details of how that role is expressed.

The Protagonist

In a game, the *protagonist* is the character the player assumes. We see the game world through this character. From a story perspective, the protagonist is the character with whom the audience is asked to identify. The remaining characters in the game are there either to try and stop the protagonist from attaining the stated goal, to help the protagonist achieve it, or perhaps as color to enhance the feeling that the game world is authentic.

After the protagonist's goal is identified, both the story and the gameplay need to provide obstacles to hinder the character's attempts to achieve it. In media other than games, the obstacles a protagonist faces can result from inner turmoil. This approach is extraordinarily difficult to make work in games, however. Although a game plot can deal with matters of inner turmoil, the majority of the obstacles the character faces must be concrete because gameplay requires activity. As such, the obstacles to a character's goal must require the player to fight, jump, and solve puzzles and other dynamic challenges. (In the best case, however, inner turmoil can always be embodied metaphorically by the challenges of the gameplay.)

In closed stories, merely defining what a character is doing is not enough. The writer must know and explain why the character is undertaking the quest it is on. Why is the protagonist doing these things? The pressure on the protagonist must be greater than the pressure from the opposing forces. If the character must put its life at stake fighting innumerable waves of zombies as occurs in the *Resident Evil* series (Capcom, 1996 onwards), then the pressure on the protagonist must be at least equal to the risk. In many of the *Resident Evil* games, the protagonists rapidly discover that they are trapped in an ongoing disaster, and thus the pressure they face is that of survival. Conversely, in *Resident Evil: Code Veronica* (Capcom, 2000), one of the game's two protagonists, Chris Redfield, comes to the island where the game is set to look for his little sister, Claire (the second of the two protagonists). This familial link provides the motivation for Chris to brave the dangers that face him.

If the pressures don't balance in favor of action in any game story, then the players will not believe in what the character is doing. If they don't believe why the character is doing what it is doing, then they won't empathize with the character. If the players do not empathize with the character, then they will have a harder time engaging with the game.

The Traditional Hero

Protagonists come in all sorts of shapes and sizes, the most famous type being the traditional hero who is strong, intelligent, and noble. They seek out adventure, right wrongs, and protect the weak. From the heroic Link of *The Legend of Zelda* series (Nintendo, 1986 onwards) to the *Tomb Raider* series' Lara Croft (Core et al, 1996 onwards), traditional heroes crave the story's challenges and do not shy from their quest.

The Reluctant Hero

Not all protagonists are as willing as the traditional hero. Many are forced to fill their role because of circumstance. In *Half-Life,* the game's protagonist Gordon Freeman is a reluctant hero, thrown into his quest when an experiment goes wrong. All he wants is to survive long enough to get out of the Black Mesa laboratory complex. This desire is blocked by many obstacles: exploding pipes, locked doors, alien invaders, and ultimately the squad of soldiers sent in to clear up both the aliens and the witnesses. These obstacles stop the protagonist from gaining the escape he craves and force him to become a hero.

Anti-heroes

Anti-heroes take the idea of the reluctant hero a stage further. Not only do they not want to be heroes, their traits are often the polar opposite of traditional heroes. Whereas the traditional hero is good looking, noble, and wise, the anti-hero is not. Circumstance forces this character to act nobly even if the character's actions and intentions are ignoble.

Tommy Vercetti in *Grand Theft Auto: Vice City* (Rockstar North, 2002) embodies the anti-heroic quality of being a central character operating as protagonist, but being largely devoid of heroic values. Indeed, as a felonious murderer seemingly lacking in any moral fiber, it is almost tempting to consider this game to be a narrative with a villain as protagonist. Nonetheless, there is an impression that somewhere beneath Vercetti's cold exterior is *something* redeeming, although exactly what that something is does not emerge in the space of the game's story.

Conversely, in *God of War*, the player character *Kratos* is a mass-murdering psychopath who kills anyone and anything he meets. However, Kratos' quest to defeat the evil God of War, restore the balance of power between the gods, and bring peace to the land is essentially a noble one. Despite this, as Kratos explores his quest, he doesn't act nobly and shows little regret for his murderous actions. Ultimately, however, unlike Vercetti, Kratos discovers that he is on a path to redemption.

As Tommy Vercetti demonstrates, it isn't necessary for all anti-heroes to be redeemed. Where they are not, however, care must be taken with the character's negative traits so that the hero does not make these negative points appear laudable. The failure to take this into account in certain *Grand Theft Auto* games was a contributing factor in the negative media furor relating to the titles in recent years.

Duos

Some characters only work as a double act. Although it is clear who the dominant heroes are in these situations, there is an impression that they would be nothing without their sidekicks. In Freudian terms, most duos operate as an id (primal needs and instincts) and an ego (the conscious self), one balancing the other. When creating a duo then, the writer must look at how the characters complement each other. What does one offer the other? What are the strengths and weaknesses that combine to make that duo interesting and effective? These strengths and weaknesses should then be reflected in the characters' purposes and personalities.

As duos rely on exploring the flaws of the partnership, they work very well in comedy titles. *Sam and Max Hit the Road* (LucasArts, 1993) sees a comic duo of straight man and the comic that provides a prominent comedy highlight in games history. Sam is analytical, methodical of pace, and capable of caring about what is going on. Max on the other hand is psychotic, energetic, and happy to dole out violence. Where a strong arm is needed, Max is there. When it's a restraining glance, Sam's your man. Each member of the duo has qualities that match and complement each other so that the pair becomes greater than the sum of its parts.

Group Protagonists

When a number of characters lead the player through a story, they provide a *group protagonist*. A narrative that uses a true group protagonist will see the story from several different perspectives, although this is less common in games because of the expense and game design problems that lie in such an approach. In principle, however, the player will be able to learn or do things with one character that the player would not with another. A group protagonist's gameplay purpose is therefore to allow a player to choose from a variety of different characters. To do well, the player must employ a combination of these characters' unique skills to overcome the obstacles in the game.

In *Project Eden* (Core, 2001), the player (or players) controls a team of specialists. Each specialist has different equipment and skills, and each also comes with a different personality. The game presents situations in which the player is invited to consider which character is best use to address a particular situation. Carter, the team leader, has better people skills than the others, and must occasionally be used to speak to specific NPCs. Minoko is the computer expert and deals with all the hacking that is required. Andre is the engineer and the person to apply to any serious technical problems—as well as occasionally needling Minoko. Amber is the brutish warrior of the group and capable of withstanding adverse environmental conditions. The base purpose of offering a range of equipment and skills is disguised by making each team member a unique personality.

Group protagonists can also occur when a game is structured as a series of vignettes. For example, in *Eternal Darkness: Sanity's Requiem* (Silicon Knights, 2002), there is a central protagonist—Alexandra Roivas—around whom the framing narrative pivots. However, the player also takes control of almost a dozen other characters for the length of a single game episode—one of whom is also the chief villain of the story. This approach allows for outcomes not normally feasible in a game—characters can die at the end of their episode, for instance, because the core protagonist, Alexandra, will remain to propel the framing narrative forward.

Differentiating Protagonists

Protagonists are not only defined by their own games. They also need to stand out from others that exist in the same type of game. Solid Snake in *Metal Gear Solid* (Konami, 1998) and Sam Fisher in *Tom Clancy's Splinter Cell* (Ubisoft, 2002) are practically interchangeable characters existing in similar worlds. However, the characters aren't quite clones of each other. If both were to approach the same problem, each would handle it in a different way. Sam Fisher is defined by his duty; whereas Solid Snake is defined by the way he rebels against his. The decision to define the character of Sam Fisher in this way was an intentional move to distinguish the later game from the earlier title.

Antagonists

An *antagonist* is someone in the way of the protagonist. In the *Mortal Kombat* series (Midway Games et al., 1993 onwards), the antagonist is the single fighter standing opposite the player; in *Rome: Total War* (Creative Assembly, 2004), the antagonists are the hordes of barbarians. However, just as protagonists benefit from purpose and personality, so do antagonists. *The Metal Gear* series sets up a number of named antagonists to stand in Solid Snake's way. These antagonists oppose the player character and will stop at nothing to succeed in their evil aims. In *Metal Gear Solid*, as the plot progresses, the actions of the antagonists impact directly on the player character, they even kill characters close to the player character. The effect of this is that while at the start of the game players simply want to succeed, as the plot unfolds, the players' engagement broadens so they seek not just success but revenge against Sniper Wolf and Liquid Snake.

A well-designed antagonist should fulfill its gameplay purpose by setting up challenging gameplay while its personality gives the player a greater emotional involvement in the story by making the player want to stop the antagonist as a character, not just as a gameplay challenge.

The key to making an antagonist engaging is the character's motivation. Many games fail their story, characters, and gameplay by creating villains who are simply "bad." The antagonist's motivation doesn't have to be complex, just explained. Be it a soldier driven by doctrine or zombies crazed with bloodlust, the player needs to know *why* the antagonist must be overcome.

In *Grand Theft Auto: San Andreas,* much of the action takes place between gangs. The player character is part of one gang—the Grove Street Family—that wants to secure family values and support the ideals of loyalty and kinship. They are even able to overcome their own prejudices to allow their sister to fall in love with a member of a rival gang. Facing the Grove Street Family, we find the Ballas, who are only interested in one thing—money. To get it, they are prepared to sell each other out, pump crack into the neighborhood, and even support the crooked policeman who becomes the player's nemesis. On the road to redemption and in his quest to rebuild his family connections, the player must help clean up the streets to return order to the neighborhood and reestablish the name of the Grove Street Family.

An engaging antagonist allows the player to not only see who the enemy is but also see the antagonist's motivation and why the antagonist must be stopped.

The Nemesis

The *nemesis* offers a single face to the opposition. The nemesis is the villain the protagonist pursues throughout the game and the one who sets obstacles in the protagonist's way. As the end of the game sees the fulfillment of the hero's desires, this can often mean the slaying of the nemesis, the frustration of the nemesis' plans, or, in more complex narratives, the metamorphosis of the relationship between these two characters.

To make the relationship between protagonist and nemesis engaging, the player needs to understand exactly what the antagonist wants and why. Again this should be defined by action. Just as the protagonist should be proactive in attaining the goal, so the antagonist should be seen to try and achieve its aims. This does not mean that the nemesis has to be physically present throughout the game, but an awareness of its existence and the effect of its actions have to.

In *San Andreas*, although C.J. starts out battling the local gang, this plot is overshadowed by that involving Officer Frank Tenpenny, a corrupt cop who seeks to use the gangs to further his own riches. Despite being crooked himself, officer Tenpenny hates the gangs, but uses the chaos they cause as cover to build his own personal fortune. On his return, C.J. appears to be a useful tool, and the player is forced to carry out missions on Tenpenny's behalf to avoid being framed for murder. As the story unfolds, Officer Tenpenny is revealed to be the spider at the center of the web. This single antagonist gives a face to the whole of the player's struggle, and players will begin to understand that their destiny is tied to that of Tenpenny. C.J. and Tenpenny must ultimately confront each other in a final showdown.

To make players interested in antagonists, the purpose and personality of nemesis characters need a set of characteristics that makes them worthy opponents. Sometimes this can mean mirroring the protagonist: a warrior for a warrior, a god for a god. On other occasions, an antagonist can be given a skill that differs from that of the protagonist, but which enables the antagonist to rival the protagonist's powers.

Group Antagonists

An antagonist doesn't have to be a single person. When playing FPS games set in a war, the ultimate villain might be the dictator commanding the opposing army, but the player doesn't generally face him in a final boss level. Instead, the antagonist is a collective entity of soldiers and machines, and victory is determined by overpowering this collective enemy. Much of this horde will remain as unnamed, unnumbered clones. Their purpose is to die, so to give them all individual characters would prove overwhelming and ultimately pointless. However, leaving this group as mere drones can lead to antagonist fatigue and the question "Why am I killing this zombie again?" The motivation of the group antagonist must be made as clear as if it were the nemesis. Where there are many, they can be treated as one if their motivation is understandable.

In this area, the use of short interjections (or barks) as in *Halo: Combat Evolved* (Bungee, 2001) can be of great assistance. Although the principle enemies—the alien Covenant—are largely a mass of faceless drones, occasionally amusing or engaging barks lend a sense of personality to what would otherwise be indistiguishable from any other alien army.

Bosses

Bosses are a mainstay of many game designs. Although sometimes overused, they do provide the possibility to add more personality to a group protagonist by singling out an individual to be confronted as an effective "Champion" of the opposing forces. By providing key members of the group (bosses) with an individual character, the actions of these individuals can be representative of the behavior of the whole. These individuals are evil, therefore the system that allows them to exist must be too. The player's emotional reaction to these characters colors their view of the whole and makes a boss confrontation have more of an impact.

Non-Player Characters (NPCs)

NPCs are the people in the street, the soldiers, and the alien traders that populate the game's universe. They are the characters that bring the story to life, drive the plot, and bring out the traits of the central character while deepening the world and the illusion of reality the player experiences. Antagonists are NPCs, but have already been covered. This section deals purely with the good or neutral characters that appear in the game.

Just as with the hordes of antagonists, the writer should look to give NPCs personality and motivation. For many NPCs, this motivation is employed to hide their gameplay purpose which is to give the player advice, sell the player a magic sword, or as with the example of the man in *God of War*, hold the bridge release mechanism that closes or opens the door to the player's progress. Because these characters can be present for just a moment, they need to be established quickly but only need to give enough information about their personalities to make them interesting. The character's personality should disguise its purpose, not overwhelm it or slow down the gameplay.

When designing games, a writer can also use NPCs to provide motivation for the player character. They can need rescuing, bring quests, and turn traitor. Even in the simplest of games, an NPC can add interest. In *Beach King Stunt Racer* (Davilex, 2003), the player drives around in a buggy completing stunts. Rather than being given a choice of different characters to play, the player is given a choice of which girl they want to impress. The girl then appears in a corner of the screen and comments on the player's actions. The aim of the game is to complete the stunts and win the girl's love. Although this is back to stretched swimsuits again, it is a novel device!

Beyond game purpose, NPCs also have a narrative purpose, presenting an opportunity for emotional depth not always achievable through the player character. Commercial arguments mean that when a player character is killed, they are frequently resurrected. The player knows this will happen, so the death of the protagonist has little emotional impact. In contrast, the death of Aeris in *Final Fantasy VII*

(Square, 1997) is one of the most talked about moments in gaming that left many players stunned. Many players report being reduced to tears by this development. When a secondary character dies, the moment can generate real emotional shock because, unlike the death of the protagonist, a secondary character's demise is final, and the character will not return.

However, care must be taken. Players can generally ascertain when a character death is narratively satisfying, and when the character has been sacrificed to the plot. Deciding to kill an NPC for emotional impact is one thing, but it must be handled appropriately to produce an emotional impact or it risks distancing the player from the story.

Lone NPCs

When dealing with individual NPCs, each must have its own unique persona. Some such characters are present throughout an entire game, whereas others appear only briefly. Creating a well-rounded NPC often requires the thought and effort that goes into a protagonist or antagonist.

If the NPC has a job, does the NPC like it? Are NPCs proud of being guards or have they been conscripted and want to go home? Do they fear the player or admire them? The character doesn't need to say much to put these things across; it is all about how they say the lines.

Although NPCs must be crafted, there is often little space (or reason) to give the player the background detail used by the writer to generate the characters. The player does not need to know every facet of an NPC's life, particularly as the important aspects of games characters are defined by their actions, not their dialogue. Overwritten characters provide the player character with reams of unnecessary dialogue that doesn't progress the plot or the game. The goal should be to give the characters depth, but keep them light on their feet.

After an NPC has been established, the NPC can change, giving the player a chance to see how the game is progressing. For example, when the player character meets an NPC for the first time, the NPC is pleased to see the player. However, when the player character returns, and the plot has framed the player for the murder of the king, the writer can demonstrate the plot through the NPC being hostile to the player. By making NPCs reactive, the writer creates a more believable universe and a deeper experience for the player. In the aforementioned *Final Fantasy VII*, the character's relationship with the two lead female characters, Aeris and Tifa, informs the player of the hero's past and how that character has changed over the years. The player's feelings about the central protagonist's journey are informed by the NPC's reaction to the central character. When Aeris and Tifa feel sad, shocked, delighted, or romantic, these are the emotions that the designers intended to infuse into the player.

Group NPCs

There is a growing trend to create an immersive game universe that teems with life. Each person the player encounters has a personality that can talk back. Providing adequate personalities to individuals on the scale required for populous worlds is currently an untenable task. Rather than seeking to create several thousand characters, games facing this problem instead create a system that allows limited resources (art, recorded voice, material, and so on) to produce the illusion of several thousand characters. This is chiefly achieved through grouping the NPCs into classes; each class of NPC can then have behavior and dialogue specified.

In the recent *Grand Theft Auto* games, pedestrians are grouped into particular classes. Each character design—drug dealer, girl in bikini, cop—has its own set of lines for if the characters are bumped into, crash, or are shot at. Each of these is styled to match the appearance of the character. The NPCs sound tough, vain, or meek depending on the character's appearance. By giving these groups of characters personalities and providing a wide range of different designs, the world is made to feel more populated.

BRINGING A CHARACTER TO LIFE

So far, this chapter has talked about the bones of the character and the purpose they serve. This section covers some of the different methods for putting flesh on those bones by creating their personality. Basic characters may only use part of this development process, whereas more complex characters require the use of an array of techniques.

Traits

Traits are what make a character an individual and work as an accessible shorthand for the character's psychological make-up. In plot terms, they inform emotion; in gameplay terms, they define action and reaction to external events. Traits represent the fastest and most widely applied technique for developing characters.

Adjectives

The most basic game characters are defined by a single adjective that represents a fundamental human emotion—they are happy, angry, or grumpy. Each character can have base emotional reactions, but return to its defined state at the end of each of these episodes. Basic characters are used when the character is only a gloss over an icon. These commonly appear in platform games where the emphasis is on gameplay and not narrative. Emotions are skin deep and generally limited to the most basic, happy, sad, angry variety.

Governing and Conflicting Traits

More complex characters should progress beyond a single adjective to competing traits. Here, each character is nominated a single behavioral feature such as bravery, cowardice, or avarice, which is the character's *governing trait*. This trait is what drives the character in day-to-day activities and defines how the character would normally react.

Matching the governing trait is a *conflicting trait*. This is a second competing trait that clashes with the character's governing trait. Sometimes this conflicting trait will save characters from themselves—they are vain, but have a streak of honor, for instance. In other characters, the balancing trait can be the Achilles heel that destroys them—perhaps the character is loyal but avaricious. This inner conflict therefore not only deepens a character but can also provide the character's journey in a closed story.

The competing trait does not have to be different from the governing trait but can arise from playing the polar ends of the same trait against the other. Honor, for instance, can be a governing and conflicting trait. Alec Guinness' character, Colonel Nicholson in the film *The Bridge on the River Kwai,* has an inflexible sense of duty that is the character's strength and weakness. At the start of the film, this sense of duty motivates Colonel Nicholson to resist his Japanese captors; however, by the end of the plot, the character's sense of duty finds him bound by his word, turning him to the point of collaboration.

Secondary Traits

After a character's governing and conflicting traits have been set out, the writer can turn to secondary traits. The character might be honorable, but is the character happy or stern? An honorable character that is tough and comical can come out with a great one-liner when cornered by the bad guy. An honorable, stern character will ooze defiance rather than spout one-liners. Secondary traits give the characters their emotional language, explaining to the writer and the player how the characters interpret their world.

Balancing the Set of Characters

No matter how basic or complex the characters are in a game, the writer must ensure that all the characters complement each other. Having two characters whose traits are functionally identical can reduce the impact of both. Therefore, if two characters replicate one another in terms of personality, then the writer must look to cut one of them or alter them to provide a more interesting counterpart to the other.

Characteristics

Whereas traits mold a character's core personality, *characteristics* are a mixture of physical and psychological factors that help define the secondary and external elements of a character. Some of these characteristics may be defined before the player turns to examine a character's traits. However, after the character's traits are established, the writer should remember that characteristics are there to add light and shade. They provide motivation for the character, inform the way others react to the character, and make the character more colorful; however, it's the character's traits that represent *who* that character is. If writers don't create the character from the character's emotional level, they won't get an emotional response from the player.

Gender and Sexuality

The gender of a character is often an early choice in a game. Sometimes this will be predetermined; for example, a game involving troops running up the beach during the D-Day landings will have a predominantly, if not exclusively, male composition. Gender and sexuality are two characteristics most often mistaken for traits. In society, men and women find divisions between them and are often defined by different interests and approaches to things. Although it is important to understand these differences, many games characters hit problems because they are defined as male or female first and then their reactions are determined.

For example, consider a character that is intended as a power monger. Gender might inform the way that a character tries to achieve a goal (i.e., through seduction), or it might be the driving force behind a character's desire to achieve that goal (i.e., to prove a woman can be as successful as a man), but it is the character's trait of "power mongering" that tells us what the character's goal is. The trait is the starting place for all the character's decisions, gender simply colors how those decisions may be carried out.

The easiest way to lapse into stereotypes is to define a character by their gender first and as a person second. This often results in games where men are stern, muscular heroes, and female characters appear as eye candy or feisty vixens. Although there is a market for such games, many players are asking for more sophisticated characters, particularly when it comes to the portrayal of women. If games are to expand to include more female players, then they must improve the way that men and women are portrayed within them. Adhering to stereotypes limits the audience and is sometimes, therefore, a bar to greater sales.

Stereotyping of all kinds (which is dealt with in the next section) can cripple characters before they leave the starting gate. They don't challenge or surprise the player and so will not engage them with the game. Subverting such stereotypes, however, and using players expectations against them can have a very positive effect.

Sexuality is an issue that has not yet been prominently featured in games, despite the general presence of gay and bisexual characters in theater, movies, and television. Perhaps it is because games are struggling to deal with the issues at the core of creating a narrative language for a nascent media that we have yet to see significant attention paid to this characteristic. It seems inevitable that it will just be a matter of time before we see a mass-market game with a homosexual protagonist, but how long that stretch of time will be is difficult to ascertain.

Race

Race is a characteristic often used and misused in the same way as gender. Just as with gender, a writer's starting position should stem from the character's traits and then examine how a character's race might affect the way that character acts in response to what their traits tell them to do. This is equally true for species. When creating a nonhuman species (such as an alien or a monstrous fantasy species), consider their culture and religion, but first consider their emotions.

Career

A character's career is more important with regard to purpose than personality and is often predetermined by the game design; for example, a war game requires a soldier. A character's career is useful shorthand for the skills a character has. If the game needs a character to be able to use guns, then time in the army or on the police force can quickly explain the character's proficiency and saves the writer from presenting this as exposition.

Career choice needn't be so conventional. The stereotypical archaeologist is a library-bound academic who dresses in Christmas sweaters and carries a trowel. In contrast, Lara Croft is a gun-toting action heroine and an upper-class British aristocrat more motivated by the desire to combat her own boredom than more scholarly motivations.

If a writer does not want to use a character's career to achieve this or is looking to add something to a character's career, then defining hobbies can provide the same cover as a career.

Wealth

A character's financial situation can provide explanation and motivation. The aforementioned Lara Croft is wealthy and therefore able to afford the travel and equipment she needs for her adventuring. In most games, the character begins poor in money, skills, and equipment and must accumulate these to progress. This gives the character motivation; if characters are poor, they have a reason for changing their world and entering the plot. Wealth opens doors to the power and abilities the character will require to complete the quest.

Family

Knowing a character's family background can help explain the character's behavior and provide story. Is the character an only child or part of a large family? Did the character live a life of luxury or have to fight for everything they possess? Does the character have relatives who can help or relatives who harass? This detail can help make a character more realistic and appealing while not impacting the character's gameplay purpose.

Stock Characters

Stock characters are off the shelf, instantly recognizable two-dimensional characters—the snarling gunslinger dressed in black or the wise, old man who gives advice. They have little depth or originality; they are stereotypes in the truest sense of the word. Most stereotypes are almost cartoon in their extreme and are instantly recognizable as fake. If the writer wants to create a realistic world, employing such characters risks instantly bursting the bubble of reality the writer has worked so hard to create.

Not all stereotypes are bad characters, however, and there are times when they can be useful tools. When an NPC is only in a game for a few seconds, the writer must establish it quickly. When entering a hotel and hearing gunshots in *Mafia* (Illusion Softworks, 2002), the player can guess that gangsters are firing and that the men in trench coats are the Mafiosi in question. The writer now no longer needs to provide any exposition; the character's job and appearance tells the players what they need to know.

Another good use for stereotypes comes by subverting them. Characters who are instantly recognizable villains can provide a fun plot twist when they turn out to be a cat-loving softies who want to help the player. Writers beware, however, as many of these subverted stereotypes have become stereotypical in their own right.

Character Sheets and Bibles

When starting a new project, many development companies produce what television companies call *bibles*. As mentioned previously, these writers' guides are manuals that explain who the characters are, describe their past, and lay out the characteristics that drive them. They codify the writer's ideas and help communicate the vision to the rest of the development team.

One technique used by writers in developing characters and communicating these characters to both the development team and the audience, is the use of *markers*. These are visual clues and shorthands that allow people to quickly understand a character without the need for reams of text.

One easy shorthand technique when faced with empty pages at the start of the development process is to think of a real person, or an existing character, and use that person as a model. This can make communication with the artists, animators, and actors easier, as long as the new character doesn't turn into libelous caricature or an exact copy. Rather, the writer should think of what similarities help communicate the new character more rapidly.

Another approach is to list the brand of clothes, trainers, or newspaper the character would buy. Saying someone reads the *National Enquirer* helps separate that character from a someone who reads *The Times*. This allows the development team to engage with characters by comparing them to people they know in real life.

Some of these markers can transfer into the game itself to demonstrate character; after all, characters are what they do, not what they say. In the world of detectives, Agatha Christie's Poirot sips from porcelain, whereas hard-nosed NYC detectives grab polystyrene cups of coffee. Knowing a Poirot-like character favors porcelain can set up comedy when he's given a cracked mug of over-stewed coffee. It can also suggest the character will need help when the investigation delves into the world of hip-hop DJs, but the character will easily solve a clue involving classical mythology. Markers allow a writer to intuit a character. They establish how a character will react to the world. However, such visual markers should be carefully selected and used sparingly to avoid overburdening the gameplay.

Having a vast wealth of information recorded in a central reference such as a writers' guide can be useful, but care must be taken because not everything is relevant. It is vital to select the information needed to tell the tale and support the gameplay. Writers should never feel obligated to use all the information they have, or they risk slowing the game down and overwriting the character.

Maintaining a Character

All the work put into creating a character is useless unless it carries over into the character's visible behavior and is consistently maintained throughout the game (or throughout the franchise for those games fortunate or unfortunate enough to warrant sequels).

Characterization Through Action

One of the more vital rules from Aristotle's *Poetics* is that a writer should ensure that drama is carried out through action not dialogue—often rendered as the adage "Show, don't tell." This means that we should see that characters are villains because they do villainous things rather than because other characters say that they are villainous. Characters are how they behave. This is more important than what they say.

Characterization Through Dialogue

Although characters' actions are more important than their dialogue, many games fail because of inferior dialogue. Although action conveys character, dialogue is often what makes the audience care about the people in the story. Flat dialogue that conveys only plot detail kills characters, and dialogue that attempts to imitate film dialogue rather than real people regularly fails to satisfy.

This is not to say that dialogue should be completely realistic. If it were, it would contain a thousand ums, ahs, and repetitions. Instead, dialogue has to sound *believable*. This means capturing the essential patterns of speech that different people use, learning their idiom and the correct terms for a particular period or career, and then condensing this down to keep its flavor but not its length. Just as a character's narrative purpose should disguise its game purpose, so dialogue's entertaining and realistic feel should hide the information it is there to convey.

Exposition describes dialogue, which simply relays bare, unconcealed information. Skillful dialogue uses subtext to conceal its purpose. This is dialogue that conveys meaning without actually saying the thing it is trying to express. So, a character that is attracted to someone could say to another character "I really like Joe." Now, as an audience we know this attraction exists, but this isn't hugely entertaining, and another route should be taken if possible. When in the same room, our character gives away her attraction in another way. Joe comments on the next-door neighbor being cute, and our character replies "She's very cute. If you like blonde and brainless." By reacting tetchily to Joe liking another character, our character has given away her secret desire for him, at least to the audience, and done it in a way that sets up conflict and tension.

One simple way to help make characters stand out from each other is to give them a dialogue tick. This is a way of speaking that is different from the other characters in the game. There are many possible approaches, including diction and accents (although as already noted, it's best to let voice actors render accents, rather than attempting to mimic the effect in prose), the use or non-use of contractions, their preferred sensory mode ("I see what you mean" versus "I hear what you're saying" versus "I feel what you're saying"—reflecting visual, auditory, and kinesthetic sensory modes respectively), their choice of pronoun (some characters may refer to themselves in the third person), or even a speech impediment (such as a stutter).

Another important factor in speech is the character's rhythm. How do they break their sentences up? Do they use 30-word sentences or struggle to assemble 6 in the right order? Where are their pauses and what elements of their vocabulary do they give emphasis? Emotion, inner conflict, and governing characteristics can all be defined by the amount characters talk and the way they break that speech down.

Lastly, characters that cannot talk can be a game writer's worst nightmare. Although characters *can* communicate by action, it is difficult for players to understand all but the broadest of a games character's motivation or for them to engage with a character that remains mute. If a writer is stuck with characters that can't communicate, the burden of their exposition must be given to another character that can communicate those thoughts instead.

CHARACTERS AND THE DEVELOPMENT TEAM

We've already seen how the game writer is only one part of the machinery by which a game comes into existence. It is not surprising, therefore, that character creation does not begin and end with the writer. If the writer is seeking to create a non-stereotypical character, and the artist creates an image that reinforces a stereotype, then the writer's job will be harder, if not impossible. Such conflicts must be resolved between the parties or through the producer. In return, the writer must seek to understand how the other members of the team go about their jobs. The writer shouldn't always give way—there are times to fight for what is narratively appropriate—but they should also be willing to compromise for the sake of the project.

Game Design

The job of the writer is to create an engaging story populated by rounded characters that serve the gameplay. The difference between a game writer and any other type of writer is the ability to focus and support the gameplay. Whereas in other media the creation of a character is shared among the writer, the director, and the actor, in games, character creation is divided among the writer, the actor, the artist, and the game designer. Where the game designer requires a character to have an ability to improve the gameplay, the writer must search for ways to alter the character to incorporate changes.

The Artist

A character's appearance has a huge impact on how the player views the character. If involved from the start of the project, then the writer needs to provide the artist with as clear a description of each character as possible. If the writer joins later in the process, then the character's appearance might already be decided, in which case, the writer must bear the character's appearance in mind when writing.

The writer must give the artists scope to practice their skills and not get caught up in unimportant detail. If a writer is set on the character having a hat solely to re-play a moment from *Raiders of the Lost Ark,* then the writer should remember that the hat was used to disguise stuntmen, and the conceit became a fun thing within the film. If the writer wants a hat, a valid argument in terms of purpose, personality, or entertainment within the game must be presented, and the writer in question must be prepared to swallow it if decisions go against them.

Voice Actors and Voice Directors

The writer's task here is to supply the director and actors with clear, concise bios for each character. These can make a huge difference when preparing for the voice recordings. Relevance is essential; the actor doesn't need to know everything about the character, but a few choice words can be extremely helpful.

CONCLUSION

The rules on character creation for games, much as with the narrative language of games as a whole, are still being written as people try different techniques, and others get to watch them succeed or fail. There is little doubt that huge strides forward are occurring, however. Characters are superseding icons in all manner of games, and the skill with which these characters are handled is also improving. The range of characters is straying away from stereotypes and injecting character twists and turns that hold players locked to their gamepad. Add to this an ever-expanding age bracket for sales and a market wanting to lure in more female gamers, and there will be an increasing pressure on developers to provide even more diverse and representative characters.

Just as important to this, character is being considered earlier and earlier in the process, allowing character reaction to be built into the gameplay, rather than tagged on to the end. Although the best game characters are still shallow when compared to the best characters in other media, this is in part owing to the player's capacity to disrupt the orderly progress of predefined narrative. This problem, in fact, is the reason why it's easier to render an anti-hero than a more complex character: if the players are likely to be engaging in anti-heroic activities with the game world, they might just as well have an anti-hero as a protagonist.

So, now that the soldiers running up the beach have been allowed doubts, dreams, and desires, and many leather-clad designs have been placed quietly back into cupboards to gather dust, it's not that the world of games will change completely. They'll just be deeper, more engaging, more fun, and a lot more emotional.

7 Cut Scenes and Scripted Events
Richard Dansky

The main body of a game's story is, by definition, told in the gameplay. The player takes the role of the protagonist and advances through a series of trials, reversals, and incidents that together comprise the story. But gameplay includes only the actions the player can perform and the choices that result, and those actions and choices are often inimical to the needs of story and characterization.

This need not be problematic. In a fast-paced science fiction FPS, it makes sense to focus on the things the game needs to do well—AI, combat models, and the like. It also makes sense for the gameplay to be the primary focus of the player's attention because this is the key element of any game.

There are times, however, when key elements of story can't be conveyed through the game itself. There are times when the player needs to be shown something, either to provide effect or information. Those are the times when it is necessary to deliver story materials outside of the gameplay, by using cut scenes and scripted events.

NONINTERACTIVE STORYTELLING

The common property between cut scenes and scripted events is that they are essentially noninteractive (although a scripted event can at times allow players some control over what they see and hear). Each has its own particular strengths and liabilities.

Cut Scenes

Cut scenes (particularly the FMV kind) are most frequently used for game intros and trailers or attract modes, ensuring that the player's first experience of the game is a visually appealing one and laying out the central conceit of the action. They are useful for making closing sequences that are appropriately spectacular and for providing intervals in the game when either high degrees of visual polish or actions that can't be shown in-game are required. They also can be used to deepen characterization, allowing for conversations between characters that the game engine can't allow for, and to establish mood and tone. Finally, cut scenes give the writer total control over events. In gameplay, characters have the annoying habit of surviving when they're not supposed to, and getting bumped off when they need to stay alive. A cut scene, however, ensures a rigid series of events. What will happen is certain to happen, and the player deals with the consequences afterwards. Often, a cut scene is the best place to kill off a supporting or allied character to the protagonist. It gives the players time to react and prevents them from becoming frustrated attempting to circumvent the inevitable in a gameplay context.

For example, the opening cinematic sequence from *Halo 2* (Bungie, 2004) accomplishes all of these goals, beginning with introducing the player to the world (Earth at war, science fiction setting, the events of the first game in the franchise mentioned in passing, and establishing the alien threat). It allows the player to see things that can't be done in game, such as the Master Chief receiving a medal or throwing himself out of an airlock, riding a bomb like Slim Pickens in *Dr. Strangelove*. By having the other characters react to the Master Chief, we get a sense of who he is and how these people feel about him, deepening the sense of characterization. And above all, it establishes the game's high production values, providing the player with a memorable entry point into the game world.

Although cut scenes are appealing and provide a broader palate of choice for the writer, they do have their drawbacks. For one thing, they break the flow of the game. A movie takes control away from the player, forcing the player into a passive role. There can also be a noticeable difference in visual quality between cut scenes and gameplay when FMV is used, and this disconnect can damage the player's immersion. Finally, there's the financial issue. Cut scenes, particularly prerendered ones, are expensive, and very few projects have unlimited budgets. In general, most game developers will allocate a certain amount of resources toward the generation of cut scenes—both in-engine and FMV—and writers will have to determine the most narratively useful manner to deploy these resources.

Scripted Events

Unlike cut scenes, scripted events don't significantly break the action. They are, instead, moments when the story takes control of either the camera (a camera case) or the camera and the action, forcing certain events. Scripted events are generally brief and used to illustrate a specific point or show off a specific effect rather than demand all of the player's attention. Those that are more than a mere camera case, are in effect related to in-engine cut scenes—with one significant difference: when a cut scene takes place, it is explicit that the player does not have control. During a scripted event, players may remain in control of their avatar and viewpoint.

There are two main difficulties with using scripted events. The first is that scripted events are limited by the game engine itself: if the game can't do it, the scripted event can't either. Often, this forces the shift to an in-engine cut scene instead because they are not bound by the limitations of the game design, only by the limitations of the game's engine. The other issue is that scripted events have to be, literally, scripted in the game engine, which can be tricky. After all, game behaviors are designed to function in the game, not for cinematic purposes. The results from even the most careful scripting can be unexpected, and getting precisely the right camera motions and events can be a time-consuming and difficult process.

To put this into perspective, the scripted event mission introductions for *Ghost Recon: Island Thunder* (Red Storm, 2002)—all of which involved a helicopter or other vehicle insertion and nothing else—took longer to script than the missions themselves and required more iterations to achieve a sufficient degree of polish.

The benefits associated with scripted events can make this investment worthwhile, however, as they allow the player to be right at the heart of key events without having to take away the player's agency (as happens with a cut scene). Nonetheless, scripted events beyond basic camera cases are the exclusive domain of more expensive game titles.

In-Game Artifacts

A third type of noninteractive storytelling technique is the use of in-game artifacts. These are among the hoariest devices in videogames, consisting of the information the player finds inside the game world, usually unveiling some combination of backstory, game knowledge, game technique, and inside jokes courtesy of the development team. In their classic form, they consist of notes, scrolls, and books the player picks up and reads to expand his knowledge and understanding. Research notes and increasingly frantic diaries in survival horror games are one well-known form, and magical books in fantasy cRPGs are another. A player can spend literally hours reading the in-game artifacts in games such as *Neverwinter Nights* (BioWare, 2002) or *The Elder Scrolls III: Morrowind* (Bethesda, 2002). More modern iterations include emails, files, and intercepted phone or radio transmissions that can be digested without ever leaving gameplay.

As graphics capabilities have improved, the ability of game developers to produce visual artifacts in their game worlds has also improved, allowing designers and writers to take advantage of everything from scrawled graffiti to significant dates on tombstones to glowing "Exit" signs that direct a player through the level without resorting to game-like elements such as mini-maps or objective indicators. Whether the effort to avoid game-like elements is genuinely beneficial is debatable, as clear communication with the player is arguably more valuable than preserving immersion. In this regard, each game project has the freedom to approach this issue in its own unique manner.

Although largely unrelated to cut scenes or scripted events, in-game artifacts are a form of noninteractive storytelling that is always worth considering simply because they are (in general terms) inexpensive to include. The cost of adding text to a game is minimal next to the cost of a cut scene, for instance, and therefore they provide a convenient method for some games to save on the cost of delivering necessary or supplemental exposition. This chapter therefore occasionally suggests an in-game artifact as a convenient alternative to the expense of a cut scene or scripted event.

TAKING CONTROL FROM THE PLAYER

The key to these techniques is taking control from the player. If players can command their own movements and thus by definition their interaction with the environment, then the scene itself cannot be controlled. No matter how elegant the scripting or clever the sequence of triggers in place, allowing the player control invariably means that no one else (even the game designers or writers) can have control at that point of the game.

Because most games strive to give the player as much control as possible, this may not immediately seem problematic. However, there are serious issues in terms of both communicating information to the player and maintaining the flow of the narrative. If the player has the choice of walking away from the NPC providing key information mid-sentence, how then does that information get conveyed to the player? If the game narrative demands that a certain character be removed from the stage, then what happens if the player can save that character? Even worse, what happens if the player can't and spends endless frustrating hours attempting the impossible when the designer has already decreed that character's inexorable fate?

It is often necessary, therefore, to take control from the players and render them spectators for at least a little while. There is a tradeoff here. On the negative side, it renders players passive when the game should be striving to be interactive. On the positive, however, plot and character can advance in preordained fashion, eliminating any possibility of the player interfering with the progression of the narrative. Furthermore, by distancing the player from action that may be potentially unpleasant—such as, say, the removal of a valued ally—removing player control renders it very clear that there is nothing the player could have done to alter the course of events, attenuating the frustration of forced failure.

Benefits of Removing Player Control

To appreciate why a game might want to remove control from the player (albeit only briefly), it is necessary to look at the benefits of doing so.

Advancing the Story

The main purpose and key benefit of taking control from the player is to advance the narrative of the game. By pausing the action, the game allows the player to absorb information that would either be hard to assimilate during core gameplay or that could not be adequately conveyed by the gameplay mechanisms themselves.

The prime example of this technique comes at the beginning of the game, with the intro cut scene or cinematic. Essentially a short film, this is most frequently used to set up the world, situation, and player goal in one step. We have already seen an example of how this can be used as an effective means of communicating general information about the game setting to the player.

Mid-game, there are multiple ways in which it is easier to advance the plot by removing control from the player. Adding or removing an item from the player's inventory is one standard example; the classic trope by which the player's progress is reset is through reversal. This technique can also be used to transmit plot-related information, as opposed to gameplay techniques. Consider the bomb detonation sequence in *The Sum of All Fears* (Red Storm, 2002), which depicts the detonation of a nuclear device that destroys Baltimore. Although it gives the player no new weapons, powers, or skills, it does advance the plot, explain the shift in locale (domestic to foreign) and enemy (backwoods militia to international terrorists), and escalate the tension (local stakes versus global ones). This particular sequence obviously could not have been delivered in an in-game context.

Cut scenes are not the only method of advancing the plot by taking control away from the player. For example, the *Metal Gear Solid* series (Konami, 1998 onwards) convey a tremendous amount of information to the player through mandatory talking heads sequences. In this regard, these games are both an example of cost effective use of resources and a warning against removing player control unnecessarily. Many players have criticized these games for the length of these talking heads sequences, which frequently take an extremely long time to deliver their narrative content.

Providing what is sometimes termed an *information dump* (*info-dump*) to the player in cinematic form packages the information in a way that the player is both familiar with and able to digest easily. Some cinematic forms provide exposition more accessibly than others. For example, consider these three forms: (1) the back-and-forth discussion of the diagnostic process on a medical show such as *House*, (2) the scrolling intonation of setting in the original *Star Wars,* and (3) the standardized technobabble explanations of the *Star Trek* shows of the 1980s and 90s. All three approaches are rapid ways of advancing the story without resorting to detailed explanations. By borrowing these forms, game narrative potentially borrows their success as well.

Ultimately, the main narrative advantage to taking control from the player in this manner is economizing the time required to provide exposition and thus advance the story. Players often want to explore, backtrack, or wander off in search of things to interact with. All of these can provide problems when the need is to advance the storyline and get information across as elegantly as possible.

Certainty of Experience

One of the biggest benefits to removing player control is ensuring the certainty and repeatability of the experience. It cannot be overstated how risky it is in game narrative and exposition to have the players running around loose, able to interfere with carefully choreographed outcomes, when they are needed front and center to hear a vital piece of game-related information. If the players are not there to hear it (or see it, or get it, or have it taken away from them), then they will lack the tools and information needed to succeed.

There are in-game ways to handle this dilemma, but these can become clunky and obvious. Having the same NPC repeat the same line of dialogue over and over while placed strategically at the exit of the level may ensure that the player hears what the character has to say, but it may undermine immersion and any illusion that the inhabitants of your game world were anything other than icons. Having multiple avenues for transmitting information or events works fine as long as the player only runs across one and isn't subjected to lethal repetition. Note, however, that different players will have different tolerances to dealing with incomplete information and degrees of repetition. As a generalization, it may be better to risk repetition of content than to risk the players having no idea what is expected of them.

Controlling the experience, on the other hand, guarantees that the players get exactly the information they require at the correct moment. There is no question of the player missing anything or being at a disadvantage if the game is structured around an unavoidable cut scene or scripted event.

A controlled experience is also one that can be fine-tuned for maximum effect. If the designer knows where the avatar will be standing at that point in the game, the camera can be placed for maximum effect with no potential for unfortunate collision or obstruction. If the designer knows precisely who's going to be alive in the scene (at both the beginning and the end—since they're not always the same), then the writer can script dialogue precisely and appropriately. The experience is guaranteed and maximized to the player's ultimate benefit.

Tutorials

Many games provide new abilities to the player as the game progresses. Although wresting control from the player for the purpose of teaching a new ability is not essential, it is sometimes necessary to ensure that the player has learned what will be required to advance through the next part of the game. However, a marked distinction exists between teaching and learning: it should not be assumed that providing a noninteractive tutorial will reliably convey information to the player. The construction of tutorials, however, is a complex issue beyond the scope of this book.

Rewards

We have already seen how a cut scene can be used as a simple reward for a player. In this context, the loss of control is not problematic. The player has just completed a section of gameplay, perhaps one that was especially challenging, and the provision of a cut scene can act as an excellent reward.

The most common use of cut scenes as rewards is showing the ultimate overthrow of a just-defeated boss. In psychological terms, this reinforces the player's dominance; pragmatically, it's nice for the player to see the bad guy go down hard and in picturesque fashion.

The reward of a cut scene can be especially strong when the player has emotional attachments to the license. *Kingdom Hearts* (Square, 2002) is a perfect example of this, pausing the action after small advances to gift the player with gorgeously rendered cut scenes and appearances by favorite Disney characters.

Rewards can also act on a smaller scale, as with the use of extravagant imbedded visual effects sequences in Japanese cRPGs such as *Grandia II* (Game Arts, 2000), *Skies of Arcadia* (Overworks, 2000), or the more recent titles in the *Final Fantasy* series (Square, 1987 onwards). These games provide extravagant light and sound shows in response to the use of magic and special abilities. The spectacle has no effect on the combat—the damage gets allocated regardless—but the player earns something interesting to watch as a reward for mastering the new spell or ability, and the mathematics of combat are hidden behind a further layer of gloss.

Foreshadowing

Taking control away from the player for foreshadowing is often a brief exercise, most often executed as a camera case that highlights an individual, a locale, or an object that will become important later. The purpose here is that the player sees the person, place, or thing so that when it appears later, there's a flash of recognition.

For example, in a game such as *007: Agent Under Fire* (EA, 2001), it is sufficient to foreshadow a future boss fight by having James Bond brush up against a villainous bruiser and then move on. The player proceeds in full knowledge that he and said bruiser will meet again over crossed swords (or guns, or powerboats, or exploding inkwells), but now anticipation is in place for that ultimate resolution. If the player had control of Bond during this introductory meeting, violence would almost inevitable ensure, thus short-circuiting the later sequences. The control that is taken from the player is both subtle and brief—just a moment of pulling back the camera and showing the villain in passing—but by the time it is returned, the stage has been set for later confrontation.

In the context of foreshadowing in videogames, however, care must be taken: the length of a typical videogame can render conventional foreshadowing techniques insufficient. There is little value in revealing something to the players in a camera case if it will not become relevant until 20 hours later because most players will have long forgotten. Either the foreshadowing must be reserved until a point closer in time to the point of relevance, or more subtle techniques must be used.

Showing Off Assets

Sometimes, there is an argument for showing something to the player simply because it looks impressive. A great particle effect, a particularly beautiful level space or character model, an impressive application of the physics engine's capabilities, or anything else that can engender a sense of wonder, beauty, or awe in the minds of the players represents a possible way for the game to provoke an emotional response (other than frustration) in the player. Because these opportunities are rarer than might perhaps be expected, it can be worthwhile to use noninteractive sequences to highlight them. If the players' experiences will be enhanced by seeing it, it's a positive benefit to make sure that they do indeed see it.

For example, there is a moment early in *Ghost Recon 2* (Red Storm, 2004) wherein the game seizes control of the camera from the player for just a moment. It pulls up and around, picking the optimum angle with which to demonstrate the effects of the player's having planted explosive charges on a bridge being used by enemy armor. When the player reaches a safe distance, the event triggers, the camera moves, and the bridge explodes spectacularly. Tanks tumble into the river gorge, smoke goes up, and concrete crumbles—all with the simulation disabled, so as not to risk the player avatar getting shot while unable to react—and then normal gameplay resumes. It takes, at most, 20 seconds, but it accomplishes a great deal.

First of all, the fact that this occurs early in the game establishes the context of the experience to follow. The game announces in no uncertain terms that it's about big explosions that the player can create, setting the stage for later action and revising any player expectation from the previous titles in the series. Second, and more important, is this: it looks cool. Players watching gain enjoyment from the carnage and satisfaction from realizing that they were responsible for this outcome—both enhance the player experience.

Dangers of Removing Player Control

The adage states that with great power comes great responsibility, and so it is with taking control from the player in a game. If a noninteractive sequence backfires, it can have devastating consequences to player enjoyment. Therefore, it's important to understand how these sequences can go wrong and recognize some of the consequences therein.

Disrupted Pacing

We have already seen how pacing is a vital aspect of narrative. The use of noninteractive sequences risks upsetting the pacing of the game. If a cut scene plays out too slowly, it can disrupt the pacing of the narrative, probably leaving the player uninterested in its development—or risking that the player might skip through a cut scene and thus lose touch with the story entirely. Equally, if cut scenes are too fast, there may be a jarring transition with the gameplay, or there may be insufficient time for the player to take in what has transpired.

A good general technique is to write out everything that needs to be said in the course of the sequence, and then work iteratively to edit out everything that can be omitted. Writers tend to default to being excessively verbose, rather than excessively terse, and hence repetitive editing usually has the desirable result of ensuring that any given scene does not outstay its welcome.

Forced Failures

A forced failure is a situation where the player cannot accomplish a certain goal, no matter what he tries. Gandalf is always going to fall off the bridge in the Mines of Moria, no matter what anyone does. The story demands it. Think, however, of how frustrating it would be to be playing Aragorn in that scenario. Imagine trying every possible way to save Gandalf and failing, time after time after time. Consider how frustrating that would be, and whether you would really want to continue playing that particular game, right after your best asset (not to mention a character you hopefully cared about) was stripped away from you.

This is the danger embodied by a forced failure. To create tension or conflict artificially, the ability of the player to succeed is artificially countermanded. Enemies are made invulnerable, player avatars are rendered helpless and stripped of their belongings off-camera, and allied characters are killed without hope of rescue. The usual motivations for forced failures are to forward the narrative, build dramatic tension, or (in rare cases) to produce an emotional response in the player, but anger and frustrations are the likely emotions to be engendered if forced failures are not handled carefully.

Stealing Rewards from the Player

Closely related to the forced failure, the theft of rewards from the player actively punishes the player for succeeding. Frequently done for the sake of a reversal, it takes all the rewards and advancements the player has earned and removes them in a way the player has no control over, frequently starting him over with no weapons, no armor, and no transportation.

A relatively benign example of this approach can be found in *No One Lives Forever* (Monolith, 2000), in which secret agent Cate Archer fights her way through a plane full of enemies, only to be inevitably knocked out by an evil henchman and stripped of her equipment. There is no way out of the level except by submitting to the inevitable knockout. Although doing this does extend gameplay—the player has to rebuild everything that was taken away, and the threat level can be ratcheted back in accordance with the player's new level of capability—it also punishes the player for succeeding. Running out of ammo is one thing; taking the gun away during a scripted sequence that the player cannot avoid is entirely another.

Removing Player Choice

Going into cut scene or scripted mode aggressively removes player choice. If the player avatar performs an action in a scripted event, there is always the chance that the very action the avatar performs is contrary to what the player would want to do in that situation. Obvious treachery that the player can't do anything about, foolish actions by allied NPCs that he can't stop, bad strategic planning while walking into a firefight just before gameplay starts again are all examples of decisions being made for the player by the game, for the sake of effect or narrative. By running the character counter to the player's vision of that character, the game creates conflict between itself and the player.

Often, it seems necessary to remove player choice in this manner. After all, if *Grand Theft Auto: Vice City*'s (Rockstar North, 2002) Tommy Vercetti rubs out the annoying lawyer Ken Rosenburg at their first meeting, that hamstrings the ability of the game to get missions and information to the player. Better, then, that Rosenburg only appears in cut scenes so that the player can't kill him and jeopardize later gameplay. It all seems very straightforward and logical, except that the player is taking the part of Tommy Vercetti, who kills lots and lots of people for far less reason than Rosenburg gives him on a regular basis. Players are kept from doing something they might want to do (and have been trained to do by the game itself), and so every nonlethal interaction with Rosenburg is a potential reminder to the players that they don't have full control of their actions in the world. Many players will not mind, but the potential for frustration is there and should be considered.

Teasing the Player

The underlying draw of many videogames is player fantasy. In the game, players can do things—cast spells, swing swords, brutally annihilate thousands of enemies with automatic weapons fire—that they can't do in real life. Where this gets dangerous, however, is when the players are shown activities in noninteractive sequences that they can't perform themselves. For example, if the game only allows the avatar to move and shoot, but the avatar gets to throw knives or perform hand-to-hand combat in scripted sequences, it devalues the player experience. Players can observe their character doing things that they cannot make the character do, which undermines the escapism of the play.

Generally, if players see their avatar carry out an action, they expect to be able to carry out that action when they are in control of the avatar. If they cannot, then the player's capacity to identify with the avatar has been somewhat lessened because they possess only a portion of the capabilities they expect to possess.

Providing Too Much Information

We know that players want to play. Burden them with too much information, however, and they may tune out and lose interest. Because the information delivered in noninteractive sequences is not player solicited, care must be taken not to provide too much at any given time.

The core of what the writer is trying to communicate should generally be something that can be explained in three sentences at most. After that, either the material being presented is too complicated, unnecessary ornamentation is being added, or the game is asking the writer to convey too much in one place. In the first case (excessive complexity), the writer can simplify. In the second case (excessive embellishment), the writer can edit. In the third case, the necessity to cram too much information into one sequence can be an early red flag for the designer and the rest of the team to restructure or resequence.

Denying the Player the Central Role

One of the biggest pitfalls of game writing, particularly for newcomers to the trade, is the temptation to write the story as if the protagonist was the hero. Rather, the form demands that the *player* be the hero. It may be Link or Pitfall Harry or Spider-Man up on the screen, but it's the players who are controlling—and in a sense, being—them.

Taking control away from the player, however, is a step on the slippery slope toward taking the narrative away from the player. It can become very tempting to use cut scenes and voice-overs to tell the writer's story, rather than the player's story. When the game starts telling the player what his character has accomplished, instead of allowing the player to accomplish it on his own, take it as a serious warning.

APPLICATIONS FOR NONINTERACTIVE SEQUENCES

Having considered the benefits and risks associated with taking control away from the player, we are ready to consider the applications of cut scenes and scripted events in the context of game narrative.

Character Development

Nongameplay elements often provide the opportunity to introduce and develop characters that fast-paced gameplay cannot. By providing characterization that's not in direct conflict with the gameplay for the player's attention, this approach allows a tighter focus on the characters and what the player should know and feel about them.

One particularly useful role in character development afforded by noninteractive sequences is in the introduction of new characters. It affords two particular advantages. First, the sequences ensure that the player won't try to shoot the new characters before learning who they are. Second, it provides time and space for exposition, letting the characters explain who they are, why they're there, and why the player shouldn't shoot them immediately after the action is restored.

The writer can also control the character's first appearance for maximum effect. It can be satisfyingly dramatic for a mysterious ally to appear out of some shadowy corner or utter a sudden one-liner directly behind the player character, but this cannot generally be achieved while the player is in control. Introducing characters in noninteractive sequences also allows writers to control the moment of introduction, rather than risking the player stumbling onto an NPC's location before the narratively appropriate moment.

Out-of-game moments can also provide an opportunity for solid, condensed character growth. This is in large part due to the fact that in cut scenes and so forth, the character can be made to do things that are not necessarily provided for in gameplay. Giving monologues, performing complex actions, or simply providing alternate body language to the motion set used in-game can all communicate a great deal about a character in a way that gameplay might not be able to.

In-game artifacts shine at this particular form of character development. Reading characters' diaries, checking out their lab notes, or watching their video recordings can allow the player to learn about characters that aren't even on the scene. Horror titles in particular make use of this technique, showing off one disturbing character revelation after another as the player dives deeper, page-by-page, into the mystery.

Finally, there is the death of a character. If a character dies in a cut scene, the players know they can't do anything about it and won't spend endless, frustrating, doomed attempts to save the character. If NPCs die—or sacrifice themselves—while the players cannot act, the players know there is no hope of rescue. This is particularly powerful for moments of self-sacrifice, such as the death of Floyd the

Robot in *Planetfall* (Infocom, 1983), widely regarded as a seminal moment in videogame storytelling.

As a further benefit, this technique lets the player get the full impact of the character's death. If an allied character goes down during a firefight, it's a tactical situation as well as an emotional one, and the player's energy is directed toward survival more than emotion. If, however, the character doesn't breathe his last until after the last enemy hits the ground, then there's time for farewells, dying requests, vows of vengeance, and transmission of vital bits of information. If handled skillfully—avoiding the now-clichéd slow-motion "Nooooo" is highly recommended—it provides a much more involving experience than simply rifling through the dead character's equipment.

Exposition

Great care must be taken with exposition because there is always a danger of dragging down the action and slowing the pace of the game. The more exposition required, the greater the break in the action and the less the player is likely to care about the meticulously detailed story that the writer is laying out. In this regard, skilled construction of noninteractive sequences can get exposition across without making the action suffer as a result.

Some games require elements in the backstory to be expanded or explained. This can be carried out in either monologue or flashback; this form of exposition catches the player up on the events in the game world that led up to the start of the gameplay. Often laying out these elements can be key to supporting player enjoyment. If players spend too much time asking "why am I doing this," they are not paying attention to the game. By laying out the backstory, the writer shores up the context of the gameplay and provides a direction for the action.

As noted previously, flashbacks are a prime method for this sort of exposition, combining the exposition of backstory with imagery. In-game documentation does this as well, most notably found in the research notes so prevalent in survival-horror games. Last but not least, it's always possible to have a character simply explain to the player what happened, but this approach can be visually uninteresting—why watch an NPC talk when you could be playing—and more often than not, these cut scenes get skipped by impatient players who are too annoyed with the medium to hold still for the message.

A superior approach may be to use a noninteractive sequence to bridge between a *playable* flashback. Although rarely used, this has the advantage of allowing the player to explore the backstory in the context of play, instead of simply hearing about it.

In general terms, however, the best thing exposition can do is advance the narrative. Telling the players what is going on allows them to buy into it, thus enhancing the meaning of their actions in the game world. Often, elements like this occur away from the game action, in locations like the villain's lair, so that the player gets to learn things the player avatar never could. One example is the short discussion in *No One Lives Forever 2* (Sierra, 2002) between the villainous Director and his reluctant henchwoman Isako. In this, the player learns the details of the relationship between the two, and that she's got a deadly, implacable enemy who might somehow still be turned from the service of the evil syndicate H.A.R.M. (This example creates a disconnect between the players' knowledge and their character's knowledge; fortunately, it is the player who benefits from the mismatch in this instance.)

Helping the Player

Although noninteractive sequences are outside of gameplay, they can still refer to it. Often, a nongameplay sequence can inform the players as to what they have to do after gameplay resumes or can make the players' task easier if they take the time to listen. The most tangible element of this is when a noninteractive element is used to provide hints to the player.

This is often the province of in-game artifacts, especially for minor hints and clues. The player doesn't need to read or even heed the hint, but putting it out there rewards the player who is paying attention. The hints provided can provide assistance with in-game abilities, puzzles, or details on specific opponents. The wooden signs in *The Legend of Zelda: The Ocarina of Time* (Nintendo, 1998) are in-game artifacts that fulfill all three of these roles.

Cut scenes can be used to provide a hint in the form of a negative example, such as the beach scenario in *Half-Life 2* (Valve, 2004). By letting the players watch scripted NPCs perform an action—in this case, trying to get off the beach without getting eaten—and fail, the game suggests to players what they *shouldn't* be doing. This is important—it is not desirable for players to discover that a particular action is fatal only through their own failure.

Sometimes a break in the action can serve to tell the player what to do next. The most egregious example of this sort is the mission briefing, which often combines a "wall of text" approach with voice-over and potentially visuals. Cut scenes and scripted events can also serve this function, with something as simple as an NPC shouting "He's getting away!" or as complex as laying out the multiple objectives a player needs to accomplish.

Depicting Action

Perhaps the most archetypal use of noninteractive sequences is in the depiction of action. This can be in the context of rewards, as we've already seen; in building the fantasy of the central role in an opening cinematic by making the central character seem impressive; or simply depicting outcomes in their most impressive light (as with the example of the demolished bridge given earlier in this chapter).

At the other end of the spectrum, the spectacle can be displayed before the action. A camera pan down the serried ranks of enemies before battle can impress on the player exactly what he's up against, as can the visualization of a boss-level foe before the action starts. Both let the players understand the enormity of what they are facing and add to the players' feeling of triumph if and when they finally achieve victory.

Cut scenes or scripted events can also be used when the writer cannot take a chance on the player not succeeding. At these moments, it's best to produce a *forced success,* which serves much the same purpose as a spectacle reward. The player has advanced to a certain point in the campaign, and the game rewards him by showing him what he has accomplished.

This can also be used to dictate the terms of a character's success, such as ensuring the player avatar allows an enemy to surrender instead of being shot randomly by a trigger-happy player. This is particularly useful if the NPC has information to give that would otherwise be lost if he died, or if the writer intends to use the character later in some capacity.

Although the depiction of action is arguably the most basic role of a cut scene or scripted event, it is important to always be certain that any such noninteractive sequence serves a purpose. All three of the other roles discussed in this section—character development, exposition, and helping the player—are more useful to the narrative and to the game than simply depicting action. If a game's cut scenes serve solely to provide exciting visuals, they risk being ultimately vacuous. Writers must be certain that the depiction of a certain action is a worthwhile use of resources before committing to the creation of expensive cut scenes or time-consuming scripted events.

WRITING MANAGEABLE CUT SCENES AND SCRIPTED EVENTS

The wonderful thing about writing scripted events, cut scenes, and the like is that while they're on the page, the sky is the limit. The writer can propose casts of thousands, rains of fire, and characters doing intense pilates workouts onscreen, going by nothing but the pictures in the writer's imagination.

However, getting it from the page to the screen can be tricky. Just because the writer can imagine it doesn't mean that the team can build the models, produce the effects, or generate the sounds necessary. Matching the scope of what's being written to the capabilities and resources of the team is vital.

Knowing Your Resources

The most important, and indeed, first step that any writer should take before writing a script is to determine what is available to work with. Knowing the extent of the resources available immediately provides dimension and scope to any proposal the writer makes. It avoids wasted work, as there won't be any time spent on proposing material that can't be composed, and it builds team unity, as team members appreciate knowing that other people are paying attention to what they're doing and realize that what they're doing is valuable.

An important secondary technique is to make any proposal scalable. It's all well and good to write to the available resources promised at the start of the project, but no plan survives contact with the enemy, and often there's a different (lesser) amount of resources available when it comes time to actually create the scene. As such, it's often helpful to compose fallback positions, and to know in advance what portions of the script are fungible. It's also important to know at what point too much will have been cut, causing the scene or event to lose its meaning. Knowing what can go and what can't and knowing it ahead of time, is vital when it comes time to debate production schedules and rewrites.

Assets

In this instance, *assets* refers to character models, other map elements, and level spaces. Often, a cinematic event requires creating new assets to tell the story properly, but this can cause friction with the people who actually have to make them. Learning what models and places are available before the script is written and trying to incorporate them rather than demanding all-new assets goes a long way toward speeding the production schedule and avoiding friction with the rest of the team. After all, assets cost time and money to build, and every bit of time spent on a cut scene or scripted event is time that doesn't get spent on the game itself.

Engine and Camera Capabilities

Game engines are finicky beasts, and camera control is one of the longest-standing problems of game design. Naturally, both are tuned for the gameplay, so figuring out what they can or can't do can provide valuable guidelines. If the writer is doing an in-engine cut scene with an engine that can only handle four characters onscreen, then crowd scenes are immediately off the menu. Conversely, if the engine can do long sightlines well and clearly, then that's an element that can be put to use.

Sound

Sound costs money. Every line of dialogue needs to be written, formatted, recorded, processed, and implemented. That's a lot of work and a lot of money. Therefore, knowing upfront how much dialogue can be included is a tremendous help. If there's no room in the budget for new characters, then creating new characters with key expository dialogue is a waste of time and effort. Instead, the writer should have a good idea of how much dialogue can be used and how many characters are available to speak it.

Schedule

Everything takes time, including scripted events and cut scenes. Knowing how much time there is and how many people are available to work on scenes also helps define what gets proposed and written. If the team is willing to outsource cut scenes, that opens a whole new world of resources. On the other hand, if they're being done in-house, that means the people doing it are potentially being taken away from other tasks. There is a limited amount of time in any game development cycle, and writing something that can't be completed—because it requires too many models, voices, or settings—is either going to result in incomplete work or crippling other aspects of the project. Writing to the schedule makes sense in that it gives writers a better chance of seeing their work realized and reduces stress on the rest of the team.

Cut Scene and Scripted Event Dialogue

Scripted events and cut scenes generally call for dialogue, and they tend to incorporate the kind of dialogue that you can't or shouldn't put into the main action of the game. There are no distractions when the scripted event is rolling; no chance that the player will be too busy to pay attention to the crucial game information intended to be passed along. Instead, the players are providing their undivided attention. This is a great opportunity, but it's also a tremendous challenge.

The format and conventions established for movie scripts can be an excellent way to think about cut scenes and scripted events because the forms can be similar in many ways. Using screenplay format allows writers to break out the elements of their noninteractive sequence, enabling them to catalogue what camera movements and assets might be needed, and, perhaps more importantly, to estimate how long it's likely to take. Using screenplays as a reference also allows the noninteractive sequence to be rendered in a language and form that should be familiar to other people working on its implementation, allowing for better useful discussion and commentary at the paper stage.

In terms of the actual dialogue, there are generally fewer restrictions with noninteractive sequences than with normal in-game dialogue. Unless the game in question has a separate conversation mode wherein conversational choices are the results of player action (as happens for instance in *Neverwinter Nights*), writers should generally aim to keep the length of in-game dialogue lines to the minimum. This is only common sense; the longer the line, the more chance there is that the player will do something (or shoot someone, or move away from the speaker) that renders it impossible to get the full import of the line.

With noninteractive dialogue, however, that's not a concern. The camera stays exactly where it needs to stay, and the controlled environment allows for lengthier lines of dialogue. In fact, scripted events are arguably the perfect place to put in lengthier bits of exposition that are vitally important to the game because you can be assured that the player will get all of it. As a result, noninteractive sequences are often used to explain backstory, set up the next quest or sequence of events, or tell the player what he has to do next—all things that generally take more than three or four words to get across.

However, such exposition should generally take place using in-engine cut scenes (which are comparatively inexpensive) rather than expensive FMV or time-consuming scripted events. Some game engines will even support specific "talking heads" in-engine cut scene modes, which are ideal for this kind of dialogue. The opportunity to expand is not a mandate to do so, however. The best scripted events are often those that are shortest and most elegant. Consider one example taken from *Tom Clancy's Rainbow Six: Lockdown* (Ubisoft, 2005). The information to be conveyed is that the enemy terrorists have managed to turn into a weapon the nanovirus they have previously stolen, and now possess the ability to throw it at the player and the player's squad-mates in the form of grenades. The player has not yet come across these weapons, so the scripted event is vital for getting across all this information, as well as the fact that the grenades are fatal.

One possibility is this:

CHAVEZ

Look sharp, people. Intel tells me that the terrorists have managed to weaponize the virus. They're using grenades for a delivery device, so if one goes off near you, you're a goner. Be careful.

Another is this:

[The camera moves into the room, showing a TERRORIST holding a VIRUS GRENADE. He flings it at the door we know RAINBOW will be coming through, then runs.]

CHAVEZ (V.O.)

Virus grenade! Down!

Both convey the same information, but the second one does it faster, more elegantly, and with fewer sound assets. In choosing between these two options, the latter is probably preferable—provided there is some confidence that the vital information is being conveyed. There is always the risk that the player will recognize that they have been in a threatening situation (a grenade has been used) but not connect it with the nanovirus plot device. It may be necessary to reinforce this exposition through other means.

Lastly, dialogue in noninteractive sequences affords opportunities that may not otherwise be plausible. For example, rapid-fire back-and-forth repartee is tricky to achieve in a gameplay context, in large part because it's difficult to guarantee that the characters engaging in witty banter are actually close, facing each other, and interested in doing so. The control afforded by a cut scene or scripted event affords an opportunity for quick exchanges, and with it opportunities for character-building and increasing tension. Having an NPC cut a character off in mid-sentence during gameplay can be difficult or even impossible and even when plausible, risks sounding stilted or artificial. Within a cut scene or scripted event, however, the pacing is controlled, allowing for the dramatic interruption to be used when it is useful to do so.

Useful Techniques

As with all game writing, constructing a scripted event has limitations outside the writers' control. This is especially true for scripted events. Because these are implemented entirely in the game engine using in-game animations, actions, and assets, there can be some pretty tight restrictions. It's useful, therefore, to learn methods for "cheating"—using the tools that are available to produce the desired affect and to minimize the risk of undesirable outcomes.

Hiding Lip-Synch

Lip-synching can be tricky. Matching up the motion of a character's mouth to the dialogue she's delivering can be expensive, time-consuming, and difficult. In some cases, the decision may be made to have the character's mouth move randomly, producing an effect similar to that seen in a badly dubbed kung fu movie. Although this is the easy way to go, it's also less than satisfying aesthetically. As a result, the other choice is often to clamp down ruthlessly on the dialogue allowed in scripted events. The fewer words there are, the fewer times the character's mouth has to be animated.

An alternative is to use the camera position to circumvent the need to lip-synch. With strong character identification and unique voices (which any writer should strive to attain), the camera doesn't necessarily need to be on the face of the character who is talking. By moving the camera to another position or switching to an over-the-shoulder or a top-down view, it is possible to conceal the faces and therefore the lips of any character. By reinforcing who is speaking with hand gestures, it is therefore possible to minimize the amount of lip-synching required.

Monologue

There is an efficacy to monologue that can make it a tempting method of delivering information. Monologue is generally faster than dialogue, it cuts down on the number of actors required, and monologues tend not to involve a lot of complicated gymnastics or camera movements.

The danger with monologue is that it risks being drab and uninteresting so it's usually desirable to break up or otherwise minimize monologue. If there are multiple characters or sources onscreen for the information, it doesn't have to be just one character delivering it. If that doesn't work, carefully timed interruptions—even ones as simple as "And then what?" or "You can't be serious!" provide an alteration to the rhythm that players will appreciate.

Trimming Dialogue

People read faster than they speak; therefore it is easy to write too many words for a script that ideally should be terse and punchy. One way writers can test their work is to have someone else read the script out loud. This provides a valuable perspective on how long the material really is, and therefore enables writers to spot opportunities for tightening the script for any noninteractive sequence. It's always desirable to achieve a shorter script earlier rather than later. Localization and recording all cost money—it is infinitely better to make changes prior to either stage, than afterwards.

Laying out what a noninteractive sequence needs to do before beginning to write dialogue for it can be hugely beneficial. What point in the game does it play, what information does it need to convey, and who needs to be there? These elements should be positioned in the script and kept there. When the time comes for the first trimming pass, these are elements that cannot be cut. Everything else is a candidate to be culled. Remove unnecessary backstory or story details first; lose one-liners if necessary.

Writers must also be wary of dialogue that includes multiple subordinate clauses and compound-complex sentences. Sentence structure should remain simple for the benefit of both voice actors and players.

In learning to trim dialogue, it's tempting to warn writers not to cut too much out of the scripts. However, in practice this is rarely the problem. Writers usually understand the story they are working on sufficiently so that they know when they have removed too much. Usually the problem is having the nerve or the insight to make the difficult subtractions that will ensure brisk dialogue.

CONCLUSION

Cut scenes and scripted events provide mechanisms for delivering story elements noninteractively. This makes it easier to advance the story and ensure certainty of experience for the player, but that comes at the risk of disrupted pacing and the reduction of player choice or agency. However, because there are strict limits to what can be achieved in terms of narrative using only the gameplay, most games must use noninteractive sequences for character development, exposition, and assisting the player.

In tackling the writing tasks associated with scripted events, the writer must fully understand the assets that are available, know the limitations of the game engine and the game camera, and develop a realistic schedule for the work. Although the possibility for more verbose dialogue is always present for a noninteractive sequence, care must be taken to preserve the pace of the story and of the game. The capability to engage in longer conversations in an in-engine cut scene does not mean that this is the best option. Concise and elegant dialogue is always more desirable than excessively long talking head sequences.

In facing cut scenes and scripted events, game writers are working in a form that on the surface most resembles other media, such as TV and movie scripts. To render these noninteractive sequences in a manner conducive to the game they relate to, it is important to keep track of their single most important element: they exist to support the narrative, and the narrative exists to support the gameplay. It follows, therefore, that they should be used only when essential, and even when essential, they should be created with brevity and efficacy as their highest ideal.

8 Writing Comedy for Videogames
Ed Kuehnel and Matt Entin

A s Robert Plant once said, "Does anybody remember laughter?" If we look back just over a decade ago, the market was flooded with a cornucopia of great comedy titles. It was the heyday of the point-and-click graphic adventure. The big two studios, LucasArts and Sierra, were churning out a string of instant-classics: *Space Quest: The Sarien Encounter* (Sierra, 1986), *Leisure Suit Larry in the Land of the Lounge Lizards* (Sierra, 1987), *The Secret of Monkey Island* (Lucasfilm Games, 1990), *Day of the Tentacle* (LucasArts, 1993), and *Sam & Max Hit the Road* (LucasArts, 1993). And then *Grim Fandango* (LucasArts, 1998) happened.

Tim Schaeffer's brilliant comic noir set a new standard for graphic adventures. It was showered with awards and critical praise, but showed miniscule profits. Marketing departments everywhere gasped, and thus ended the reign of the graphic adventure (at least outside of Scandinavia which has hardly been the industry's most fertile ground for comic hijinks). A handful of comedy titles appear now and again, perhaps most prominently the low brow, scatological action-adventure *Conker's Bad Fur Day* (Rare, 2001), but for the most part games as a forum for laughter were largely forgotten.

There is no doubt that humor does have an audience in games; in fact, the astonishingly successful *Grand Theft Auto: Vice City* and *San Andreas* (Rockstar North, 2002 & 2004) feature comedic elements prominently, from the burlesque of the Love Fist bomb-in-the-car mission in *Vice City* to the slapstick of blind triad boss Wu Zi Mu (Woozie) in *San Andreas*, both games feature prominent attempts at humor, albeit fairly unsophisticated. However, there are definite signs that publishers have been wary of comedy games since the decline of the point-and-click adventures. Perhaps a new game genre is required to act as a vehicle for comedy; in this regard, we can only wait and see what the future holds.

The purpose of this chapter is to give practical advice to those who aspire to write a genuinely funny videogame. This chapter will not attempt to teach you how to *be funny*, but rather it will relate practical advice so that aspiring comedy writers who seek work in the games industry will have some guidance to the unique problems of adapting comedy to an interactive experience.

CHOOSING WRITERS

The biggest roadblock to producing comedies in the games industry is the lack of available writing talent. On the surface, this claim seems specious: there is a wealth of talented comedy writers in Hollywood available for hire, right? Writers for TV shows such as *The Simpsons* and *Futurama* have been used successfully in the past to create funny games based on those intellectual properties. Elsewhere there is no shortage of game writers, including people who have made a career writing science-fiction, fantasy-adventure, horror-survival, or military stories for games, but alas, few comedies. The problems with using Hollywood writers are economic and practical; the problem with using career game writers is mostly an issue of mismatched talent. In this section, we'll discuss the pros and cons of both, what situations work, and how aspiring game writers can use this knowledge to their advantage.

Using TV Writers

If a developer is making a game based on a popular show such as *The Simpsons*, *South Park*, or *Family Guy*, it makes great sense to hire writers who have worked on those shows. They have a proven track-record, are familiar with the characters and comedic style, and fans and publishers alike will rest easy with the knowledge that a professional is on the case. Nothing is as critical to the success of a game purporting itself to be a comedy than the writing and voice acting.

There are issues, however, when using Hollywood professionals. The first is cost: as testament to how rare truly talented comedy writers are, Hollywood pays them a substantial amount of money. It would not be unusual for a top comedy writer in Hollywood to make as much in a month as most freelance game writers make in a year. Some games have as much dialogue as an entire season of television and can take months to write, making the cost of using Hollywood writers significant. Although game budgets are ever increasing in our industry, matching Tinsel Town dollar for dollar to lure away their best comedy writers is impractical, with some exceptions. With *The Simpsons* for example, it's very possible that the game's publisher, a media conglomerate that likely owns both the show and the rights to make the game, will have access to the show's writers (more likely "junior writers") at a reduced rate, or you may get lucky and find top Hollywood writers who just really love games and are willing to take a cut in pay. In general, however, without the money to hire Hollywood's best, it's much more likely that the average developer will end up dealing with mediocre talent driven to games by financial necessity alone.

As an example of the problem, consider this episode from our personal experience. On our first title, mostly to help put our publisher's mind at ease, we interviewed some professional writers they had lined up to do some potential "punch-up" work on our scripts. The first pair had some fleeting association with a sports talk show, worked sporadically on other Hollywood projects, and wrote wedding toasts. The next worked on such long-cancelled programs as *Perfect Strangers* and *Step by Step...* and hadn't worked much since. The last person we interviewed was not a writer but a producer who had some great stories about Drew Barrymore and had little else to offer. We asked all three to write a scene for our game and read it out loud to us and were unanimously disappointed by the results. Their advantage lay solely in the fact that the words "Hollywood Writer" were used to describe them, and in an age where the games industry is obsessed with being viewed as an equal to film and television, this can be a powerful enticement for publishers and developers.

In addition to the financial cost of using Hollywood comedy writers, there is also a considerable skills gap to consider. We have already encountered numerous examples of areas in which writing for games is a completely different exercise from writing in other media, and these issues are equally relevant when writing comedy for games. As an example (once again taken from our personal experience), one pair of Hollywood writers, when performing for us the scene they had written as part of their audition, had our lead character perusing a grocery store with a potential love interest. A wacky series of events lead the girl to shove a "giant sausage" down his pants, a near impossibility for our artists to animate at the time. There are many frustrations in store for the writer accustomed to working with fewer constraints than what most game engines have to offer. Later in this chapter, we'll identify those of particular interest to people writing comedy for games.

Using Game Writers

Given that top Hollywood comedy writers are too expensive for the average developer, an obvious alternative is to hire professional game writers, people who have devoted their career to writing interactive narrative and are familiar with the limitations of 3D technology. There is no shortage of professional game writers who are capable of exemplary work, but few have experience with comedy. Furthermore, many professional game writers, and most traditional game designers, producers, or (in some cases) programmers who fall into the role of game writer are not necessarily suited for the task. The games industry culture has historically been, for lack of a better word, nerdy. This is one area where conventional media has the advantage over games. Jokes involving goblin archers and elf mages don't really speak to a wide "casual" audience. Unless a comedy is specifically targeted toward likeminded geeks, as with the remake of *The Bard's Tale* (InXile, 2004), it is unlikely that such niche comedy is going to succeed on a large scale.

This is not to say that it isn't possible for comedy in games to originate solely from a game writer. The best-selling European comedy adventure game *Discworld* (Perfect 10 Productions/Teeny Weeny Games, 1995) was written by one-time game writer Paul Kidd, and the hugely popular and successful Sierra and LucasArts adventures mentioned in the opening to this chapter were all written by writers firmly entrenched in the games medium. Whether the comedy in these games would succeed in the modern games market, however, is open to debate.

In-Between Solutions

If hiring direct from Hollywood is not by itself a solution, and a professional game writer might not be competent at comedy (although as ever, there are exceptions), the available solutions for writing comedy for games are by necessity somewhat hybridized.

Draft with Hollywood Writers, Adapt with Game Writers

One possible solution is to hire top-notch Hollywood comedy writers, and accept the prohibitive fees this implies. These writers can be given rough story outlines, from which they can write the most important dialogue, such as the major cut scenes and key dialogue sequences. The additional lines of dialogue (which are likely to be an order of magnitude more numerous than the key narrative elements) can be written by a professional game writer, who can also adapt the Hollywood writers' material into game form.

This is a workable solution, but it necessarily gambles upon both the Hollywood writers' ability to write material suitable for adaptation to a game and the game writers' ability to maintain and expand the original comedic tone to cover the entire game. It is also an extremely expensive solution, probably only suitable for a AAA game (the upper tier of game development budgets).

Draft with New Talent, Edit with Hollywood Writers

An alternative solution is to recruit some genuinely talented comedy writers outside of Hollywood. Recent college graduates with degrees in English or Television Writing or even Game Design can be a good place to start. They have the talent to make it in Hollywood, but their passion is games. They are game-literate, but their comic sensibilities run more toward the mainstream. They understand the technical limitations inherent in writing comedy for games and what advantages a nonlinear medium gives to the writer. They write all the dialogue, and the developer can then use top-tier Hollywood talent sparingly as an "extra set of eyeballs" for important scenes. Freed from thinking about technical limitations or bogged down by unimportant work, these Hollywood writers are allowed to do what they do best: punch-up scripts. Any odds and ends are handled by the developer and the synthesis between the two groups yields more fruit than in the previous case.

The assumption in this solution is that new talent is more game-literate and more able to adapt to the needs of game writing, than other writers. The cost of this solution, however, is still probably too high for anything other than a AAA game intended for the mass market.

Draft with Comedy Writers, Adapt with Game Writers

A cheaper alternative may be to create a partnership between comedy writers from outside of Hollywood—stand up comedians, for instance—and then adapt their work for a game format by using game writers. This approach has the huge advantage of being significantly cheaper than the previous two suggestions, by virtue of not having to foot the bill for Hollywood talent.

As an example of something close to this approach, consider the radio content in the recent *Grand Theft Auto* games, arguably the most successful comedic elements in these games. The commercials, frequently used to inject humor, were constructed for *Grand Theft Auto III* (DMA Designs, 2001) by Dan Houser (now creative director at Rockstar North, and one of the principle writers on all the recent games in the series) and radio personality Lazlo Jones, the host of syndicated radio show *Technofile*. Combining talent from different media in this way seems a viable, and comparatively cost effective, solution to the problem of constructing comedy for games.

MAKING COMEDY GAMES

After writers have been chosen for a comedy game project, the process can begin in earnest. Early on, progress will be slow and (for many projects) committee-driven. After a firm direction has been established, writing will need to be finished quickly and will undergo heavy scrutiny. The rest of this chapter aims at giving more practical advice on how to meet the high expectations placed upon a game writer by coworkers, publishers, and the consumer audience.

Choosing a Style

First, it's important to determine the type of humor the game will focus on. During the writing process, the script will likely sidetrack into all types of humor; but for the sake of consistency, game writers should determine their general comedic theme. Is the goal to be witty and urbane like *Grim Fandango* or gross-out like *Conker's Bad Fur Day*? Are you slapstick like *Crash Twinsanity* (Traveller's Tales, 2004) or a parody like *The Bard's Tale*? This decision helps the comedic game writer create a framework from which to build a brand of humor and decide which audience to focus on, although when working with a license or an established series this will often be predetermined. In the case of *Leisure Suit Larry: Magna Cum Laude* (High Voltage, 2004), "witty and urbane" would not fit the bill. The *Leisure Suit*

Larry series has an established precedent for adult (albeit sophomoric) humor, replete with the attendant sexual innuendos and rude one-liners.

Because it's not possible to be all things to all people, the game writer must ascertain the game's comedic intent from the outset. This provides the development team a bull's-eye to aim for and the publisher a good idea of what to expect, thus hopefully avoiding any huge surprises as the project progresses.

Choosing a Story

Most comedy games are story-driven to some extent. For any story-driven game, narrative and gameplay cannot be separated. Writers must work arm-in-arm with game designers from the very beginning to ensure a fluid, cohesive, and most of all, fun experience for the player. Because gameplay and narrative must interrelate, the writer cannot leave game designers out of the story-creation process. No matter how hilarious a story might be, if it doesn't lend itself well to gameplay and interactivity, it will necessarily become savagely altered later in development, much to its detriment. This is true for all games, but it is especially important to remember when writing comedy.

The early development process inevitably produces no shortage of truly funny ideas that the writing team will grow extremely attached to, but the realities of the development process mean that many of these ideas probably shouldn't make into the finished game. A lengthy courtroom scene in which the hero cross-examines a merkin supplier might be extremely funny, but if the player is left with nothing to do during that scene but watch a six-minute cut scene, it should be reconsidered. Remember the important distinction between games and other media: games are interactive. A *Simpsons* fan who is content to sit perfectly still and watch a half-hour episode on TV will likely become fidgety and anxious if expected to sit and watch more than 90 seconds of cut scene during a game based on the show.

Stories for comedy games should have three goals:

- They must lend themselves to the use of the game mechanics.
- They should involve a minimum loss of player control (the audience should spend as little time as possible watching cut scenes).
- They must be funny to the game's audience, and ideally (although less importantly) to the majority of the development team and the publisher as well.

If the concept for the game's story cannot by itself raise a few laughs, then there is probably a problem—although in more subtle parodies this may not apply. The story for *Discworld Noir* (Perfect Entertainment, 1999)—a private detective in the fantasy city of Ankh-Morpork investigates a series of gruesome and bizarre murders—is not likely to raise a smile, but the final game still achieves a certain degree of comedy through its pastiches of film noir and fantasy stereotypes.

Research

The process of solidifying a story starts with a high-level outline, which should be a few paragraphs at most. The outline should make clear what the major goals are for the player, and it should be obvious where key features come into play. It should avoid a lengthy list of places and characters beyond what is definitely required. The opportunity for humor should be evident, and although people should find the story concept amusing, the summary itself may not necessarily elicit a lot of laughter (jokes are funny, joke summaries usually are not).

The importance of research cannot be underestimated. Mostly, this is likely to involve watching movies because this is one of the primary sources of comedies in modern culture. One basic method for research is to find as many films as possible within the relevant subgenre, to watch these, and to produce copious notes. For example, suppose the team has settled on an alpine setting for the game, and on winter sports to supply the bulk of the gameplay. The brainstorm list of game features includes downhill skiing, the long jump, snowmobile racing, snowboarding, and the like. A trip to a local video store demonstrates that Hollywood has drawn from this well a number of times, producing a large number of movies of questionable quality including *Ski School*, *Ski School 2*, *Ski Patrol*, *Snowboard Academy*, *Downhill Willie*, and *Hot Dog: The Movie*. Seeing what works and what doesn't in these admittedly subpar films can still provide a game writer's imagination enough fuel to create a basic outline that offers both great comedic potential and lends itself well to the aforementioned gameplay features. Any film that blends action and comedy well, or at least has a similar setting, may be worth examining during this phase of the project.

The Internet can also be an invaluable resource. In the example of an alpine-based game, there is a wealth of information on winter sports: the fashion, the equipment, the lingo. Writers can browse catalogues, watch ski lessons, and read blogs. Anything, no matter how trivial, could be useful. Although the Internet is a less reliable source of information than, say, the local library, it has a tremendous capacity to deliver its information in a rapid and readily digestible form, which allows the game writer to explore and become familiar with an entire subject area quickly. The research enables the game writer to sound knowledgeable when speaking about, and lampooning, the topic in question. Comedy benefits substantially from a thorough understanding of its premise; it allows the writer to move beyond broad clichés to hopefully capture the many subtleties and nuances of any given subject.

Keeping the Story Simple

Keep in mind that although the story must lend itself well to humor and gameplay, it need not be overly complicated. In fact, it can be argued somewhat convincingly that it is better to err on the side of being overly simplistic than trying to write the *Annie Hall* of videogames. The story itself will never be as important as how it is executed. Many successful comedic films have thrived with stories that serve mostly as clotheslines from which to hang jokes.

There are other reasons to keep things simple. Story-driven games need to have clear goals for the player. For example, while "score seven girls' panties in a week" isn't exactly something Woody Allen would write; it's simple, easy, and lends itself well to a nonlinear medium such as games. The player is now free to comb the mountain in search of seven beautiful women, each with her own self-contained mini-plot. Also, under this structure, the player could pursue the girls in parallel, with the freedom to go back and forth between different storylines and modes of play; pursuing only those goals most intriguing to them.

In general terms, simpler stories tend to lend themselves more to action. If the players understand that their primary goal is to score with girls, and a girl tells them snowmobile racing gets her hot, it doesn't take much in the way of direction before the player is whooshing past the competition in a race to be the first to cross the finish line. Self-contained mini-plots have other advantages: should the project fall behind schedule, it's possible to cut one or more mini-plots without leaving gaps in the story.

After a solid story outline is in place, it's time for the story to be reviewed by the rest of the development team, in particular, the producer or creative director, the lead artist, the lead programmer, and the lead game designer. Game writers must be prepared to take criticisms and suggestions in stride. It is easy to become discouraged when you have to go back to the drawing board several times, but it's far better to develop a story that the majority of project leads are pleased with and will feel invested in, than to press forward with a vision that lacks support.

After the outline has been approved, the writer can begin fleshing out the details. Again, this is where a simple story has its advantages. For example, suppose the lead character, a party-crazed ski instructor named Radster, has made a bet with Wolfgang, an arrogant rival instructor with a thick German accent. Whoever students earn the best collective score on the final ski exam gets the mountain all to himself and earns the chance to win the heart of Sunny, the beautiful girl-next-door-type and daughter of the financially troubled resort owner. The loser leaves town forever.

This seems like a simple and formulaic starting point, but many questions are raised by this outline. How many students can be modeled, based on the schedule? How many levels? What will be the final core feature list? Can the player choose to play Sunny instead of Radster (giving the player a choice of avatar gender)? If so, does the story have to be structured to make the gameplay work with either Radster or Sunny in each section, or must two parallel stories be developed? Will completely separate animations be needed for both Radster and Sunny or can some be reused?

After the leads have come to an agreement, the game writer is free to begin the next stage of brainstorming. At this point, it's a good idea to get the rest of the team involved, for several reasons. First, it gives the rest of the team a chance to get acquainted with the story and raise any objections they might have. Second, it's likely that the project team will be a source of some great additional ideas. For example, you might have a team-wide brainstorming session to come up with ideas for different students the player will have to train (Olympic-hopeful, daredevil, war criminal, and so on). Third, letting the rest of the team in on the creative process is also a good way to give them some vested interest in the story, further cementing people's loyalty to it and ensuring a higher degree of cooperation further down the road.

Having established the answers to more detailed questions about the logistics of implementation, it's then necessary to revise the outline. Each act of the story, or in the case of the current example each student, requires an overview. These will ultimately need to be broken down scene-by-scene during a series of meetings with the project leads. For example, talking to the daredevil initiates a brief cut scene, which leads to a game in which the player must lead him through a slalom course. Wolfgang lays a trap for the player, which leads to some platforming and some puzzle solving. The concepts behind each scene should have everyone in the room laughing and excited about their prospects.

Eventually the documentation will include a breakdown of every scene in the game, each with its own amusing concept. A schedule can now be put together for the writing staff members who are free to move on to writing dialogue.

Infusing Humor

After a game's story, characters, and setting are firmly in place, the writers need to give serious thought to infusing both character and world interaction with plenty of humor. Although much attention is paid in this chapter to the type of writing to undertake for the story's sake, that is, cut scenes; equally if not more important is the work invested in making exploration and interaction amusing.

A logical place to begin is with the major NPCs. What kinds of things will they be doing in the world when not interacting with the player? (Almost no one should be standing around doing nothing in the game world.) The (unreleased) follow-up to *Magna Cum Laude* featured an "ice cream salesman" on the beach, an aging hippie who had perfected the art of selling marijuana-laden frozen treats right under the collective noses of the island's police. When left alone by the player, he would hawk his wares to college students by saying "Get your Acapulco Gold Crunch here! Acapulco Gold Crunch!," he would interact with incidental characters by telling "uncool" middle-aged tourists "Naw man, sorry. All I got is vanilla," and hit on girls less than half his age.

It's vital to decide early on (with the help of the game designers) what types and what level of interactivity will be available to the player. If the player can pee on them, run them over, or hit them in the head with a coconut, the game should have some sort of humorous response in each case. These reactions can help flesh out a character and the world, help tell the story, or be completely silly and random. In *Magna Cum Laude*, a lot of positive feedback was received on the exchanges written between NPCs for the player to eavesdrop on. At times they would provide hints to the player about how to progress, and at times they were a complete non sequitur. Either way, they were a method with which to make people laugh without forcing them to watch cut scenes.

If exploration is a big part of the game, it will be necessary to work closely with the level artists and level designers to make this as pleasing as possible to the intended audience. Wherever possible, filler should be used advantageously. For example, an outdoor level may have nondescript storefronts not meant to be accessed by the player, but that might prove fertile ground for sight gags. If memory constraints prevent the artists from putting much in the way of resources toward making this happen, it might be possible to allow the player to listen at an open window and overhear a funny confrontation between the storeowners and their landlord. Opportunities can be found everywhere in the game world. Can something funny be done with the fountain in front of the courthouse or the vending machine in the library? What kinds of collectibles will the game use? These can in themselves be made comedic. Signs, posters, and other 2D art similarly provides additional opportunities for humor. The goal here is not to cram jokes into every conceivable square inch or have things feel forced, but to fully explore every avenue of interactivity and exploration open to the player and make sure that they contribute heavily to the overall comedic experience.

The Authority of the Writer

Much of this chapter has focused on working with team members to get their feedback at each level of story detail. At first glance, this may seem excessive, but there are several reasons why this process should be made as transparent as possible. When working on a comedy, the writing will naturally undergo an enormous amount of scrutiny. A comedy that isn't funny is a waste of time (and money). It is to everyone's benefit then, that the team, along with the publisher, has confidence in the story before any detailed writing begins. It would be a potential disaster to spend months constructing a detailed line-by-line script without the necessary approvals, only to later have to discard the entire script and start from scratch.

It is important not to mistake the job of game writer as a purely artistic role. Like television shows and most movies, a videogame is a commercial medium made for entertainment not for the fulfillment of artistic goals. In an industry where large, interdependent teams are the norm, and every second on the schedule counts, there is little time for second-guessing or infighting. Comedy game writers would be wise to champion concepts that entertain and excite the entire team and that inspire confidence in the people funding development.

The downside to the necessary consensus-building is compromise. In the best case, the project manager has staffed the team with people whose personalities mesh well with the style of humor that has been chosen for the game. Even then, the game writer will likely endure a considerable volume of bad suggestions from many well-meaning people. Writers should endeavor to be open-minded, but ultimately they must execute these concepts, which is hard to do if they lose faith in their own story. These are tricky waters to navigate as people tend to think egocentrically in regard to their sense of humor: if they find something funny, so should everyone else. If they despise something, then no one else could ever possibly find it funny.

Comedy game writers must work hard to entertain using their ideas and then trust the creative process: if writers can get a conference room full of people laughing at something, chances are it will work with the audience. If the writers can't, it's perhaps a sign they are on the wrong track. Realize also that a writer can never please everyone with every idea, but here too, having an audience can be advantageous: if three people find a particular joke funny, and one doesn't, chances are the concept will make it into the final story, even if that one person is higher up on the organizational chart.

If writers really believe in something strongly, regardless of the reaction it gets, they can push to give it a chance. As noted previously, the proof will be in the execution. The team should be aware that if the idea doesn't come together, it can and will be scrapped for something else later. Also, ensure that team members realize that story details are subject to change after writing begins, as concepts that seemed ripe with opportunity weeks ago may prove fruitless when implemented.

In this regard, game writers are much like any other contributor to a game project: they have authority over their domain of expertise (writing), but they must still function as part of the team to ensure that the game is completed to a high standard. Just as the game writer trusts the expert opinion of the artists, programmers, and game designers, so these professionals must trust that the writers know what they are doing—subject to the omnipresent possibility of human error, from which no one can escape.

Game writers should always bear in mind that at the end of the day, their name will appear in the credits under "Written by," and if something in the game isn't working, people will hold them responsible, not whomever came up with the idea in the first place.

External Editors

Publishers commonly want to use Hollywood writers in addition to a developer's internal writing staff to ensure quality and give executives some peace of mind. This is often a waste of the publisher's money, as it seldom results in any significant improvements, for reasons we have already examined. Nonetheless, for all but the small independent game projects, the publisher is fronting considerable finance to the project and has the right to take whatever steps considered necessary to protect the investment. If writers have been diligent in testing out their story ideas, performing scripts, and revising based on feedback, they should have nothing to fear. Outside writers operating as external editors should be considered just one more tool to increase the final quality of the writing.

If an external editor is used to "punch things up," the editor should be sent finished scripts only. It won't help to have them work on scenes that are going to change anyway. The editors should also receive scripts in a format that is easy to edit. For example, game scripts are commonly rendered in a spreadsheet format. The lines as currently written can be put into the first column, explanatory notes (when applicable) into the next column, with a third column for the consulting editors to add alternatives they feel constitute improvement. Such a format makes comparing things easy for all involved, but ultimately, it should be up to the writer to decide which lines make the final cut.

Script Reviews

After the outline has been refined sufficiently that there is a scene-by-scene breakdown of the entire story, writers can finally begin the process of writing the game script. Before beginning, the writer should establish the process by which scripts will reach completion. For a game aiming at comedy, one of the best approaches is to hold script reviews. In essence, a script review is a private reading of part of the script for any and all necessary leads on the project, as well as anyone whose opinion the writers respect. Performing the scripts out loud for the benefit of a captive audience is an excellent opportunity to determine whether the comedy is on track. If the audience laughs hysterically, the script is probably on track. An uncomfortable silence is usually a bad sign. With any first draft, writers should expect to hear both reactions. This is always helpful, as it allows the writer to know what to expand upon or what to cut from the scene.

This kind of script reviews work well for several reasons:

- Reading the scripts out loud will do much more to get across humor than having people read the words on paper.
- Having a small group from which to get feedback from reduces the likelihood that a single senior individual will act as the vessel through which all the script's

comedy is judged. This can be especially problematic if that one person, although higher up on the organizational chart, is vastly unqualified to make these decisions. If five out of six people laugh hysterically at something in the script, it will be hard for that sixth person to justify rewriting it, even if the person happens to outrank everyone else at the meeting.

■ Many things will come to light during the writing process. Concepts may change, scenes will call for the addition of art or sound assets not previously defined, even new functionality might be necessary. Project leads must remain abreast of the latest version of the script to fully understand what resources are necessary to pull it off.

After each script review, writers should allow the people present to comment, while taking notes. The temptation to argue with any point raised must be quashed: it will not encourage open discussion if people feel that they must debate every point. Comedy rarely emerges from vociferous disagreement. Writers should decline to make firm decisions on revisions at the script review; these should be made afterwards when they have to time to carefully consider the merits of each piece of feedback. The most successful script segments may undergo six or seven reviews before they are finished, and some scripts may have to be tossed out even after a considerable investment of time if they cannot be made to work.

As equally important as having the leads present at a script review are the presence of people whose personalities closely resemble those of your target market. These people should be used as often as possible to make sure the writing is on the right track and should be on-hand to provide "fresh ears" at each reading.

Although regular script reviews are the best case, they can also be time consuming. It may not be possible to involve a large group of the development staff in regular script reviews, and in this case, some compromises are inevitable. At the very least, the script segments that relate to key moments in the narrative, probably those which will be rendered as cut scenes, warrant the extra scrutiny implied by a script review process.

Focus Tests

There are many negative opinions about focus groups, and it is certainly dangerous for anyone to base all development decisions on the feedback from a group of strangers. That said, from the perspective of publishers, focus tests serve as a reasonable predictor of how a wider audience will react to the humor in the game. Writers must be open-minded and *prepared* for any such tests. It would be an obvious mistake to show anything to a focus group that isn't already highly polished.

Tests should be done later in the project, when the professional voice acting, character models, music, sound-effects, and so forth are in place, and every little kink that might somehow throw off the presentation has been worked out. If the writers have been diligent in testing their material during script reviews, the feedback should be positive. Having an outside perspective on what has been done always serves as a sanity check and can be especially reassuring to those who aren't involved with the process on a daily basis.

Showing Off the Game

Even after the game is complete, the game writer's role is not necessarily complete. Almost all games require promotion, and perhaps the most important part of this phase is showing the game to the trade press. Although it's possible for a game to succeed without the support of videogame magazines, this is rare, and it's certainly easier to succeed with the support of magazine reviewers than it is to sell a game they deride.

Because the game is already complete (or mostly complete) at this stage, and the assumption is that the writers have more than adequately discharged their duties, however, the game should be able to sell itself. Even so, comedy begins with a state of mind: people will be disinclined to find a game funny if they approach it with a negative mindset. Therefore, even little things such as meeting with game journalists and maintaining an upbeat and friendly relationship with them during promotional exercises can make a great difference to a game's ultimate success. If a writer can make a journalist laugh before even seeing the game, the journalist will be far more inclined to be receptive to the game's humor when he finally sees it running.

TIPS

By creating a hilarious concept, backing it up with a sound script review process, and putting in a considerable amount of work, a comedy game can have its best chance of success. This final section considers a few tips that are worth bearing in mind.

Working with a Team

Even story-based games with a short play time, say 6 to 8 hours, will probably require the talents of more than one writer. (In regard to game length, a shorter length is more desirable than a 40-hour saga when writing comedy for games.) Fortunately, writing in teams tends to produce a higher quality of work than when writers work in isolation. If the chemistry is good, small groups of writers will have each other to riff off of, to show off in front of, to push, and to get each other laughing. After the dialogue in each scene has been fleshed out, individual writers can go off on their own and fill in the blanks. Afterwards they can edit each other's material before it's reviewed and assist each other when blocked.

Multiple writers will also help the game stay on schedule. The time available to complete scripts is usually short, as little work on the game's cut scenes can begin until scripts are locked down and dialogue recorded. Having more than one writer can speed things up considerably.

Technical Issues

Professional game writers work with far more constraints than their Hollywood cousins. Some of these technical limitations become especially irritating when writing comedy.

Facial Expressions

The capacity to render faces has advanced immeasurably in a very short period of time. It will be a long time however, before 3D characters are able to mimic the slight nuances and body language that great comedic actors use to their advantage. Motion capture, too, is helping narrow the gap, but writers should avoid writing scenes that depend heavily on subtle physical comedy. This is something that usually lies beyond the scope of a videogame to render convincingly.

Keep Assets Manageable

Even with a fully fleshed out concept for each scene of the game, there still exists practically infinite possibilities within each scene (especially because logic and consistency need rarely apply in most comedies). In addition, characters will need a lot of props to riff off of: objects, music, places, other characters, and so on. The sheer volume of art and sound assets that a script can generate if writers go unchecked is amazing. Some additional assets will be necessary, and therefore writers should ensure that the producer leaves time in the schedule for their creation. Many will simply represent nice ideas, and writers should check themselves against the temptation to write material that requires excessive quantities of new assets to get the humor across. All assets cost money and time to make, and even the most cutting-edge consoles have memory and other constraints. A script that uses fewer assets is almost always superior to one that requires excessive additional materials.

Timing

Writers should become familiar with their game's audio engine. Sitcom-like timing is reasonable and should be expected, but any cut scenes that are not prerendered (FMV) may suffer from timing issues that occur while the game streams audio directly from the disc. This may affect slightly the way that in-engine cut scenes are written versus FMV.

More general timing issues must also be addressed. If the audio engine can only deliver one line of dialogue at a time (a common restriction), then there is no hope of having multiple characters talk at the same time. Any scene requiring such an exchange must be rewritten. Similarly, because each line of dialogue must be read from media in the general case, writing lines where one character interrupts another is dangerous. It may only take a fraction of a second for the second line to load, but that is enough to make it sound stilted and artificial.

Character Interaction

Although highly detailed character interaction is possible in videogames, that doesn't mean it's going to necessarily look good. If a scene is written to depend on complicated interaction between two or more characters, writers must work with animators to see what's achievable. If a scene doesn't look right, it will be necessary to try something else. Certain animations are still difficult to implement—for example, cloth deformation (someone taking off their shirt, for example) is still fairly cutting edge. It may be best to avoid any complications rather than investing time developing material that must later be replaced. As technology becomes more advanced, these constraints will lessen considerably, but even in the future, it's likely that there will be underlying cost issues to consider. As ever, communication between different members of the team (between writers and artists in this instance) will go a long way to preventing problems.

Working Blue

For the most part, games are still largely perceived as being solely children's fare. Although this has not been accurate for some time (the average age of the gamer is said to be 29), it will be a long while before popular culture catches on to this. Until then, comedy writers should be on notice: retailers such as Wal-Mart and Best Buy, while perfectly content to peddle games filled with decapitation, dismemberment, and buckets of blood, are much more squeamish when it comes to sex, sexual content, adult language, and adult themes. Because retail chains can mean the difference between success and failure, publishers will be more inclined to listen to what they hear from the retailer than what they hear from the developer.

It may seem, based upon what can be made to work in TV shows such as *South Park* or *Family Guy*, that the sky is the limit in comedy. Although this may be true in more established media, games and TV are two radically different media. What is accepted in one context will not be accepted in another.

For example, the console release of *Leisure Suit Larry: Magna Cum Laude* was banned from Wal-Mart, Best Buy, and the entire continent of Australia: roughly 60 percent of the retail chain. There was a recognition from the publisher, Vivendi Universal Games, that a *Leisure Suit Larry* game could not possibly make it onto

Wal-Mart's shelves while retaining that which is attractive to fans of the series: bouncing breasts, sexual innuendo, and adult situations. This alone protected it from the worst excesses of censorship.

Top executives at both the publisher and developer side need to be comfortable with the style of humor and the consequences it may bring when the game ships to retail. Savvy writers take risks, but prepare themselves for the inevitable last-minute panic from the publisher's marketing arm when it comes time to show the game to retail executives or the Entertainment Software Ratings Board. Writers should always take the sensible precaution of writing and recording alternate material for anything that is highly likely to be perceived as offensive, risqué, or taboo.

Legal Issues

Even parody, protected by the First Amendment in the United States (and by equivalent laws in many other countries), is a gray area when it comes to games. Although there is no legal precedent for denying games the right to parody, lawyers of videogame publishers can be skittish on exercising this right. Perhaps the root of this problem is that games remain a second-class medium in the eyes of many people, and therefore writers working in games must often accept limitations that would be intolerable in other media. As an example, when High Voltage Software began to pursue development of a *Family Guy* game, they were told to avoid parody altogether. Considering that at least two thirds of the humor inherent to the license originates in parody, this presents obvious problems for any writer working on the project.

CONCLUSION

For those with the talent, sense of humor, and determination, the ever-expanding games industry represents a great opportunity. Games are becoming more and more sophisticated, and publishers are looking further for ways to make them accessible to wider and more diverse audiences than in the past. Cream-of-the-crop Hollywood writers are generally too expensive, and most professional game writers lack the experience and sensibilities to connect comedically with a mainstream audience.

As with all game writing, there is no way to go it alone: writers of comedy games need to entertain and inspire an entire team with their concepts and wrangle solid ideas from their coworkers while deftly avoiding too much compromise. The ego of a game writer is always at risk of being trounced upon, and especially so when writing comedy, so a thick skin is highly desirable. The rewards for success, however, are great. The market is starved for genuinely funny games and when executed to a high standard, they immediately stand out among the sea of derivative titles. They're also about the most fun a writer can have developing a game. Given the overwhelming popularity of comedy on TV and in movies, it can surely only be a matter of time before comedic games establish themselves once again as a viable and creative market.

9 Writing for Licenses

James Swallow

"The Franchise" is often regarded in creative circles as something of a dirty word. The concept of a product based upon another creation is frequently looked down upon as unworthy, uninspired, and unchallenging. However, in the entertainment industry, the franchise is the holy grail of Hollywood executives and game developers alike as the ideal of the concept, the game, the character that cannot only become a star in its own media, but also make the leap to others and rake in profits from whole new audiences. Although it might seem like a poor creative choice and a path toward slapping a brand name on a substandard game and pushing it out the door, it can in fact be a rewarding exercise for both the writer and the end user with the right amount of care and attention to the source material.

The traditional perception of a licensed game is something produced on a thin budget and tight timeframe that sells by the label, not by the substance of the title. However, a game writer with respect for the material can challenge that stereotype and help produce a memorable product. At the core of franchise thinking is the *license*, the right granted to one group by another to take an intellectual property (IP), which could be anything from a movie plotline to a comic book character or a rock band—and translate it into a new medium. In the games industry, the migration of IP has been a two-way street for many years, but by far the greatest success has come from games developers taking on board a franchise and making it into a gaming hit. Licensed titles have been and still remain a major part of the gaming industry's landscape; in the month of December 2005 alone, more than a half (24 out of 40) of the games listed on ChartTrack's Top 40 PlayStation 2 chart for the UK were based on existing licenses from other media. A similar analysis of the US sales data for December 2002 shows almost half (18 out of 40) of the top 40 best selling console games for this month were based on existing licenses from other media, collectively responsible for 46 percent of the unit sales this month. These figures may be skewed slightly by Christmas sales factors, but the underlying message is the same.

For a game writer, writing for a licensed project presents a whole new series of concerns above and beyond the usual creative challenges of developing engaging worlds, compelling characters, and a gripping story. What on the surface might appear to be an easy gig—after all, the writer is being handed the whole concept on a plate, right?—can, in fact, be an obstacle course of continuity, approvals, and unforgiving deadlines. The licensed game provides the writer with a box of toys that arrive with backstory and history built in and ready for use, sometimes with the chance to take on cherished characters and worlds and bring new life to them. That same toy box also comes with rules and restrictions that will challenge a storyteller in ways that writing for a conventional, original IP does not. In this chapter, we'll look at the needs and the pitfalls of writing narrative and story elements within a licensed game world, and the unique hurdles that a writer will encounter in the process of transferring an existing IP from other media to the game environment.

IP OR NOT IP?

What is the definition of an intellectual property (IP)? In its most basic incarnation, IP is an idea, the concept and creation of a given agency; in the arena of game design, it could be the character of Indiana Jones or James Bond, the *Star Trek* milieu or the Marvel Comics universe, a movie such as *The Godfather,* or toy lines such as Barbie or Bionicle. IPs as diverse as the rock band Aerosmith and the Crazy Frog cellular telephone ring tone character have migrated to videogames. In essence, the licensed IP is the material for which a developer pays an external creator a fee to use in a product. Often, a percentage royalty based on sales of the licensed product will follow the initial license fee. IP contracts between developers and licensors can vary greatly from single-use deals to long indentures covering multiple titles over several years.

What attracts a game developer to an IP-based product? By far the greatest appeal of license is that it comes with a ready-made audience. Brand loyalty, whether to a sports team or a television series, a toy or an iconic character, is at the heart of the franchise. Followers of a given franchise will migrate to a game title that connects to the brand they have invested time and energy in, in some cases even crossing into the games marketplace for the first time after the release of a tie-in title. When *Battlestar Galactica* (Warthog, 2003) was released for the Xbox and PlayStation 2, for example, many long-time fans of the television series purchased consoles just to play the title based on their favorite show.

Current or emerging popularity of a given franchise is another important factor. Feature films in production or television series rating highly may interest a developer, as well as longer-term, less event-based IPs, such as comic books, novels, sports teams or toy lines. In an uncertain market where purchasers are fickle and trends can vary broadly, the IP represents the closest thing to a safe bet in terms of consumer share. When Electronic Arts released its first videogame based on the *Harry Potter* franchise in 2001, they knew that an audience for that IP already existed, thanks to the popularity of the source novels and the feature film. While not every *Harry Potter* fan would buy their game, the crossover between the core audience for the franchise and EA's target market was more than enough to make it a dramatic success (selling around 8 million units).

However, the conceit of a "timely" release is not the only one that allows a franchise to find a preexisting audience. To give two examples, *The Warriors* (Rockstar Toronto, 2005) and *Blade Runner* (Westwood Studios, 1997) were based on cult movies from 1979 and 1982, respectively, and their releases were not tied to the source films in any way; if anything, the original films benefited from the game releases by stimulating a reissue of the movies to sell to gamers, whose interest in the original IP had been piqued. Both the *Warriors* and *Blade Runner* games were able to sell not only to gamers who were fans of the original films, but they were also able to attract an audience of players who knew the source IP on a more vague level—a brand familiarity rather than an outright brand loyalty—capitalizing on that element of goodwill, no matter how slight, to tip a consumer toward buying that game over another. The trend in Hollywood toward remaking old television shows for a new audience (*Starsky and Hutch*, *Charlie's Angels*, *The Dukes of Hazzard*) is a prime example of the same recognition factor in play across the movie industry. When Rockstar North's *Grand Theft Auto III* was released in 2002, the 1977 car-chase movie *Grand Theft Auto* (which despite the name was only an inspiration and *not* the IP for the game) was re-released on DVD with packaging very similar to the videogame to capitalize on the game's notoriety.

Of course, an IP doesn't automatically equate a license to print money. Tying a game to a franchise that performs poorly will damage the title's sales no matter what the quality of the game might be—the flop of the animated children's movie *Shark Tale* sent the game of the film straight into the chum bucket of discount stores nationwide—and a publisher who incorrectly gauges the interest of the audience can find itself out of pocket. Perhaps the most notorious example of the latter was the disastrous game project *E.T. The Extra-Terrestrial* (Midway, 1982) released for the Atari 2600 VCS. The first ever movie-to-game tie-in, more than six million *E.T.* cartridges were produced despite the fact that there were only around five million Atari VCS consoles in the marketplace; this oversight, coupled with what was widely regarded as a very poor game, resulted in the bulk of the title's production run being turned into landfill in New Mexico.

One would hope that this proves a poorly executed game will not be saved by its relationship to a box office blockbuster, but the reverse can be true. Despite receiving a critical mauling in the games press, *Star Wars Episode III: Revenge of the Sith* (The Collective, 2005) nevertheless managed to remain in the top slot on sales charts while the movie it was based on ran in crowded cinemas. But for every

Revenge of the Sith, there is a *Star Wars: Dark Forces* (Lucasarts, 1995), for every *Star Trek Pinball* (Avalon Interactive, 1998) a *GoldenEye 007* (Rare, 1997); these tie-in titles leave a lasting impression on players and prove that franchise-based games can reach the same heights of excellence as "original" titles.

For the franchise holder, the relationship with the game developer—and by extension, the game writer—may be anything from hands-off to draconian in the extreme (an issue discussed later in this chapter), but in their interest, the game tie-in will likely be of only tangential consequence to their marketing machine. For the most part, licensing departments see a videogame as an opportunity to place a dozen advertisements (as in the box art) into game stores in every shopping mall, increasing awareness of the source IP, often in the run-up to a major release event. In this manner, the game serves the same function as the novelization in a bookstore, the T-shirt, the lunchbox, and the Happy Meal. This is the cold, hard, money-making end of the franchise machine, and the realization that the licensor may give a game project no more regard than a coffee mug with a logo can be hard to swallow.

As the media of games continues to outpace the movie and television industries in terms of growth of turnover, this mercenary viewpoint is waning, gradually being replaced by one where franchise holders understand that good licensed games will reflect better on their IP and broaden the audience experience for the fan base. Many major film and television studios, having seen the burgeoning power of the games media as an earnings generator, have formed developer divisions of their own, such as Fox Interactive and Warner Brothers Games. To the savvy licensor, a high-quality game based upon a core franchise not only raises consumer awareness of a movie/TV show/book/product, but also brings a gamer audience into their orbit, drawing in a new revenue stream. The cross-pollination of game license and original franchise can be seen in the development of games based on the movie IPs of *The Matrix, The Chronicles of Riddick,* and *King Kong. Enter the Matrix* (Shiny, 2003), *Escape from Butcher Bay* (Starbreeze Studios & Tigon Studios, 2004), and *Peter Jackson's King Kong: The Official Game of the Film* (Ubisoft, 2005) have all benefited to a greater or lesser extent from direct involvement by the writers and directors of the motion picture source material, building on the experience of the feature films. The future for licensed games looks brighter than ever, and we can hope that the days of the second-rate cash-in are numbered.

WHAT MAKES A LICENSED TITLE WORK?

The stigma attached to licensed videogames—which, sad as it is to admit, is sometimes well deserved—is that they are poorly executed knock-offs of inferior quality made to capitalize on a current trend and turn a quick buck. Their detractors point to how some developers take an existing game engine and do little more than layer in some artwork and character design from the source IP, cobble together a narrative from the original subject matter, and kick the game out the door with the franchise logo looming large from the cover. *You've Seen The Movie/Read The Book/Heard The Song? Now Play The Game!* This sort of shortsighted approach cheapens and damages the reputations of not only the developer but the licensor, and sours gamers and fans of the franchise alike. What is missing from these low-grade tie-ins is a respect for the source material, and without that, a licensed title is doomed to be at best forgettable and at worst derided.

So how can a licensed title raise its worth? What are the factors that make a licensed game a good one? Consider what gamers and fans want from a licensed title; a good gameplay experience is a given, and largely this nuts-and-bolts aspect of the game design will be outside the remit of the game writer. But what consumers want when they purchase a game based on an existing property is to become part of that world, to step into environments from their favorite saga, to engage with iconic characters, to be surrounded by the props, the sounds, and the essential *texture* of the source IP. The key appeal of playing a game based on a film, a book, or a television show is the immersion factor. In the movie theater, you experience the adventures of swashbuckling archeologist Indiana Jones second-hand, watching passively as he dodges giant boulders and battles bloodthirsty cultists. You are along for the ride with Indy as he makes his choices and courts danger at every turn; but when you play *Indiana Jones and the Emperor's Tomb* (The Collective, 2003), you *are* the hero, not just an observer. You choose whether to use the bullwhip or the pistol to fight off that attacker and you decide whether to swing from a vine or swim for it. Suddenly, you are there, living and breathing inside the fictional world of the big-screen champion. When you make a difficult jump, the "Raiders March" music swells just as it would if Harrison Ford had performed it. The design of the *Emperor's Tomb* game world looks and feels like an *Indiana Jones* movie; you play it and are immersed in it. You become Indy.

As such, the single overriding rule for the writer when embarking on any game project based on a license is that the game must mesh with the original IP *as closely as possible*. Licensed games fail most egregiously when the narrative bubble pops, and the immersion in the fictional world is lost. No amount of great gameplay or flashy graphics can overcome a moment where a focal character behaves against type or where a known element of the storyline is contradicted. If the world of the game does not match the world of the source IP, the power and presence of the license is lost, ultimately defeating the entire object of the game's intent.

THE VOICE OF THE WORLD

We've just considered the *texture* of the IP, which is the core of a licensed game, the ephemeral look and feel of a franchise that must be translated to the game world if the title is to have any chance of success. To create an engaging game narrative within a license, a game writer must have both a respect for and an understanding of the fictional reality behind the game. For the writer to find this "voice of the world" requires a level of investment that differs markedly from that needed to write a wholly original game. The mélange of elements that make up the characteristics of a licensed world are diverse, and they can vary from something as simple as the sound effect of a door opening to the complex color palette of a vast landscape. The points in which a game writer can impact the consistency of a game world are at the heart of the narrative and in the tone of key characters. It's a given that if a game features established fictional characters, your dialogue and direction of those characters should match the source; however, the same must be true for the world around them, especially if the licensed game is *not* using established characters in central roles. For example, the NPC crewmen aboard a starship in the *Alien* universe would differ greatly in personality and manner from those on the Starship Enterprise; these incidental elements, like the door sounds or the landscape, are as much a part of the texture of their world as foreground hero figures such as Ripley or Captain Kirk.

This is the area where licensed games most often fail to satisfy, at the point of intersection where the gamer is drawn into the world of the IP. Characters that sound wrong in comparison to their original versions or plotlines that do not follow the same sensibilities of the franchise will break the illusion of immersion. In addition, some licensed titles evoke a sense of taking place in a vacuum, without any genuine relationship to the source IP. Whereas gamers progressing through an *Alias* videogame will not affect the continuity of the ongoing TV show by their actions in play, a well-crafted game based on that IP will—if even only on a subconscious level—lull them into the impression that they *could*.

One simple and subtle way to cement the sense of participation in the franchise is to ensure "kisses with continuity" throughout the narrative, which can be anything from an off-hand reference in dialogue to the appearance of a notable location or supporting character. In the original design document for the game *Star Trek Invasion* (Warthog, 2000), several planets were given generic sci-fi names that had no relation to the *Star Trek* mythos. Although these locales were never visited in the game and only referred to in mission briefing voice-overs, changing a handful of them to the names of alien worlds that had already been established in *Star Trek* television episodes helped strengthen the illusion that the game took place in the same fictional setting. The best continuity references are those that will delight the dedicated fan and grant them a sense of inclusion, but which will not draw so much attention that they derail the enjoyment of more casual players.

The primary components of any IP can be boiled down to three elements: the tone, the world, and the characters. The game writer that fails to grasp any of these fully will find it difficult to extend the franchise into the gaming environment. The tone of a given IP can be the most ephemeral and the hardest to pin down; essentially, it's the outlook that prevails in the fictional setting. Is it a grim, dark milieu where danger lurks around every corner? Is the world of the license a bright, welcoming place or is it clinical and cold? Utopian or dystopian? Are the stories in the IP's world aspirational or downbeat? In particular, minor characters and NPCs will be exemplars of this aspect, building the sense of place through their actions and speech as well the more static props of the narrative environment itself. Depending on the type of game and the manner in which the licensed title is tied to the franchise, the world of the IP may be either the focus of or the backdrop for the storyline.

In many *Star Wars* videogames, the heroes of the saga play supporting roles around a player avatar, and the worlds and locations of the "galaxy far, far away" are the key element of IP in-game; in fact, these sorts of games could almost be considered as a form of fantasy tourism. These *Star Wars* places—the swamp world Dagobah, the ice planet of Hoth, and so on—are the "stars" of the game, and the player appeal comes from the chance to visit these locations and take part in adventures around them. Conversely, in a game such as *Ultimate Spider-Man* (Treyarch Invention, 2005), the location is a stylized version of a real place—New York City—that serves only as a background for the focal role of the titular webslinger. Lastly, the characters from the IP form the final part of this narrative triad. The *Spider-Man* game just mentioned is an excellent example of a franchise where the persona is king; players are attracted to the gameplay experience because they want to be that character and engage with other iconic Marvel Comics personalities. Within the bounds of the source material, the setting for Spider-Man's adventures could be almost anywhere, but the character himself remains inviolate. In particular, in IPs based around characters aimed at a younger age group—*Mickey Mouse, Tom & Jerry,* or *Hello Kitty,* for example—the game's background world may be totally malleable.

The *Die Hard: Nakatomi Plaza* (Piranha Games, 2002) FPS game developed for the PC platform is an example of a licensed title that, at first glance, appears to achieve the right level of parity to the feature film source. On closer inspection, however, the all-important "you are there" effect is largely absent. Like the original *Die Hard* film, the game locks the player-hero in an office tower filled with terrorists and hostages, and challenges him to save the day. But what makes *Die Hard* the film an engaging piece of cinema is the tight plotting, the hi-octane mixture of action, gunplay, and dark humor throughout. The game fails by providing the flying bullets but not the quips or narrative tension, and the experience soon devolves into just another generic FPS. In addition, the *Die Hard* franchise has little in the way of iconic imagery—the movie's key figure, of the bloodied and bevested policeman John McClane, is barely seen in the first-person perspective game. Thus, the experience of being in that fictional world is lessened even more.

Compare this to *X-Wing Vs. TIE Fighter* (Totally Games, 1997), a space combat shooter set in the *Star Wars* universe. *X-Wing* (in all its incarnations) is steeped in the texture of the IP universe, with soundtrack music from the films, authentic dialogue, sound effects, and visual elements drawn from the movie mythos. Nothing can detract from the feeling of being part of that reality when one is flying an attack run over a mammoth Star Destroyer or fending off Imperial pursuit while your robot co-pilot chirps and beeps. Whereas *Die Hard: Nakatomi Plaza* attempts to ape the story of the movie it was based on, *X-Wing Vs. TIE Fighter* instead uses its source IP as a springboard to create new narrative threads that touch on the movie plotlines, but do not contradict them. We'll address this point in greater detail later in this chapter.

If the original IP upon which the license is based is an established franchise, depending on its popularity or age, the game writer may be using anything from a handful of books and comics to decades of television episodes and films as resource material. Franchises with large fan bases and strong pedigrees may have ranks of other spin-off materials and publications that accompany them—contemporary examples are the *Star Trek*, *Star Wars*, and James Bond IPs—and the writer may have an embarrassment of riches to draw upon. A writer working on a game based on an established and popular character such as DC Comics icon Superman would have little difficulty finding comic books, complete histories, biographies, and reference guides, as well as numerous films, television shows, cartoons, and reams of online material penned by dedicated fans. Other IPs may be much narrower in aspect, with only a handful of works as resources, perhaps just a single book or film. As part of the development process, the licensor may be able to provide the writer with certain resources (such as a product bible or similar reference), or it may be necessary for the writer to seek them out alone. If the game writer comes to the licensed assignment "cold" and largely unfamiliar with the source material, research time becomes a consideration that should be factored into the project duration. In other cases, the licensed game may be based upon a relatively new IP or one that has even yet to be completed, such as a forthcoming feature film or an ongoing television series.

With a movie, matters of security may complicate the issue of source material for the writer; film studios are notoriously tight-fisted when it comes to releasing screening copies, scripts, story documentation, and production artwork prior to a premiere date. In a worst-case scenario, the game writer may be forced to write a narrative with little or no knowledge of the actual source IP! If the IP belongs to a series, the writer may be able to draw from earlier storylines; for example, the *Blade II* (Mucky Foot, 2002) videogame bore little resemblance to the sequel movie, clearly drawing its inspirations from the first *Blade* film. But if there is nothing to take inspiration from, the situation may become untenable, and any game so created would have little or no connective matter to the source IP, and thus defeat the object of a license in the first place. In such a case, the game writer should discuss the situation with the developer and the licensor, securing as much access to as much material as possible at the earliest contract stage, and be willing to accept a raft of legally binding nondisclosure agreements.

In writing a game based on an ongoing television series, a different hurdle is encountered. For a show with one or more seasons under its belt, the writer should track down and watch as much of the series as possible, but with plot threads and narratives being continually written for the TV series, the writer must be wary of stories that may conflict with the intentions of the show's producers; consider if a game writer were to create a plot featuring the return of a long-lost supporting character, only to have that character return on the series before the release of the tie-in and render the game's plotline null. In all things with licensed titles, the IP is the canonical, incontrovertible source and all tie-in storylines must spin off from and serve that narrative. If the licensor is open to a greater level of participation, the game writer may be able to submit story concepts through the developer to the series producers for evaluation to avoid any conflict of ideas. With a newer, less developed television IP, the concern becomes the lack of definition of the series world and its characters. In this instance, documents such as episode scripts and writers guides (bibles) can help a game writer understand the direction and texture of the fictional world. Based on shows with several years of episodes, games such as *Buffy The Vampire Slayer: Chaos Bleeds* (Eurocom, 2003), *The X Files Game* (Hyperbole Studios, 1998), and *Alias* (Acclaim, 2004) skirted any thorny issues of series/game continuity by setting the narratives of each title in the earlier seasons of their series, casting them as lost episodes. Each of these titles is also notable for the involvement of actual writers from the television shows, helping to translate the feel of the source IP into the game environment. Although it is unlikely that the plotline from a game tie-in will ever directly impact the core aspects of a franchise, the narrative must be created as if it will, so that when players step into the game world, they accept that it exists in the same "universe" as the franchise.

In all things, the writer must constantly strive to immerse the player in the fictional game world—true enough with any title, licensed or otherwise—but with a game based upon an existing franchise, the writer does not have the luxury of building that world from the ground up and gradually introducing it to the player. A gamer who purchases a title based on a license is most likely to already be familiar with that fictional world, and indeed may be very loyal to that brand and highly knowledgeable about its minutiae. Thus, a writer must show a strong degree of narrative rigor, yet also maintain a storyline that will be accessible to more casual fans of the franchise. This is the greatest challenge in writing for a license; to think inside the box, and yet be able to push against the walls of it to map out new and engaging stories.

BEYOND THE FRANCHISE

After the landscape of the IP and its core elements are mapped out in the writer's mind, the next question addressing the development of a game narrative arises. Looking back to the earliest tie-in titles, licensed videogames of the past were primarily concerned with delivering a gameplay experience that directly mirrored the source material. Consider *The Empire Strikes Back* (Parker Brothers, 1982) for the Atari 2600 VCS, which took a single scene from the film—the snowspeeder attack on the walkers—and built a game from it. This model, of following the source IP's narrative directly, remains in place in licensed games to this date; however, as games and gamers have developed in sophistication, the experience of simply replaying the same scenes and tracking the same narrative line has come to be seen as the poorer creative choice. In an age where the audience has grown to expect extra content for its entertainment dollar, games based on plotlines that the players will already have experienced in a different medium must bring more to the table to engage them.

Licensed games fall into three categories of relation to their IP narrative; like the *Empire* game, there are those that follow the source with little or no variation; then there are those that mingle an existing plotline with extra scenes and subplots to build up the narrative, such as *From Russia With Love* (EA, 2005); and finally, there are games that create a completely new narrative within the world of the IP, such as *Tron 2.0* (Monolith, 2003). By far, those that meet with the strongest positive critical response are the games that use the IP as a springboard to tell new stories and are not hidebound by it. However, creating such a narrative inside a licensed game requires considerably more application of effort and time than, for example, the construction of game levels and story following the beats of an existing feature film script. For the game writer, the structure of the game story may already be determined based on factors such as timing, budget, and licensor flexibility.

In developing a linear "mirror" or expanded version of an IP plotline, the writer's primary source is, as ever, the original material. The task of turning a storyline into a series of discrete levels or sections for a game involves breaking the source narrative into manageable chunks, and studying them for points in which player interaction can take place. Look for natural lulls in the story, scene transitions, points where the gamer can take a breather, or places where a cut scene may be required/requested to move the narrative forward outside the game engine. Expanding on the narrative can be trickier; the amount of new material that can be added will depend on the degree of freedom provided to the writer by the licensor, and care should be taken that the core storyline does not become overshadowed by the new additions. You may have an idea for a climactic level that trumps the ending of the source IP, but to include it will disrupt the flow of the narrative and rob the original storyline of its power; additional narrative elements must serve the core plotline and mesh with it, not work against it. A good expanded scene draws upon existing factors from the core story; for example, in a film narrative where a hero transitions from one location to another through means of a cut, in game terms this can be played out in full, as the gamer takes the character on the unshown journey between the two scenes with all the challenges it might entail.

If a line of dialogue refers to an unseen event, consider making that sequence a gameplay component. Jarring changes in location and continuity are difficult to manage—the common dramatic device of the flashback is rarely deployed well in the game medium—and should be used with utmost care to avoid derailing the flow of the core narrative. In some cases, the game writer may be able to recover deleted story elements from earlier versions of the IP plotline—scenes rescued, in a literal sense, from the cutting room floor. If the game writer is in communication with the creators of the original IP, there may be the opportunity to question them on sequences or concepts that they were unable to include.

The *Revenge of the Sith* videogame used this method to add in extra gameplay elements by drawing not only from scenes in the finished version of the movie but also from sequences that were scripted but were ultimately never committed to film; the opening stages of the game feature an extended race through chambers filled with leaking fuel inspired directly by the first draft of the *Revenge* movie script. The key to making expanded scenes seamless once again falls to the writer's understanding of the source IP; know the texture of the IP, and it will become clear what fits and what does not.

With a game that goes beyond the set narrative and opens up new territory within the IP world, the writer faces a different set of challenges. On one level, the props and characters of the IP world provide a safety net and a spur toward story ideas; but they are also a restriction that prevents the game writer from crafting a completely original narrative. It is important to look upon the guidelines of the IP world not as limitations, but as opportunities; especially in a franchise that may already have been well mined, these "rules" can serve as signposts toward potential story threads. Some franchises, in particular television shows, follow a formula model—consider the problem-investigation-solution format of procedural dramas such as *CSI* or *E.R.* versus the character arc narratives of *Deadwood* or *Six Feet Under*.

In developing a game around a formula-based franchise, the format provides a narrative framework to start from, although a creative writer will want to stretch against such boundaries. With a licensed game, however, it is important to first make the player and the franchise fan comfortable with the game world by reflecting the core themes and structure of the source material. After this groundwork is laid, the game is free to expand beyond the confines of the formula. Sequels or prequels are as popular in the games industry as they are in the film business, and licensed games are a good arena for these kinds of narratives. For a fan of the franchise, a sequel/prequel game has the added interest of direct connection to an existing piece of the IP world, and this facet also assists in marketing if the release of the title connects to a related release in the core franchise.

The *Star Trek* adventure title *Hidden Evil* (Presto Studios, 1999) has a narrative that forms a direct sequel to the feature film *Star Trek Insurrection* and was released in the wake of the movie. Similarly, *Escape from Butcher Bay*, featuring the titular anti-hero from the film *The Chronicles of Riddick* was released just prior to the launch of that motion picture. *Hidden Evil* picks up where *Insurrection* ends, extending the experience of that story forward, whereas *Butcher Bay* forms the first part of a quartet of stories comprising Riddick's adventures (along with the *Chronicles* movie, the preceding *Pitch Black,* and the animated feature *Dark Fury*). Fans who wanted to "buy into" these narratives would feel compelled to take up the game so that they could experience the entirety of the storyline.

A similar concept is the *side story*, a narrative that takes place alongside the core IP plot, interacting with it on several points of connection but unfolding as a story in its own right. *Enter The Matrix*, which parallels the storyline of *The Matrix Reloaded* and *The Matrix Revolutions,* is a recent exemplar of the type. However, these kinds of narratives run the risk of over-connecting with the source IP; the writer must take care not to become too deeply immersed in the minutiae of the franchise while fashioning the plotline. A game story that hinges on an obscure point of interest in a single scene will not make compelling play for someone with only a passing familiarity with the source.

Although it may seem odd to talk of "completely original" narratives within an IP-based universe, writers have the most freedom to expand a franchise world when they can create brand new stories that extend the fictional milieu. We continue to return over and over to the golden rule that applies across the world of licensed titles: *serve the IP*. Although game writers might be tempted to take up the threads of an existing franchise world and remake it as they see fit, such an approach is highly unlikely to be approved by the license owner! Instead, writers are challenged to bring their own voice and their own creative edge to the storyline, while still keeping within the boundaries of the IP environment. Going beyond the limits of the franchise is an excellent way to draw in the fandom of an IP, enticing them with the prospect of new adventures featuring their favorite characters. Electronic Arts and the James Bond license show both the strengths and weaknesses of going outside established continuity. 007 games such as *Agent Under Fire* (EA, 2001), *Nightfire* (Eurocom & Savage Entertainment, 2002), and *Everything or Nothing* (EA, 2004) earned varying critical success with wholly original plotlines that straight movie adaptation games such as *Tomorrow Never Dies* (Black Ops, 1999) and *The World is Not Enough* (Eurocom, 2000) did not. Fans of the Bond franchise came to the games in the periods between the big screen films for a fix of their favorite super-spy, drawn by the appeal of stories that did not exist in other Bond media such as books, comics, or movies. Yet, when EA took the franchise too far from the source material with poorly conceived titles such as *007 Racing* (Eutechnyx, 2000) and the villain-themed *GoldenEye: Rogue Agent* (EA & Savage Entertainment, 2004), the audience response was negative. It is telling that EA has since moved back to the expanded adaptation narrative model of the Nintendo 64 success *GoldenEye* with its latest Bond title, *From Russia With Love*.

The process of creating new stories for an existing franchise is not dissimilar to that experienced by freelance writers working in episodic television, who come to a series that has been well established and must create stories that merge smoothly with the flow of the show. As well as plot, game writers may also be called upon to create new characters and new story elements that in some cases may become a fixture of the IP; events and characters in several of the early *Star Wars* games have since gone on to become part of that franchise's central canon, referred to elsewhere by the authors of spin-off comics and novels—although such inclusion is usually the exception rather than the norm. As with all other elements in the game, such new creations will be scrutinized by the licensor to ensure a good fit with the IP's worldview and may be subject to several revisions dependent on the license holder's level of involvement. Stories that radically alter portions of the IP world or transform focal characters in major ways are likely to be shot down at a very early stage. The writer that shows a reverence and knowledge of the franchise will find the licensor to be more receptive when fighting their corner over plot points. Tie-in works may seem unrewarding; after all, the creators of the core IP are under absolutely no obligation to be informed by the game writer's work or to even acknowledge its existence elsewhere in the fictional universe, and the restrictions placed on the writer may at times seem overly limiting. But the appeal of working with cherished characters or exciting new properties is a great draw and the heightened level of consumer awareness that comes with a tie-in will raise the profile of a writer involved with the project. We'll consider some of the restrictions inherent with licensed games in greater detail in the next section of this chapter.

JUMPING THROUGH HOOPS

For the license-holder, the IP is their precious resource; it may be the avatar of a massive franchise that has been part of their corporate identity for years, or it may be a new creation that they hope to grow into the games market. However you slice it, the licensor is likely to be very protective of the IP, and it will be a rare occasion when the game writer is granted a free hand to alter and reimagine the tenets of an IP with no interference from the owners.

With any project, the game writer will pass through a series of approval stages at the developer and publisher levels. When a licensed IP is involved, there may be one or more additional tiers of approval and oversight added to the production, slowing the process and adding the weight of extra opinions for consideration. Depending on the nature of the IP, the licensor's participation may be cursory or highly involved. At its most basic level, the IP owner will have a licensing executive whose sole responsibility is to ensure the correct presentation of the IP in all its spin-off incarnations; but there may be requirements that involve other licensor staff as well. For example, a game based upon a television series may require approval not only from the licensing agent at the TV studio but also from the production department for the series itself (to ensure no crossover of plotlines), the office of the show's executive producer, and perhaps even the actors who may want to ensure their characters are correctly portrayed.

For the most part, the game writer will not be in any position to directly impact the comments and changes brought down from the IP owner level—typically, the license to produce the tie-in game will give the licensor power of veto over any and all aspects of production. The writers may be forced to accept changes that sit badly with them, but once again we return to a core rule of licensed projects—what the owner says is law. The best way to avoid any friction at the licensor review stage is, as stated previously, to work as closely as possible to the model of the IP itself. To avoid confusion in rewrites, the game writers should be sure that they report to a single person as the developer on these matters; multiple, and possibly conflicting changes coming in from multiple sources will cause problems down the line during revision stages.

Some licensors will enforce strict rules about the presentation and the nature of the IP as it appears in the game world; these may be as simple as defining the colors of the clothes a given character wears to tight restrictions on the use of language and narrative subjects. The licensor will be fully within its rights to demand, say, that a character never eat, or use a weapon. In particular, IPs with a strong appeal to a younger audience may have to adhere to age guidelines that prevent allusions to violence, sex, or other mature themes. The writer may have an edict demanding that the hero never be seen to take a life or be seen to die if they fail during gameplay. The latter, sometimes known as *script immunity*, presents problems if the game narrative features action and jeopardy. Given the tangential nature of game tie-ins, in particular if they are released parallel to an ongoing series, the licensor may also impose a no changes rule that requires the game writer to return the fictional world of the IP to the same state it was in at the start of the game story, resetting events so that nothing in the game can impact the reality of the core fictional world. Generally, the game writer will not interface directly with the licensor, but deal with them through the developer; however, the game writer should have a channel of communication in place where any serious concerns can be addressed if the quality of the end product is threatened.

As well as the additional sets of approvals, licensed games often have rigid and inflexible production schedules. Although tight timetables are nothing new in the games industry, with a licensed title, the dates for delivery may be locked into a release schedule tied to the licensed IP. If a game is a spin-off from a new movie, it is essential that the title be in stores before the film is in theaters, so that the licensed product can raise awareness of the core IP for the licensor. The license holder wants to entice the consumer into seeing the movie, and then to buy into the IP by purchasing products related to it. If the game of the film arrives in stores too late, the potential audience interest is gone, moved on to the next big release, and the game's sales will suffer. Shipping before or after the all-important release date can mean success or failure for a tie-in. However, the mercurial nature of Hollywood box office and the entertainment business in general means that rapid changes in release schedule are not uncommon; films in particular are subject to delays or shifting premiere dates, all of which may impact the work timetable for a licensed tie-in.

Although these extra conditions may add pressure to the writer's life, the involvement of an IP licensor in the development process also adds an extra level of quality control that helps bring the licensed tie-in closer to the intent of the franchise. A good licensor will not just sign off on a product that fulfills the basic requirements, but will actually contribute to the process and enhance the finished game. At the end of the day, the licensor is the authority on their IP, and with their help, the game writer can create a narrative that truly extends that fictional world into the gaming realm.

THE GAME AS IP

We've already considered the matters that stem from taking an external IP and turning it into a videogame; however, after an original game concept has been developed, the opportunity presents itself for the game to become an IP in its own right, spawning sequels and migrating from its medium to other avenues. For the game writer, these are opportunities to carry a storyline into new arenas.

The most obvious extension of a game license is into other games, whether they are sequels or spin-offs. A game writer involved with a title should seriously consider during their tenure on a project the possibility of a sequel and address the matter with the developer if they want to be involved in any follow-ups; alternatively, a game writer may be recruited to work on a game sequel having had no experience of the original title. If a developer found the storyline or script of a title to be the subject of criticism, they may want to address that concern by bringing in outside writer talent to craft a better script for the sequel. In such a case, the game writer must follow the same guidelines laid down earlier in this chapter (in the "The Voice of the World" section); with a game sequel, it is imperative to play through and absorb as much of the original game as possible and to understand the changes (if any) that the developer requires for the follow-up. A clear understanding of where the game IP has been will allow you to grasp the direction it needs to grow in. Finding the tone and texture of the previous game(s) is important, as the loyalty of gamers who enjoyed the original will bring them back for the return experience—and they will expect to encounter new narratives in a game world that is seamless with those that came before. The game writer involved in a sequel should also make time to research critical opinions and reviews of the original game to gain an insight into the successes and failures of that title.

Most games developers and publishers have little connection with the book publishing industry, but like the games business, the book business also understands the value and appeal of a licensed product. The feature film novelization, the TV tie-in, the spin-off "new adventure" are all regular fixtures in bookstores, trading on the same recognition factor as licensed games. Acknowledging the popularity of the games industry, publishers have taken up game licenses in recent years to bring players into the reading marketplace. Dozens of game IPs have made the transition from screen to page, among them *Tomb Raider, Halo, X-Com, Shadow Warrior, Unreal, Resident Evil, WarCraft, Splinter Cell, StarCraft, Crimson Skies, Brute Force, Perfect Dark,* and *Wing Commander* to name but a few; even games with such limited narratives as *Doom* have been translated into novel form.

For game writers with authorial experience (or who want to gain some), taking the plotline of the game script and turning it into a prose novel may be an ideal opportunity. However, writers new to writing prose fiction may find a difficult road ahead of them, especially if the book publisher has a stable of experienced tie-in authors ready to pick up the game IP and run with it. Licensed books share many of the same restrictions and concerns that licensed games do, and an untried author may be rejected in favor of a writer that has proven ability for penning good material on a short publishing deadline. Game writers with prose on their resume are in a far stronger position to campaign for the role of tie-in novelist. Additionally, as the release of a tie-in book is typically scheduled around the release date of the IP subject, the game writer may not even have time to write the novel! However, many tie-in books are released after the fact, often on the back of a games franchise that has multiple incarnations and is a proven brand. Generally, the book publisher approaches the game publisher with interest in an IP, although increasingly games companies are looking to be proactive with their franchises and sell their brands. If you as a game writer feel that a novel is a viable spin-off concept, consider approaching the game publisher's marketing department with an outline.

Similar in process to novel tie-ins, although with a shorter turn-around and more visual appeal, are comic books. Game franchises have been part of the world of comics since the early days of videogames; in fact, in Japan, it is rare to find a popular videogame release that doesn't have a comic book adaptation in the marketplace. In the West, IPs such as *City of Heroes, Gunlok, Mortal Kombat, Tomb Raider, Killzone, Street Fighter,* and *Crimson Skies* have been made into comics. Like novels, generally the comic book publisher approaches the game developer, but increasingly comic tie-ins are produced to coincide with game launches to broaden the franchise across the entertainment spectrum.

The highest profile translations of game IP come from feature films; to a large extent, the only successful television adaptations of videogame franchises have been in the area of cartoons (everything from *Pac-Man* to *Tekken*). The question of the merit of videogame movie adaptations is open to debate, but the fact remains that Hollywood continues to tap the games industry for new film franchises. *Resident Evil, Tomb Raider,* and *Doom* have all been turned into expensive blockbuster movies, whereas other films such as *Bloodrayne, Mortal Kombat, Alone in the Dark,* and *Super Mario Brothers* have had variable levels of success. At the time of writing, the game-to-movie migration shows no sign of slowing, with big screen versions of *Hitman, Splinter Cell,* and *Halo* on the horizon, and the film adaptation of *Silent Hill* due to open shortly. The likelihood that game writers will be involved in the development of a film version of their game is slim; it is more probable that the studio developing the IP will assign writers from their own stable, although there may be an opportunity for game writers to become involved on a consultancy level, perhaps even to receive a credit as the creator of the original concept. However, generally a game writer will sign away the rights to be involved with spin-offs as part of the initial contract with the game developer. The writer keen to exploit the potential of any future tie-ins should consider this at the negotiation stages.

CONCLUSION

Game writers come from many avenues of experience—from novels, film, animation, television, and other roles within the games industry—and the skills they bring with them from those disciplines enrich the stories of the games they create. In working on licensed titles, game writers must embrace a whole slew of restrictions and creative limitations that do not exist with original works. These challenges are demanding in a way that no other project can be, tasking the writers to adapt their voice and sensibilities to match the tone of an established fictional world, and yet still retain their innate creative spark and craft compelling, engaging game stories. Writing for licenses can be a safety net and it can be a noose, but beyond all these things it can also be a road toward raising your profile, and becoming part of a popular franchise respected on a global level; a chance to bring your work to a whole new audience.

10 The Needs of the Audience
Rhianna Pratchett

In 1972, the Magnavox Odyssey, the world's first home console, gave birth to a new entertainment form and with it spawned a fresh breed of leisure hedonists—the videogamers. As gaming started to grow and take shape, it rolled through the back-bedrooms of the world picking up devotees like the beginnings of a ball in *Katamari Damacy* (Namco, 2004). A number of these devotees were to go on to make their own games for others, just like themselves. And so the ball kept on rolling.

But now, nearly three and a half decades later, the devotees are still out there, stuck to that ball, still making the games and playing them. Overall, however, the audience landscape is very different. Hardcore gamers are still important to the videogames industry, especially as early adopters in the wake of new console launches. But as the drive to make the industry more mainstream continues, our gaming evangelists are slowly slipping out of the top spot in many publishers' eyes. Instead, the goal has become to stretch the demographic range of videogames and reach out to those groups who had previously been, both intentionally and unintentionally, excluded.

This chapter examines the new and evolving audience demographics and their views on gaming, using the UK as a case study, as well as looking at how developers can better cater to the gaming needs and desires of these new players. It will also look at how the story-driven elements of videogames are particularly pertinent when it comes to fulfilling these needs. We will also be examining how issues of gender, ethnicity, and accessibility for players with disabilities should be addressed as part of this process.

Game stories, like other works of commercial fiction, must be written for the audience. This certainly isn't an excuse for poor games writing, but instead should be seen as a challenge in its own right.

WHO IS IN THE AUDIENCE?

For some time now, the games industry has been steadily moving away from being purely the preserve of teenage male geeks, although the perception from many quarters lags behind considerably. Now a demographic chart that once spiked around the 10- to 18-year-olds males section has flattened out, like an umbrella sat on by an elephant, to cover all ages and both genders. But it's not only popular perception that needs reevaluation but also our perception from within the industry as well.

The demographic make-up of the videogames industry, however, has not changed nearly as quickly as that of its audience. Videogame development, for reasons too numerous to go into here, still remains a predominantly male preserve, many of whom are proud (and rightly so) of being in the first wave of gaming devotees. It is consequently unsurprising that the "making games for me (and my friends)" mentality still permeates the industry—after all, it has been a solid foundation for many years.

When addressing the hardcore gamer market, this approach can still work to a certain degree. After all, nobody knows hardcore devotee gamers like hardcore devotee developers. But as the games climate shifts and new gamers are brought into the fold, games studios can no longer afford to ignore the needs of the growing mainstream and casual audiences. More importantly, they cannot ignore the fact that they are no longer making games solely to appeal to their own demographic. As the budget for the most expensive games skyrocket, courting a solely hardcore audience is a luxury that mass market games developers can't afford if they want to make back their costs in sales.

CASE STUDY: GAMING IN THE UNITED KINGDOM

The advantage of using the United Kingdom as a case study for examining the games audience lies chiefly in its comparatively small population of approximately 60 million people, compared to the United States population of approximately 300 hundred million people. The smaller population and smaller physical size make gathering data on the UK market a considerably more manageable task. The buying habits in the UK are similar in general terms to the general trends in the US, and the major European markets are all similar in some respects to the UK market (although for most games, the UK is generally considered the primary market, with Germany, France, Italy, and Spain lagging behind by various degrees). The UK is uniquely positioned, therefore, as a potential microcosm of the global games industry.

In 2005, the British Broadcasting Corporation (BBC) conducted a survey entitled *Gamers in the UK: Digital play, digital lifestyles*, which examined the habits of UK gamers across the country. The survey found that approximately 59 percent of the UK population between the ages of 6- and 65-year-olds are gamers—a *gamer* being classified as someone who had played a console, PC, handheld (that is, GBA-SP, DS, PSP) mobile, or Interactive TV game at least once in the last six months. The paper surveyed six different age brackets: 6 to 10, 11 to 15, 16 to 24, 25 to 35, 36 to 50, and 51 to 65. The results also showed that not only were UK gamers fairly equally split between males and females (which we will discuss later) but also evenly spread across all income brackets [BBC05].

Unsurprisingly, it was the two youngest groups that put a lot of value on gaming as a pastime, and they cited it as their number one entertainment form. As the audience age increased, the perceived value went down until it was relegated into seventh place (behind entertainment forms such as television, watching movies, and reading) for the 50 to 65 year olds. It was also in the three oldest age groups where the more traditionally story-orientated game genres started to emerge higher up the favorite and most-played lists. Role-playing games were in fact the top genre of choice for the 51 to 65 age group and third favorite for the 35 to 50s. These older age groups reported that the videogames market in the UK was oversaturated with fighting, shooting, and driving games. This may well be the key to why this group tends toward playing less twitch-orientated and more traditionally cerebral genres.

The survey also found that 100 percent of the youngest age bracket (6 to 10) are gamers, and this dedication suggests that they are going to continue playing games throughout their lives. But as they advance in years, trends from this survey indicate that so will their gaming needs and desires, and the videogames industry is going to have to keep pace if it wants to reap the benefits.

From this data alone, it seems apparent that game developers and game players no longer share the common demographic bond they once did. But assessing the needs of the new audience isn't about burning our bridges and putting the old school out to pasture. As mentioned earlier, the goal is reevaluating our audience perception and reeducating ourselves. It's also about thinking beyond the hardcore and casual audiences we already have, but also the ones who rarely touch or simply shy away from games altogether. In the case of the UK, the BBC's survey estimated that 41 percent do not play games—a huge potential audience that the videogames industry hasn't been able to touch. This is not to suggest that reaching out to the wider audience will be easy; it's often hard enough to get an established audience to buy a particular game, let alone attempting to target audience members that don't even know they want it!

THE MAINSTREAMING OF GAMING

Whether we really like it or not *mainstreaming* has become the current watchword of the modern games industry over the past few years. Many would argue that it has become, in part, what currently defines the modern games industry. But actually pinning down what mainstreaming means when it comes to designing and marketing a finished product has been a much harder task than we may have first imagined.

Titles such as *The Sims* (Maxis, 2000), *Nintendogs* (Nintendo, 2005), and the *Grand Theft Auto* series (DMA Design et al., 1997 onwards), along with accessible family-friendly entertainment technology such as *EyeToy* (Sony, 2003), *Singstar* (Sony, 2004), and *Buzz!* (Sony, 2005) have proven that relatively untapped audiences are out there that will come in droves given the right products. Most of the aforementioned games (with the exception of *GTA*) aren't particularly story driven. Certainly *The Sims* and *Nintendogs* have created the all-important realistic world that allows the players to tell the stories themselves; however, through a combination of shrewd design and marketing (and in the case of *The Sims*, getting the once-in-a-lifetime gift of being the right product at the right time), games like these have helped grow the videogaming audience.

This growth in particular is an important factor for all games developers. Now our audience pool is filling up with new fish, demanding fresh and exciting sustenance; it's not going to be just about replicating what Sony has done with *Buzz* or Nintendo has done with *Nintendogs*. Trends come and go, and audiences can be fickle. Instead, there are many different ways for developers to fish this pool. Creating strong stories, characters, and narrative, as has been proven with other entertainment forms, can be enticing bait.

Big companies such as Sony and Nintendo have a relatively firm grasp on some of the ways to attract and keep casual and mainstream gamers of both genders and all ages. But a large portion of the games industry is struggling to follow suit. Of course, having tons of money and studios the world over can help you grasp most things! These are turbulent times for the games industry, which is hardly surprising when you consider that we are still very much in our adolescence as an entertainment form.

Comparing the development of the games industry with that of the film industry can be useful. The initial roots of film predate the late nineteenth century. However, the first real steps in turning what was initially perceived as gimmick, into the beginnings of an actual entertainment industry came in 1895 when Louis Lumière used his newly invented cinematograph to present the first projected, moving pictures to a paying audience. Scroll forward 34 years (the same amount of time as between the Magnavox Odyssey's release and now), and the motion picture industry had matured enough to show its first full-length color talkie *On With the Show*, and the Marx Brothers had just made their first movie *The Cocoanuts*. In those terms, the games industry has a long way to go to reach its full potential. Becoming accepted as a full mainstream entertainment media is just one, relatively small, step.

Some have argued that mainstreaming simply means dumbing down games, but when it comes to game writing, it's more likely to imply increasing sophistication of narrative. We are now seeking to develop games for audiences that are saturated with high-quality entertainment at every turn. They are used to, and expect, good stories, strong characters, and engaging dialogue when they make their entertainment choices. If games don't come up to par, the games industry loses out.

Basic stories and poorly written dialogue, usually provided by whichever overworked designer had drawn the short straw, may have sufficed while the games industry was finding its feet and its audience was enraptured by what this unique and wondrous industry could provide. Now, if the games industry is to truly stand nose-to-nose with the entertainment big boys, it needs the stories and engaging content to back it up. Although gameplay is, and will always be, the meat and potatoes of a game, good stories and characters provide the much-needed gravy that enriches the overall product.

GENDER AND ETHNICITY CONSIDERATIONS

As the videogame audience has become larger and more evenly spread out, so too has it become more diverse in its physical make-up. Gender and ethnicity are two particularly important areas to consider when thinking about who your current audience and potential audience are.

Gender

The female gamer's needs have been the subject of much debate, particularly over the past five years or so. Many vehemently dislike the so called "pinking" of games to make them more appealing to the fairer sex and find it often patronizing and ineffective. However, this has undoubtedly proved successful in some cases, certainly when it comes to attracting younger female gamers. The success of Her Interactive and girl-centric licenses such as the *Barbie* and *Bratz* games, are testament to that.

Others believe many females are playing the games that already exist, regardless of whether they have been geared to them or not. For example, *The Sims* was not specifically designed with female gamers in mind. Some use this as evidence to claim that the games industry is already doing a decent job of attracting female players, according to logic that claims "If it ain't broke, don't fix it!" It is generally easier to hide behind such assumptions than to consider the benefits of change.

Despite the rather short-sightedness of this argument, there is some truth in it. Looking back to the BBC's report, of the six age brackets surveyed, the gender split was, surprisingly, fairly balanced. The most even divide, 52 percent male to 48 percent female, was between the 6 to 10s and the 51 to 65s age groups. Even the greatest gender divide, which was between the 16 to 24s and the 25 to 35s, was only 56 percent male to 44 percent female.

However, the female gamers in the BBC's survey showed a strong preference toward collaborative and less-violent titles, particularly puzzle and adventure games. The survey also showed that although females were active gamers, they weren't playing for as long as their male counterparts and suggested that the saturation of shooting, fighting, and sports games might be one reason for this. Surely it's no fluke that some of the most successful products to come out of Her Interactive have been the story-heavy Nancy Drew adventure games.

The European Leisure Software Publishers Association (ELSPA) report published in September 2004 highlighted the fact that female gamers actively prefer a greater depth of story and characterization in their games. The paper also suggested that when female gamers play character-driven games, they like to identify with their lead protagonist, whether the lead is male or female [ELSPA04].

It's no secret that female gamers, particularly hardcore ones, tend to be vocal when it comes to airing their opinions about games characters of both sexes. Some of the more prolific female-oriented Web sites have even carried detailed character breakdown and analysis on a game-by-game basis. The representation of women in games is also a popular topic in the wider-press, even though the actual content of such articles seems to be regurgitated annually. Sheri Graner Ray has gone so far as to suggest that the provision of a female avatar for players is an essential step to providing a gender-neutral games market, stating that male avatars are highly unappealing to many female players, whereas female avatars are no less appealing to male players [Ray03].

It is possible that the recent drive to attract more female gamers is responsible for the influx of female lead protagonists over the past few years, but whether this has had a positive impact on bolstering the number of female gamers is uncertain. It seems certain that some female gamers were encouraged to play *Tomb Raider* (Core, 1996) because the female lead, Lara Croft, was a more appealing character than the typical macho stereotypes that had been circulating prior to this point. Even though the game had little characterization surrounding Lara, she made for a refreshing and, at the time, an unconventional avatar. Anecdotal evidence suggests that for many female players, the *Tomb Raider* games were their first encounter with modern videogames, and this capacity to reach outside the conventional hardcore audience almost certainly contributed to the market success of the franchise, especially *Tomb Raider 2: The Dagger of Xian* (Core, 1997), which sold more than 8 million units.

In the wake of *Tomb Raider's* success, it seems female protagonists and "sassy girl" sidekicks abound. But due to poor character design and writing (and more obviously a certain artistic over-exuberance in representing the overtly femaleness of an avatar), many of them flounder as actual characters and just get remembered for having laughingly inappropriate clothing. This is not a desirable impression to be putting across to the existing audience for games, and it is certainly not the view to be presenting to those who could be potential gamers. To an audience not fully acclimatized to the world of videogames, this makes videogames look at worst very sexist, and at best rather archaic. It may only be perception, and not an entirely accurate one at that, but common perceptions, even when inaccurate, are pointers to problems that need to be addressed.

Although Ms. Croft has experienced rare success as a game character, having been portrayed in two movies (at least one of which was moderately successful), the specter of her ample bosom cleavage has had a limiting effect, as embodied by her appearance in *Playboy*. Consequently, her interest to female gamers and potential gamers has dwindled from something interesting and unique to something more akin to a virtual boys' toy. This does not reflect a problem with the games industry's capacity to portray female characters so much as a problem with the games industry's portraying believable characters at all. Often this means that game characters are so lacking in depth and realism that it's all too easy to just boil them down to their visual basics. It need not be this way, and the increasing involvement of professional game writers in the development process can only serve to improve the situation.

Ethnicity

The way videogames represent ethnicity is still very much a growing issue in this industry, although it doesn't normally get the coverage that the representation of women and the views of female gamers do. A few papers have been written on the subject, some of which claim that not only are the majority of videogame protagonists white, but also that the representation of other ethnic groups, such as African Americans, Asians, and Hispanics, often tend to be stereotypical and sometimes even bordering on offensive.

This is another area where videogames are still lagging a fair way behind other entertainment industries. In 1982, the videogame industry shouted from the rooftops about its first black protagonist in the Commodore 64's *Cyborg* (Sentient Software, 1982), although this was 19 years after Sidney Poitier won an Oscar for *Lilies of the Fields* and 11 years after *Shaft* first hit our screens. (It was still some time after this that the first African-American actress won an Oscar, however.) Since 2001, things have improved, and there have been a few more nonwhite protagonists in starring roles in videogames, most notable of which have been the Carl Johnson (African-American) character in *Grand Theft Auto: San Andreas* (Rockstar North, 2004) and Nick Kang (Chinese-American) in *True Crime: Streets of LA* (Luxoflux, 2003).

There have been several titles with nonwhite player-characters that stem from real life stars, namely the *Tiger Woods* golf series (EA, 1998 onwards) and *50 Cent: Bulletproof* (Genuine Games, 2005), although in these cases it must be acknowledged that the marketing value of the licensed star name is what made the games possible. It is unfortunate in examining the roles of nonwhite characters in games that only the Tiger Woods games are not ultra-violent shooting/driving games. Although we can be grateful that there is some representation for different ethnicities, there is still a long way to go before we reach a level playing field.

When it comes to portrayal of both gender and ethnicity, videogames also seem to be stuck in depicting the same type of characters over and over again: the tough, African-American weapons expert; the sexy female sniper; the lithe female Chinese/Japanese assassin. Although mainstream media can hardly be described as a bastion of political correctness, most other entertainment forms have made great improvements in this area. Sadly, the videogames industry appears to hang onto clichés and stereotypes for longer than other media. Given that so much narrative material that appears in games is derivative of other media, this is an especially sad state of affairs.

There are some signs of improvement. The *GTA* franchise, putting aside issues relating to the violent gameplay, has given its audience stories with slightly more meat and realism to them, with more interesting protagonists and more memorable NPCs. The series has certainly improved the representation of ethnicity in games, even if their general narrative content is still fairly low brow, and the humor is rather juvenile. It is unfortunate that there is no equivalent franchise to mark out as a figurehead for better representation of women in game narratives.

Better representation of ethnicity in games is essential for breaking out of the same old stories with the same old protagonists and mirroring the scope that other entertainment forms already have. Given that the audience for videogames is ethnically diverse, there is no viable excuse for not seeing the same diversity echoed in the representation of game characters.

ACCESSIBILITY

The first hour of play in a game is generally considered to be the most important when it comes to hooking the audience. This is the make or break time that can be the difference between cultivating a beautiful friendship between game and player and sending a frustrated player back to the shop demanding a refund. Establishing a strong narrative hook at this point is an extremely effective way of ensuring that players continue playing.

Maintaining Hardcore Interest

The games industry has generally become proficient at addressing the needs of the hardcore audience, although this is in no way a guarantee of successful games sales.

A tremendous volume of games that are produced each year are sequels to previously successful games; in games, the trend is for sequels to attract a larger audience, whereas in films, sequels are assumed to capture only a fraction of the previous audience. Facing a market largely comprised of sequels, it's no wonder that even hardcore gamers are looking for something a bit off the very well beaten track. Upping the narrative and emotional engagement are approaches that have the potential to work very well in this context.

Consider, for example, the development of the *Age of Empires* franchise (Ensemble Studios, 1997 onwards). These strategy games are largely only of interest to a hardcore audience, but even with this limited target audience, there has been a need for Ensemble to reconsider the narrative implications of the games. Prior to 2002, Ensemble hadn't concerned itself very much with narrative or story in this franchise, aside from a little history. However, with *Age of Mythology* (Ensemble, 2002), the third game in the series, the developers decided it was necessary to provide a more in-depth and character-driven narrative in the main single-player campaign. Central to this was putting a story at the core of the game structure, and the results were well received by the hardcore audience for the game.

With *Age of Empires III* (Ensemble, 2005), the developer returned to the more traditional style of play seen in the earlier games in the franchise. However, they opted to maintain a strong story element. The narrative was structured around three generations of a particular family during the discovery and colonization of the New World. After the studio saw how popular the story side of *Age of Mythology* was with the players, they knew it was going to form a big part of the new title. As a result they decided to structure the main portion of the game around fictional characters during real historical events, blending what actually happened with what might have happened. Once again, the game was well received by its audience.

Despite some hardcore gamers' protestations that "games don't need stories," it remains the case that those games that include a narrative element have found it easier to maintain their audience. Narrative elements allow the actions in the gameplay to have meaning in a wider context, and even in a basic strategy game, the implicit narratives of a game's battles become stronger when placed in the context of an explicit narrative structure.

Attracting New Players

Pleasing hardcore gamers and still making a title accessible to newcomers can be a difficult challenge. If players aren't familiar with a particular game, then their first port of call is likely to be the (often obligatory) tutorial. This means that, unless the opening cinematic or a brand attachment has won the loyalty of the new player, the developer is gambling on the tutorial to engage the player. Unfortunately, most game tutorials manage to be the least appealing part of the game, creating a significant problem.

Time spent integrating tutorial features into the main gameplay in such a way that the player almost forgets that they are playing a game is almost always worthwhile. The ideal is to be able to do this in such a way that the experience actually overrides the perceived learning curve.

Consider *The Chronicles of Narnia: The Lion, the Witch and the Wardrobe* (Traveller's Tales, 2005); given that this game was developed from an existing popular book license, and released to coincide with the theatrical release of the film based upon this license, this is clearly a game expecting to attract primarily an audience of casual players. The game, therefore, has a significant burden of accessibility to address.

In the game, the player begins in the middle of dramatic action. It's the height of WWII, London is being bombed, and the Pevensie family is stuck in the midst of it with their family home literally falling down around them. As soon as the player gains control of the first character, Peter Pevensie, they are tasked with using him to round up his siblings and help them escape to the air-raid shelter. At the same time, the game also introduces the various abilities of each child.

Because of the way the developers designed this first part of the story and situated it in a level that is full of noise, chaos, and a palpable sense of urgency, players feel like they are pulled into the game right from the start. As well as conveying basic instructions successfully, it brings home one of the story's underlying themes—that the children escape one war only to find themselves in the middle of another.

This is an example of dovetailing the encumbrance of a tutorial with the establishment of the game narrative, a technique that is gradually becoming standardized in titles expecting to reach a wider audience. In the best cases, any notion of a tutorial vanishes, and the player is placed in a situation whose resolution will naturally reveal the necessary controls, which are flagged only when needed. The recent *Grand Theft Auto* games have tended toward this approach, which can be found in many of the recent high-profile releases, including *Resident Evil 4* (Capcom, 2005). *Resident Evil 4* commences with a narrative episode surrounding a cabin in the woods that has been structured to introduce the player to the core controls in situ. Most players do not even notice that they are being taught how to play the game, so effective is the disguising of tutorial features as part of the narrative and gameplay. Such tutorials ease casual players into the control scheme gently, while avoiding the frustration many hardcore players experience in being taught to play in too rigid and lethargic a fashion.

Players with Disabilities

In the previous sections, we have looked at accessibility in the context of a game's attempt to hook in players with the early part of the game and the game's story. However, another aspect of accessibility that warrants examination is what gamers with a range of physical or sensory handicaps need to play the games. A whitepaper by the International Game Developers' Association (IGDA) identifies many such disabilities ranging from profound hearing and sight loss, to attention deficit disorder and dyslexia. Just to give an approximation of the size of the international audience we're talking about here, the paper cited a report from the US Census Bureau in 1997, which reveals that 23 percent of Americans over the age of 15 considered themselves to be disabled (to varying degrees)—constituting some 48 million people in America alone [IGDA04]. Poor accessibility for disabled players therefore has the potential to cost mass-market games a significant proportion of their potential audience, putting aside any ethical consideration to provide games that are accessible to all comers.

In addressing the needs of players with disabilities, it is necessary to ensure that the game does not depend upon faculties that should not be taken for granted—including hearing, the ability to distinguish one color from another, or the capacity to read small text. To quote the paper: "Gamers play games for entertainment, not to experience a sense of frustration. Unfortunately, once a player gets shot for the tenth time because they can't hear the footsteps of someone coming up behind them, they are not likely to be entertained. It's more likely that they are angry or confused."

With particular reference to the story and narrative in a game, the paper highlights certain areas for improvement. Captions over spoken dialogue and cut scenes for hearing-impaired gamers should be essential for any mass-market game. Customizable fonts and standard text presentation are other features that while fairly easy to implement are yet rarely included in games. These features would make a world of difference for visually impaired players. Likewise, visual descriptions of nonspoken action within a game would also make a big difference to this group, and would also create more work for game writers at the same time.

Although small companies are doing research and developing technology in this area, the paper is very pragmatic about the problems inherent in addressing the needs of this audience. Especially when it comes to mainstream games, this is a question of finance and time. There is clearly a need for greater research into this area so the problems can be accurately identified and addressed. Some are already making inroads into this area, with good results. Valve was widely praised at deafgamer.com for putting captions into *Half-Life 2* (Valve, 2004). They also used different color codes to represent the speech of individual characters and subtitled some of the more important noises in the game. This is definite food for thought when it comes to designing the speech-to-text ratio in games, in particular considering how the story and characters can be made accessible to those with varying physical and sensory ability levels.

MEETING PLAYER EXPECTATIONS

Games are extremely effective at eliciting a certain narrow range of emotional responses from their players. When it comes to engaging players on wider emotional levels, however, games fall behind other media. This is an area where the games industry has yet to become fully proficient, and also an area that presumably the audience at large is particularly interested in. This final section considers how games can meet (and exceed) player expectations, and the importance of game narrative in achieving these goals.

How Gamers Evaluate a Game Brand

In 2004, videogame market-research specialist GameVision Europe put together its European Consumer Intelligence Report, in which it asked European gamers from Great Britain, France, Germany, Italy, and Spain to list how they evaluated a new gaming brand. GameVision defined a gamer as someone living in a household with an active games platform who has purchased or been given games on that platform at least once in the past 12 months. In addition, GameVision defined an active games platform as one that has been purchased in the past 12 months or that had a game purchased for it in the past 12 months.

The results of this research identified 22 key factors that influenced a player's choice of brand [GameVision04]. They are, in order of overall importance to the group examined:

1. Genre
2. Gameplay
3. Graphical execution
4. Console availability
5. Multiplayer
6. Innovation
7. Narrative (particularly linearity/free-roaming)
8. Entry learning curve
9. Length
10. Level of violence
11. Recognizable publisher
12. Online
13. Who is it for? (age rating)
14. Difficulty
15. Universe (coherence/immersion)
16. Universe size
17. Characters

18. Speed
19. Film license or celebrity involvement
20. Soundtrack
21. Morality
22. Use of technology

What is particularly interesting to note here is that narrative comes out relatively high up the scale. In fact, it's of greater importance in evaluating a brand than factors that might well be perceived as being higher up in many developer and publisher's minds—such as level of violence, difficulty, length, and whether a game is tied in with a film license or celebrity. With this in mind, it's slightly strange to see 'characters' only listed at number 17. Were we dealing with a TV program, film, or even a book evaluation, you would expect to see characters listed in the first or second highest slot. This can be arguably seen as an indictment of the quality of game characters; perhaps we're not creating enough memorable characters for gamers to really consider them as being a pertinent factor when evaluating a new brand.

When it comes to suggesting how feedback such as this can be used in the future to bolster the quality of narrative and storylines within games, Sean Dromgoole, CEO of GameVision Europe, believes that it's about the medium developing a more streamlined approach to creating entertainment: "The successful companies are delivering gameplay that is less challenging but delivers a wider range of entertainment experience and are coming closer towards delivering quite complex emotional experiences."

Publishers often want a more film-like feel to their games. But Dromgoole believes that if the industry is looking to ape another entertainment medium in the future, as far as stories and narrative structure are concerned, then it may well be better off looking toward television, rather than the film world. He is also of the opinion that because videogames are generally becoming shorter, rather than longer, they are already becoming more like TV. "We can learn a lot of tricks from television writers, like the art of creating good narrative questions and cliff hangers. These could work well in videogames given the right application. I think we'll eventually see that disc you buy for a lot of money, that you never know you're going to complete, being replaced by regular episodic content. The kind that's produced by hardworking, fast working teams of people, in much the same way that television series are put together."

Coherent Worlds

The audience needs more than just better stories or better characters from videogames; the audience wants a better overall depth of realism, which in part embodies the first two desires. They get it from TV, films, and books and now they just need it in their games as well.

Richard Cobbett, veteran UK games journalist, firmly believes that "improved density" within videogames is becoming an increasing vital element in making game worlds more appealing to both new and old audiences. Cobbett elaborates: "Overheard guards, news reports continuing the story (*San Andreas* did this particularly well), sketches on radio and television sets such as *Vampire the Masquerade: Bloodlines'* (Troika, 2004) 'Deb of Night' segment, or the 'Dick Justice' running gag in *Max Payne 2* (Remedy, 2003), chatter from NPCs, hints from home-base, reactions from onlookers etc. All of these are small elements in themselves, but together they are a crucial part of making a succession of city-shaped 3D meshes feel like a real world, with consequences and scope beyond the small part that the player is actually interacting with."

GameVision Europe also believes in the importance of realism in videogames and claims that gamers value realism highly as well. This is as true for depicting a world based on our reality, such as *GTA*, as for a fantasy world, such as in *Neverwinter Nights* (BioWare, 2002). In its Spring 2004 Report, GameVision Europe neatly summed up the different levels of realism. They are listed here in an order that emphasizes their importance to the narrative and story content of videogames [GameVision04]:

Verisimilitude in graphics—How real do the graphics look? This has been a significant issue throughout the history of videogames. Not surprisingly this also comes in at number three in the previous game brand evaluation list. Although not particularly important to writers, unless they are contributing ideas to the overall atmosphere of a game, the appearance of the game is a key factor in the player's enjoyment of the story materials.

Everything works—Everything in the game world works in the way a player would expect it to. This can also be linked to coherence, discussed later in this list.

Accuracy of simulation—This considers issues such as kinetic realism, rag-doll physics, movement of cloth, plastic sheeting, and so on. Again this is of primary concern to artists and programmers.

Coherence——Everything fits together. This is where story designers and writers come into play because creating a coherent game is as much about the way characters talk and interact, or the way a story pans out, as it is about making the graphics look believable. Coherence and "everything works" are two of the key factors behind the success of simulation-based titles such as *Nintendogs* and *The Sims*. The beauty of these games is that they feel like very accurate representations of the real world, which in turn influenced and created much of the gameplay.

Credibility—Everything is believable. Again this is another area in which story, dialogue, and characters are important. It's also an area where many games fall down. Partly this is because poorly written dialogue doesn't sound like it is being spoken by a real character or even been written by someone with a good grasp of the subtleties of human communication, such as subtext, nuances, and how what people don't say is as important as what they do say.

Voice acting (discussed in a later chapter) is also becoming increasing important in creating credibility. The industry can no longer tolerate poor quality voice acting in mass-market products, especially because there is no shortage of talented voice actors available in a wide range of price scales.

Although realism is not a necessary element of a videogame, in the context of appealing to a wider market, there will always be a greater demand for games that provide players with a coherent world within which to lose themselves. Immersion, in this sense, can only be aided by greater attention to the construction of narrative materials, such as setting, character, and plot.

CONCLUSION

This chapter looked at how the modern audience for videogames has changed over the last few years and is continuing to evolve. It also looked at how game writing can play a big part in helping entertain this new audience and also play a major role in growing the demographics even more.

The need for better writing in games and more believable characters and worlds is at the heart of broadening the appeal of videogames. In the drive to become more mainstream, it's important to keep "dumbing down" from becoming just plain dumb. Understanding the existing audience for games, whether through audience profiling or regularly maintained fan communities, is vitally important for any company looking to maintain a brand. By endeavoring to understand the audience, companies can gain vital clues concerning how to steer their game franchises in the future.

Audience perceptions aren't only shaped by the games we've produced over the past three decades, but they're also shaped by players' experiences in the many other entertainment media at their disposal. It is no longer acceptable to deliver a subpar story in games. The audience expects more. If the games industry is ever going to truly emerge as a mainstream entertainment force, everyone involved must step up to the challenge. Nowhere is there a greater need for improvement than in the quality of videogame stories.

There will always be a certain audience for games in the forms that we have become accustomed to (and with the well-worn clichés of those forms), but finding new audiences means taking new risks. Not only risks with gameplay and stories, but with our own preconceived ideas as well. The audiences are there, even if they don't know it yet, and it's up to the game writers and game developers working in partnership to convince the audience that its next great entertainment experience will come from playing a videogame.

11 Beware of the Localization
Tim Langdell

Two of the fastest growing trends in the game industry are the greater importance of story (and hence of writing) and the rapid growth of international sales. These two trends combine—one might say collide—to make the historically consistently important issue of localization now one of vital concern. Having devised a game in one language with one particular culture in mind, it is important to know if it will work in other languages and for other cultures. Not only is the writer faced with fundamental differences between languages, such as how long a given equivalent word is (and thus, will it still fit in the assigned space on the screen?), but also will the subtleties, humor, and connotations of words and phrases in the original "design language" easily translate into new target languages?

With few exceptions, if a writer knows a game is going to be available in more than one language, it is far better to design the game with this in mind from the start—allowing for all the different language variations—than it is to complete the game in one language before trying to convert it to the others. For this reason alone, the design team should include the writers—both those in-house and those who might be part of any third-party translation and localization team—because their input is going to be vital on a number of levels.

Some of the localization issues will be fairly evident, and others will be more subtle. For instance, if the original design team has relied on the use of short two- to four-letter English words to populate a crowded head-up display (HUD), then major problems are likely to occur if a German-language version of the game is required when the team finds—as they typically will—that the German equivalent of the English words are considerably longer. Similar obvious problems are likely to be met in translating such a game to markets such as Japan and China, where the characters that must be used onscreen will require significantly different design and formatting from the original English. But the problems can be far less obvious: a joke told in one language will often not work if translated literally into another. Humor and common idiomatic phrases may be far more specific to the writers' culture than they may be aware. Worse, a phrase that means one thing in the writer's culture may mean something quite different (sometimes the opposite or some-times something rude!) when translated into another language.

These issues are increasingly relevant in game development, and writers work-ing in games have an obligation to understand the problems inherent to localiza-tion if they are to deliver their work to the highest professional standards. This chapter examines some of the key problems and suggests ways in which writers can avoid the worst of the pitfalls.

TRANSLATION NOTES

If a development team is designing a game entirely in English without thought for how translation to other languages will impact the game, they must bear in mind that the team on the receiving end of translating and localizing the game will likely have to get up to speed on several years of development in only a matter of hours or days.

Writers working on the originating team have a number of things they can do to make life easier for the translation team. First, they can resist trends in the orig-inal design that they are aware may present problems in translation. We've already mentioned the problems that can arise from trying to fit too many very short Eng-lish words into an onscreen display and issues that arise when converting from English to a language with a different set of characters. Writers can also make com-prehensive notes on why writing decisions were made that can be of invaluable help in localization—explaining in simple terms what an idiomatic phrase means, clar-ifying where something is meant as humor, or pointing out which phrases are game-critical and which are not. Perhaps, for instance, the text they have written is integral to the player solving a puzzle in that part of the game—they will need to en-sure the localization team knows how the text relates to game play, and hence let the translators know they cannot do a loose translation that will cause that part of the game to be at best opaque and at worst insoluble.

The writers' annotation of a game can thus make all the difference to the process of translating it for different territories, and often just a little forethought about the issues that will be raised with different languages can turn a nightmare project into a relatively smooth one. In general, writers should err on the side of writing too copious notes on their choice of words so that their downstream writ-ing colleagues can determine the best compromise between translation of meaning and all the other factors (such as physical space available on the screen, memory limitations, and so on).

The more writers know about various other potential target markets and lan-guages, the better equipped they will be to write the original so that it may be more easily localized. For instance, if they know a game is likely to be launched in areas of

Europe where Romance languages are common (such as French), then they should think twice about making gender-neutral language key to the original American English game script. Otherwise, they present the translators with choices between poor translations or clumsy word choices, simply because they are working in a language where words have gender variants or where there may be no gender-neutral equivalents to what was written in the original.

LOST IN TRANSLATION

One of the best-known casualties of translation was the phrase "all your base are belong to us" that appeared in the early videogame *Zero Wing* (Toaplan, 1991) for the Sega Megadrive console (known as the Sega Genesis in the United States). So poorly translated was the European English version of the original Japanese game, that *Zero Wing* achieved cult status for the terrible word choices throughout the game that often verged on the hilarious. Outright poor translation can be avoided simply by using a qualified team to undertake the localization. Even competent teams can get caught by failing to be fully conversant with cultural, ethnic, and regional idioms. A phrase such as "You've messed with me one too many times—you're going down boy" could easily fall foul of a too-literal translation, as could the British English phrase "I say chaps, don't blow a gasket but I've got some bad news." Without conveying that "chaps" means men and "to blow one's gasket" is to get upset, some rather comical or at the least very confusing translations could result!

Despite a sizable percentage of all games sold worldwide being either originally designed or sold in English, there can be some serious differences between even American and British English word usage. To "keep your pecker up" may mean "stay cheery" in British English, but it has quite a different connotation in the US! As Winston Churchill is credited with saying, the US and UK are "two nations joined by a common sea, but divided by a common language." Students at the University of Southern California were puzzled by why the British soldiers in *Call of Duty 2*, an Activision title, kept calling out for someone named "Jerry" and asked if it was a common first name either in the UK or in Germany. Only when it was explained to them that "Jerry" was a slang word for "German" did they fully appreciate precisely what it was that the British soldiers in the game were saying.

Even simple assumptions that feel fairly safe when designing in English, say having an "N" button to click for "No" and a "Y" one for "Yes," can hit problems beyond the obvious that the words for yes and no in other languages do not begin with the letters Y or N. For instance, in some languages, it is not appropriate to indicate yes or no with a single letter. Writers must be cautious of assumptions about what is and is not universal practice.

AVOID CONCATENATION

Often in games there are a number of player choices that might lead to outcomes expressed in phrases based upon variations of just a few words. "You pick up the red stone," "You pick up the green stone," and so forth, depending on which of the stones the player character has picked up. Not infrequently, game programmers will see that in English there is little point in storing all these phrases separately when they can simply concatenate the words together, switching out the color of the stone that has been picked up. But in many languages, simple concatenation does not work as it does in English, because the grammatical constructions of many languages are very different.

For example, in Japanese, the grammar for "You pick up the red stone" would be more commonly (without translating the words into Japanese) "The red stone pick up," as the object usually comes first in a sentence, the subject of a sentence in Japanese is usually implied, and the verb usually comes last. You could, of course, construct code to concatenate the Japanese text, but Japanese would require different concatenation code to English and from most other languages.

The safest solution is to avoid using text concatenation in any game that will be translated into other languages. If, for any reason, concatenation is vital to the game design, either a redesign is required, or the translators will need to consult on the design of the concatenation system.

LIP SYNCH

Dealing with the simple fact that words in different languages can be substantially different lengths can impact many aspects of a game. Not only can these differences cause havoc to neatly designed onscreen displays, but buttons that had text on them that worked easily in English can also need to be resized and repositioned to accommodate the translated text. To some degree, differences in word length can be offset by changing different font sizes and styles, but the impact of varying the length of spoken dialogue and narrative can be even harder to deal with.

In many cutting-edge game engines, characters' mouth movements are algorithmically generated based on the vocal string that is fed to the animation engine, thus enabling the developer to put any vocal track into it and the facial animations will be in synch with what is being said. In less sophisticated game engines, a more common solution is a cycle of animations that mimic general mouth movements that in turn mimic lip-synch when none really exists. Many games have used this trick to some degree or other simply by having the mouth movement animation start when the audio file starts and end when it ends, thus giving the illusion of lip-synch. However, this will only work in most games if the translated text is at least reasonably close in length to the original. If the translated audio is far longer, which a literal translation will often produce if English is the original language, then the onscreen character may not have finished speaking before the next action in the game is queued to start.

Sometimes, a development team will attempt to lip-synch animations to dialogue by hand. In essence, the writer times the source dialogue, and then passes those times to the animators to animate character mouth movements. Avoid this approach at all costs! Most projects following this approach hit huge problems when, after hours of such hard-wired animation has been completed, the script gets changed and the animations no longer fit the new text. When the implications of these static animations on the localized versions of the games are considered, you can see that this approach is highly undesirable.

LOCAL COLOR

The use of good voice-over artists who can give a local feel to the game can be of great value—ideally a game should not appear to have been translated from some other language or intended for a different initial audience, but created locally and intended for the local audience. Clearly, if a game is called *True Crime: Streets of L.A.* (Luxoflux, 2003), then players will realize it was not originally written for a local audience. But even so, careful choices in who is used as voice talent can mean that the game features are not just technically well-translated audio, but also that the dialogue and narrative show a deep appreciation of local accents and idioms.

The advantage that may be gained from making a game seem "truly local" can be destroyed if the game has built into the core logic some reliance on American English—for instance, the need to find a particular password that just happens to be in English. In this, as in all localization issues, it pays for the game writer to always keep in mind that the game will ultimately need to be translated for other cultures.

CULTURAL DIFFERENCES

Attention to cultural factors is also important in achieving a good translation—some cultures do not take to the depiction of violence in the way the American audience of an original game design might. Countries such as Germany have strict rules about not depicting blood and gore onscreen, and this can seep over into acceptable and unacceptable dialogue and story as well. Germany also does not permit the use of certain World War II text—thus if your game relies on such text, you will have to come up with an inventive alternate for that territory's version.

Remember that good localization is far more than just selecting the best words to replace the language of the original game design. Games are being adapted to entertain completely different cultures.

Sexual content, and in particular sexually explicit wording, is a further example of a topic and theme where it may be necessary to rewrite for certain territories before translation of the game can start in earnest. Furthermore, depiction of crime and the use of drugs can be deemed offensive in some cultures or even outlawed. Depending on the game, then, writers may have to plan for substantial rewrites prior to translation. Usually, the publishers will be aware of any such issues and will be keen to advise the developer as to anything that must be avoided, reworked, or reconsidered.

Cultural differences may take on even more subtle hues; for instance, a game character who is very colorful in every sense of the term (both visually and in the language she uses) may have to be changed for the Japanese market to make her an attractive protagonist—one that culture's game players can relate to. Be careful, too, of using fashions and trends in a particular culture only to then find that these do not translate at all into other cultural contexts. These considerations can be as simple as the descriptions (and visual characterizations) of how characters dress, to the way they speak, to what they do and do not find trendy. Further examples of these cultural differences can be found in the way emotion is expressed or repressed.

Some developers may decide that these considerations suggest a too fundamental change to the game design to be worth undertaking, preferring to exclude the game from any market that requires such radical rethinking. However, publishers increasingly expect games to be suitable for an international audience.

GAME-LITERATE TRANSLATORS

Although it is clearly important to have people involved in the localization of game writing who are very familiar with the target language and associated culture, idioms, and other important factors, it is at least as essential to have translators who are familiar with playing games and the terms that game players are familiar with in that territory. Videogame players can spot a mile away when a nongameplaying third party has been involved in translating key elements of a game's text or user interface.

Variations on a territory-by-territory basis as to what keys or buttons are usual for any given action or response and how to refer to those keys and buttons can be crucial to conveying the image of a professionally localized game—one that ideally the player cannot tell did not originate locally. This is equally true of the language choices that translators need to make to arrive at the best compromise for a given phrase or term. No single phrase will likely be a perfect fit, either because the literal translated phrase is too long or because the literal translation does not convey the subtext and implied meanings of the original because it misses the idiomatic way the original was phrased. Arriving at the ideal translation of any given phrase or word, then, can sometimes be a complex mix of decisions by the localization team, and a key factor in their making the best choice will be how well versed they are in game playing terminology for that territory.

Always endeavor to use translators who are game literate. This will minimize the risk of the localized versions of the game falling prey of inappropriate language choice. Either stick to companies or individuals who have worked on translating games previously, or at least confirm that the translators have some experience with the genre of game being translated.

The Importance of QA

Sufficient time must be allocated for proper testing of the translated game. Localization adds layers of potential problems to a game that can be even harder to error check than with the original language design. The people who know the game best are on the development team, and they are highly unlikely to be able to play the translated version at all (except in very rare circumstances). The upshot of this is that game testers for localized versions of a game are likely to be based in the target territory and hence are very unlikely to be people the developer has worked with, barring a long term relationship with the companies involved. Time must be allocated to allow for the QA (quality assurance) process to be carried out in all the destination languages for the game.

A further reason that adequate QA time is essential lies in the potential for small errors to creep into development. Even though a development team may believe they have kept the translated text and audio tracks separate from the rest of the game, that does not mean that changes made during the localization process may not have caused problems with the game or even fatal errors that could cause the game to freeze. Common problems include when programmers are confident they have a sufficiently flexible routine for accepting an audio file only to discover that they placed a timer in a loop that did not allow for the translated text to be much longer than the original as it was—thus causing the game to crash.

Moreover, even the clearest annotations to the text and audio for translation will likely not be perfect. Until someone can actually play through a game in its localized form, it is impossible to be certain that no key errors of translation will make the game unplayable (or unsolvable). Look for text translations that are not displayed properly onscreen because they were previously missed by those checking the user interface, HUD, or other displayed text and failed to appreciate that the foreign text was cut off on one side. Always ensure that someone checks that any foreign character sets are not incomplete or improperly displayed (especially a problem with Chinese and Japanese kanji characters, whose meaning can change completely with just a slight alteration to how they are displayed).

CONCLUSION

Taking translation into account during the initial design phase is the key to good localization of a game. The original team should not rely upon completing an original, say, American English version first before setting about deciding what languages to translate the game into. The latter course will lead to far greater errors because the underlying code is not created in a "localization friendly" way and, in some cases, may have been done in ways that do not easily lend themselves to translation at all.

Numerous considerations must be taken into account when localizing a game, far beyond merely selecting appropriate words to translate the English original— there are considerations of the length of translated words both for whether they will fit onscreen or in the audio for spoken text, issues such as the way different cultures express ideas, and cultural differences in phrasing and idiom that can make conveying the subtlety of narrative and dialogue, and especially conveying humor, extremely difficult. In addition, localization teams must not only be excellent at translation but also knowledgeable about gaming terms. Finally, providing adequate testing time for each of the localized versions of the game can make the difference between good localization and faulty localization.

Game writers have to learn to work with translators. The sooner they commit themselves to understanding the differences in language and culture that apply, the sooner they will be prepared for the challenges this process entails.

12 Adding Magic–The Voice Actors

Coray Seifert

Increasingly, most, if not all, of the material written for a game is ultimately recorded by voice actors. Working with voice actors is a radically different process than writing a screenplay for actors who will be working on set with other actors. Voice actors need direction that tells them clearly and concisely how a line can be read. Good voice actors—and there are hundreds, perhaps thousands, of such people—are a game writer's greatest allies. They can make an average script sound good, and they can make a good script sound sensational.

This chapter features practical information regarding the core skills and techniques of writing for voice actors. Elements of each phase of voice-over (VO) recording are addressed, and you will come away from this chapter with a better understanding of how to write, produce, and direct VO recording sessions. Research from this chapter comes from writers, producers, directors, and audio engineers currently working in the game development field.

WRITING FOR VOICE ACTORS

Great dialogue starts with a great script. Accordingly, this section covers the core skills and techniques essential to game writers for creating VO scripts. This section applies directly to writers, although producers and directors involved in the writing process can also benefit.

Writing the Spoken Word

One of the most challenging disciplines of writing is crafting words that are read aloud. When writing for a static medium, such as onscreen text or Web copy, the only interpreter of the information is the reader. When writing for VOs, the message must be much clearer because there are multiple interpreters of the writing. After the writer has crafted the script, the performer must interpret how to say the line, the director must interpret the actor's performance, the sound engineer must interpret the desired tonal qualities of the character's voice, and finally, the player must interpret the final in-game presentation of the script. With so many variables, it is essential to make clear how the writer intends for every word and every line to be interpreted.

Marty O'Donnell is the award-winning audio director for Bungie Studios, creators of the *Halo* franchise (Bungie, 2001 onwards), the *Myth* series (Bungie et al., 1997 onwards), *Oni* (Bungie, 2001), and many other titles. He advises writers to "make the scripts clear and easy to read. Keep it brief and to the point. Simple emotive cues like 'happy, sad, intense, crazy' can be more effective than long motivational descriptions. Underlining for emphasis is an easy way to show which word you want accented in any line."

In addition to writing clear, readable scripts, the following sections provide suggestions for creating dialogue for the spoken word.

Accommodate for the Human Voice

Always keep in mind the final medium through which your words will be communicated. Humans have an extremely dynamic range of sounds and noises that our vocal structures can produce. That said, the human voice also possesses a number of distinct limitations. Crafting dialogue with these limitations in mind will result in tighter, more compelling copy that is better suited for the medium of videogames.

Raison Varner, a composer and sound designer for Human Head Studios, creators of *Prey* (2006), points out that "a lot of the time a line will *read* better than it *sounds*." He encourages writers to "say the lines out loud or at least think about what it would be like if someone *said* this line to them."

O'Donnell echoes these sentiments. "If you're writing dialogue, please read it out loud and get others to read it out loud so you hear it long before you get actors in the recording booth."

Actually hearing the words is the best way to find out if your script will hold water when performed during the recording session. Find a quiet corner and read your script out loud—not always a simple task in a busy office. If you are unfamiliar with the acting process, see if you can schedule one of your actors for a prerecording session read-through. If you do not have access to your actors before the primary recording session, sitting down with a producer or designer for a read-through can be nearly as beneficial.

In addition, Kyle Peschel, producer and VO director for *Timeshift* (Saber, 2006) encourages writers to "read your script backwards. Seriously, stop at the bottom and read up line by line. See if each line is tight enough before you understand the context. Also try printing out your script and having someone else read it aloud to you. It is amazing how different people pronounce and read your work. If they aren't getting it, you better add more context, otherwise the game might take on a different personality than what you are expecting."

Sometimes, characters need to convey complex ideas such as a battle plan, an explanation of a scientific phenomenon, or a string of expository plot details. The tendency of many writers is to devise an elegant sentence that combines a lot of ideas. It may be better, however, to divide these ideas into multiple sentences. No matter what the decision, the writer must write with the human body in mind.

Humans possess dynamic and adaptable vocal structures. However, when stressed, only the most elite and experienced voice actors can maintain this dynamic range. Outside of excessive fatigue, long sentences are the primary culprit of stress on the vocal structures. Stressing the vocal limits of your actors will often lead to sloppy, flat VO recordings, so writing short, crisp sentences is an absolutely essential part of writing good VO. The one exception to this rule is dialogue that, in your game world, would be delivered by a character that is out of breath or gasping for air. In this case, it is worth remembering to note this as voice direction (for example, out of breath).

Keep It Simple

An easy trap to fall into when writing dialogue is to add flowery or unusual verbiage to clarify the meaning of a phrase. Although the temptation to flex your linguistic muscles is very tempting, VO scripts should be written using the most simple, universally understood language possible. The elegance of a VO script lies not in its complexity but in its simplicity, as the player must be able to understand exactly what your actor is communicating the first time they hear it. Very few gamers will break out a thesaurus and reload from their last save point just to make sure they understood a complex cut scene.

Newspaper and magazine articles are frequently edited for length, where sections toward the end are the first to be cut. Accordingly, print writers often adhere to an *inverted pyramid* style, where all essential information is featured in the beginning of the article, with supporting facts and detail included toward the end. Because game dialogue is often trimmed in the same way, by the player more frequently skipping later parts of the cut scene, game writers can also benefit from using the inverted pyramid.

Further, writing the tightest copy often results in the most compelling recorded dialogue. Longer sentences and thoughts may sound awkward and may not accurately mimic the natural flow of human conversation. Shorter sentences tend to sound more proactive, exciting, and dynamic.

Nick Laing, a producer and VO director at Electronic Arts, encourages writers to "always go for *fewer words*. Forcing in too many words is the downfall of many scenes. Keep it short, keep it organized, and remember that writing concise copy is an iterative process."

Allow for Redundancy

Back up your plot points and expository details with material in other parts of your script or game copy. Unlike other media, where readers explore written material in a linear or near-linear fashion, game writing can be read repeatedly, out of order, or not at all. Dialogue writers must prepare accordingly.

As Peschel points out, "You need to have redundancy. Who knows when the player skipped a cut scene or stopped paying attention during a moment of key character development. Your scope is very limited in most games, unless you are creating a role-playing game, so you'll want to keep to the point. I am often fond of radio script writers because they understand how to put as much content into five minutes as possible."

Supply Context

All the talented professionals interviewed on this topic agreed that it is essential for writers to include a great deal of contextual information in their scripts. Contextual information refers to notes on inflection, emphasis cues, or script notes that give the actor and director reading the script a more complete knowledge of how each line should be read.

When writing cut scene scripts, a script format similar to that used for screenplays may be used. However, much game dialogue will not be for cut scenes, but for use in-game. These lines are generally harder to provide context for. Making the voice actors completely understand the game context behind a line is not efficient, especially for the hundreds of barks and other short interjections often required for a game.

With this in mind, one of the most efficient ways to convey context in a general game script is to provide framing details at the levels required. This can be seen at three levels:

Character Descriptions: Providing a brief but complete description of each character in the notes at the front of a recording script allows the voice actors to immediately understand who they are supposed to be playing. However, only the relevant details should be used. For a description of a main character, 100 words is an acceptable length, but for a peon whose only role is as cannon fodder, anything longer than a 10-word description is a waste of time.

Game Context Descriptions: Game scripts should be grouped according to the purpose that the dialogue fulfills. Barks for use in combat should be presented in one block, brief character conversations should be elsewhere, and cut scenes probably merit being scripted in something closer to a screenplay format. Each section requires an introduction to establish its context. The shorter the description, the easier it will be to use. Use 100 words as the maximum, with a few sentences being a better target.

Voice direction: Individual lines may require voice direction to specify the tone or emotion at use in the line. Rather than forcing the voice actor to interpolate the context, it is generally superior to state how the line should be spoken. Instructions such as "angry," "hurried," "nervous, then angry," generally suffice—voice actors know their trade well.

The amount of context supplied can be less if someone from the writing team will also be present in the recording sessions to provide supporting direction (which is always desirable). If a writer who worked on the script cannot be in the recording studio, the voice director will require adequate notes to support all the material. There is generally no need to provide this supporting information in the voice actor's scripts, although some voice actors will request this material, so it is worth making it available.

Although it is ultimately necessary to trust that your actors and VO director will correctly interpret your script, you can always make that task easier by ensuring that they have all the requisite information.

Duke Clement, sound designer for SNK Playmore USA, shares his thoughts on contextual information, saying "dialogue writers can make life easier by communicating as completely as possible the intent of every single line, to everyone involved in the production process. The better everyone in the process understands the motivation behind every line spoken in the game, the more likely the intent of the game's storyline will remain strong and congruent."

To reach those not directly involved in the recording session, Mark Rudolph, director of marketing for SNK Playmore USA, asks writers to "consider if the dialogue was written in Japanese. Not only do you have to translate and localize the dialogue, you must also consider the cultural differences of your audience."

Make Preparations

Preparation is the key to a productive recording session. The days and weeks leading up to the session are where the bulk of the quality—or lack thereof—of your recording session will be derived. Because of the massive amount of variables writers have to contend with, creating a simple checklist to work through often helps this process immensely.

Kyle Peschel uses a checklist of details in checking each line of a script. This process allows for a high degree of attention to detail, and is reproduced here as a helpful guide.

Context: "Context is *everything*, especially when an actor has fifty different ways to say 'Yes'—calmly, yelling over gun fire, sarcastically, depressed, and so on."

Speaker: "The character who is saying the line. An obvious but often forgotten detail that can be essential when dealing with characters speaking over a phone or radio."

Target: "Who is the character talking to? An essential detail when determining intonation and inflection, plus, localization will love you if you supply this information."

Filter: "Is the speaker wearing a full faced helmet or speaking through a radio? What type of audio filter needs to be applied to the line? You need to specify exactly what this filter should do to the character's voice so that your audio engineer can make the appropriate modifications."

Length: "When dealing with FMV or other timed sessions, how long does the character have to say this line?"

Line Count: "Your voice-over studio will want to quote your studio time based on this. Some studios allow as much as 150 lines per hour."

Word Count: "Again, localization will love you as they will know how much it will cost per conversation if they want to cut out chunks of the game."

Filename: "Never assume your VO studio will know how to deliver your files and name them. Never. Seriously... *Never*."

This list clearly demonstrates the degree of preparation that can be applied to get the best results out of voice recording sessions. Often, there will only be one round of recording sessions, so it is vital that they proceed smoothly. In this regard, there is arguably no such thing as excessive preparation.

Conveying Emotional States

Portraying your characters' feelings in a natural and convincing style is one of the most difficult, and most important, balancing acts facing the game writer. Emotional impact starts with sound word choice, but also includes the volume, timbre, and intensity that a voice actor will apply to a line. Go too far and your VO recording will sound forced and disingenuous; not far enough, and the subtleties of human emotion will be lost in the action and ambiance of the interactive experience. Finding the middle ground will create compelling dialogue that gives the primary action in your game even more impact and realism.

In story-driven games, effective, balanced dialogue begins with a strong story, populated with characters the player cares about who are (generally) engaged in conflict that initiates a call to action. These characters are the anchor for your script and will provide a great deal of the motivation and inspiration for your voice actors.

"The best way to convey emotion in game dialogue is the same way you convey emotion through any writing; by creating character and conflict," says O'Donnell.

"If strong emotions are in the writing, the actors will bring it out in their performance, artists will show it on the screen, and composers will drive it home with music."

Introducing the player to a character's hopes and desires brings the player closer to that character. Give that character a future in the fictional world, and you are instantly providing the character with more depth. Convince the player that the character's goals and aspirations will be positively or negatively affected by the player's actions in the game, and you are giving the player a direct call to action and making that character's fate even more important to the player.

Kyle Peschel notes "strife and relationships to other characters are essential when conveying emotion. Establish this, and your voice actors will have a head start on creating an impact on your player."

In games that are less story-driven, or in sections of game scripts that are not part of the focus of the narrative, conveying emotional states can be considerably harder. Dialogue tends to be short, situational, and not connected in any coherent fashion to a definitive narrative context. Consider the conversations between non-combatant NPCs in a battle zone in an arbitrary game. The player will usually be moving around constantly, so there is little room for conversations. Rather, characters must make offhand remarks that are appropriate to the situation. The writer has no choice in this context but to trust the voice actors, and simply express the emotional state that is required in voice direction. Voice actors are professionals and will know how to put many different twists on the same line.

As a simple guide to possible voice directions relating to emotion, consider this list of emotions identified by a psychologist specializing in research in this area [Ekman03], presented here in a form suitable for listing as simple voice direction (either as adverbs or as present-tense verbs):

- Sadly
- Agonized
- Angry
- Surprised
- Afraid
- Disgusted
- Contemptuous
- Sensuously (experiencing sensory pleasure)
- Amused
- Contented
- Excited
- Relieved
- Amazed (experiencing wonderment; or awed, if mixed with fear)
- Ecstatic

- Triumphant (experiencing the emotion *fiero*, personal triumph over adversity)
- Proudly (experiencing the emotion *naches*, pride in the accomplishment of a child or student)
- Uplifted (experiencing the emotion elevation)
- Grateful
- Gloating (experiencing *shadenfreude*, delight in suffering of enemies)
- Guiltily
- Ashamed
- Embarrassed
- Envious

This list describes 23 entirely different emotional states. The number of potential voice directions is many times more than this, but this demonstrates how the choice of a single word capturing an emotional state can supply considerable information to a voice actor just by itself.

Prototype and Iterate

Two areas of game development that are too frequently overlooked in the early stages of production are writing and audio. Getting placeholder prototype copy and dialogue into a game can reveal a great deal about how effective the material is within the structure of the game. The quality of this rough draft is less important than getting *something* in place. The earlier you get material that reflects the final script concepts into the game, the better your final results and the smoother your terminal production processes will go. This often means recording scratch vocals for all of your characters yourself.

Laing highlights the importance of early implementation of game dialogue. "I have lost an entire feature due to a bad recording or writing session. Audio often gets considered last, after it is too late to do any pickup sessions or any reasonable tweaking. This is unfortunate because the sound and VO of a game truly brings it to life, and the process to do so is relatively simple and should be easy to plan for."

Peschel echoes these sentiments. "Never leave VO recording to the last minute. Too many times I've allowed a project to progress past the ideal point for recording VO. It later went on to upset FMV lip-synching technology, localization, testing, and overall quality as a whole."

The most effective way to ensure that you have usable copy early in the development process is to set, or have your producer set, an early deadline for a first pass at game copy and dialogue recording implementation. Although it can be very difficult to craft quality dialogue in this timeframe, it can ultimately be the saving grace of a project. You will later have to apply the many levels of editing and iteration that is the hallmark of any good script, but sprinting toward an early deadline keeps you ahead of the production curve and saves you many headaches near the end of the development process.

Inflections

Often, games set in unique locales or featuring local flavors require distinct dialects and accents. In this case, the "less is more" catchall is definitely appropriate. A subtle accent that isn't exactly identifiable within the first few syllables is much more desirable than an overblown, overdone accent that gets annoying after being heard 10,000 times by an experienced player. Often, the elongation of a single vowel or the use of one or two colloquialisms in a sentence is enough to communicate the desired effect.

Generally, however, writing scripts in colloquial form is a bad idea. The voice actors will not necessarily be able to decode your chosen means of transliterating the accent or dialect and will instead be uncertain what exactly they are being asked to read aloud. Write the dialogue in plain language. Provide descriptions of inflections as voice direction (for example, NY accent—said as "yoot" instead of "youth") or, better still, state the required accent in the character descriptions at the start of the script. Provided the voice actors know the accent or dialect required—which should be determined as part of the casting process—they will be more than capable of applying the necessary intonation in the recording sessions.

You can also work with the recording engineer to apply additional effects to the voice to provide character. For example, lowering the timbre or pitch or applying a mild distortion effect to a character playing a salty, veteran marine can give an actor's voice more texture, depth, and realism. When using effects however, the less is more rule also applies. Nothing sounds worse than an overmodulated, over-processed line of dialogue—unless it's also performed with a bad accent.

Ham with Care

Some games and genres call for an over-the-top acting style to create humorous, lighthearted situations for the player to enjoy. The writer's job is to make sure that the copy for these games does not go too far.

Tom Sloper, a game design and production consultant and member of the games industry for more than 20 years warns VO directors "be careful. I encouraged hamminess in the 1992 game *Leather Goddesses of Phobos 2: Gas Pump Girls Meet the Pulsating Inconvenience From Planet X* (Infocom, 1992). I thought hamminess was appropriate for a comedic spoof of sci-fi B-movies. But the game got bad reviews because the actors were so hammy, even though voice-overs were cutting-edge technology then. You might think hamminess is appropriate, but the reviewers might not share your opinion."

Write for Your Talent

Just as your actors must have voices appropriate to the parts they are playing, your script must be appropriate for both your characters and the actors you have hired. Often it is impossible to know whom you'll be writing for. However, if you do know, you have a huge advantage because you can see what things that actor does well, what things they have trouble with, and what nuances that actor brings to the character. Further, if you are working with a familiar actor or established character, your writing will benefit from a prior body of work or set of established details about the character.

In most cases, however, you'll need to accommodate for a given level of unfamiliarity with your actors. One effective way to do this is by supplying ample contextual information, as discussed previously. Peschel advises VO writers to "supply a ton of context in the script. I have never been in a studio at 10:00 pm and said, 'Gee... My writer just gave me way too much context. This is going way too easy.' I have however been in a situation where I wish my writer were around to stab in the eye for not thinking ahead. It's essential to remember that each actor is typically only supplied with their character's lines, so entire scenes can blend together if there is no conversation context."

As intimated before, having one of the writers who worked on a game script attend the voice recording sessions can be an invaluable aid. There is usually a tremendous quantity of secondary context that is not noted in even the most voluminously annotated script, such as the likely possible game situations at which a line will occur. This is information that can be impossible to convey in text, and only the experience of working on the script will suffice.

Finally, it is very tempting to write copy with the best voice actors in mind. Instead, you should focus on the limitations of an amateur actor's voice. Your script should be so well written that even an inexperienced actor can give a compelling and effective performance. This way, if an experienced actor performs your material, their performance will take your script to the next level.

Script QA

With myriad nuances inherent in human communication come myriad possibilities for contradictions, awkward phrases, and other problems that aren't immediately apparent to the author of a script. Therefore, putting your script through the quality assurance (QA) process like any other development asset can reveal potential improvements and unaddressed issues.

One method of putting your script through QA is to get the opinions of other developers, writers, or game-writing professionals. Duke Clement encourages VO writers to "Meet with the producer and the different teams to read through the script. Act out the parts with the members on the production team. Soon everyone will understand the intent of your script."

Bringing in someone unfamiliar with the script will provide the most honest assessment of the work. Therefore, maintaining a trusted circle of friends that you can QA your script with is essential for creating a top-quality finished product. Note that you should always check with your friendly local producer to make sure that you will not be sued for showing this material to someone outside of the project. You always have the option to hire an external writer for a brief script check. This shouldn't be expensive, and the benefits can be immeasurable.

When all is said and done, however, you are the writer and you are responsible for ensuring the high quality of your own work. You are putting your name on that script, so you should make any final choices about the specific implementation of your script.

BETWEEN SCRIPT AND RECORDING

The success of a VO recording session is directly related to the talent you are working with. Fortunately, thanks to the extensive use of voice actors and directors in other media, including animation for TV and film, plenty of talented individuals are available in this regard—many more, in fact, than there are experienced game writers. However, to get the most out of this talent pool, the right choices must be made in casting and appropriate preparatory steps must be taken. This section focuses on practical elements of preparing voice actors for a recording session. These tasks will not always fall in the remit of the writer, but it is not uncommon for the writer to also serve as voice director, and indeed game writers often find themselves involved with or in charge of any and all aspects of this process.

Voice Casting

The best script, the most expensive equipment, and the most talented director are all useless if you have the wrong talent for your recording session. Working with experienced, talented voice actors is always the best way to ensure that your recording session will produce the highest quality dialogue. That said, experience often correlates to expense, so you will not always have the luxury of hiring the most experienced voice actors. Accordingly, following a few basic rules for finding top talent will greatly increase your chances of securing the best people for your session.

Typecasting Is Okay

Ultimately, hiring decisions should be based on vocal range and skill. However, you will often get very good results if you can find an actor whose voice closely matches the tone of the character you envisioned while writing the part.

Sloper observes that "actors should sound right for the part. If you've got a part for a young boy, get an actor who sounds like a young boy. They must sound endearing, enthusiastic, and appropriate for the role. Conversely, an actress playing a drill sergeant must have an instantly recognizable air of authority to her voice."

Most voice actors will have a demo reel consisting of samples of their work. Although this won't provide a complete description of an actor's range, it is a good guideline. If they already have a sample of their work that is appropriate to the role being cast, they are probably a good bet.

Ignore Appearances

Note that the most appropriate performer for your role may not look the part. It is absolutely essential to separate a performer's visual impact from their vocal personality. Often, a huge part of a performer's impact is their body language, which in the world of game development, is placed solely in the capable hands of your animation team.

O'Donnell explains, "The best voice actors usually have a face made for radio. Just because an actor looks great or even acts great onscreen doesn't mean they have a great voice or have experience performing all alone in a soundproof booth with a microphone and headphones."

Usually, casting is carried out by listening to samples of work and demo reels, so this issue will not present much of a problem. Nonetheless, prejudices can creep in. As a useful example to bear in mind, the voice of Bart Simpson, a ten-year-old boy character, is provided by Nancy Cartright, an actress in her forties.

Hire Professionals

No matter what the budget of your game is, it is essential to work with consummate professionals throughout your recording session. The art of acting has a core set of skills that translate across all mediums, and a professional actor—even a relatively inexperienced one—will always deliver better results than an amateur or hobbyist. The most desirable professionals, however, are those who have done game work before, even if their overall body of work is limited.

Varner explains "I've always felt that it's important to look for actors that have experience doing VO for videogames. If they are gamers themselves, that's even better. They will understand how the dialogue is played in games, and how their performance will be played back. The better they understand the process, the easier your recording session will go."

Even if the budget is tight, hiring talent based on vocal range and skill means that you will, ideally, have good actors that will accommodate to any role and may be able to cover multiple roles.

Peschel comments on what he looks for in his voice actors: "In short, range. Ideally you are trying to save money, so you want to have someone do more then one voice. Some actors can do three or four voices, but I personally believe that is going too far. I typically use two voices per actor. Beyond that, you start wrecking their voice with a bunch of dying grunts and your third voice is utter trash. I also cast my big character roles first. Often your main character doesn't have the most lines, so be mindful of not wasting the best actor on the player's character if you won't hear him often. Also, look through your script and see who will be talking to whom during the game. You don't want to have five policemen and always hear two low pitched guys' voices talking over one another. Pairing up voices in games is essential."

Enthusiasm Is Key

As with designers, programmers, and artists, the talent you hire for a VO recording session must be excited about the work they're doing. Part of filling a role effectively is the ability of performers to lose themselves in the role. Inexperienced actors often have difficulty immersing themselves in a role. If you can find performers who are particularly effective at making roles their own, that is a big plus.

Clement points out that "the ability to express thoughts and emotions with conviction is extremely important."

Laing expands on these thoughts: "Actors must have enthusiasm, beyond just the right sound of voice. They are going to have to talk an awful lot before everything is said and done."

Most voice actors experience a wide variety of roles as part of their day-to-day work, starting in the unglamorous world of advertising voice-over and working up to the choicest roles in animation. Try to get a voice actor who considers games to be a worthwhile media. If voice actors believe what they are doing is unimportant, it will be harder to get a strong performance out of them.

Hire Based on Performance, Not Recommendation

Auditions are the most sure-fire way of ensuring that a performer will be right for your part. Although hiring based on a performer's reputation can be an effective way to save time during the hiring process, it is risky. Personal loyalties, owed favors, and rounds at the bar can skew the judgment of even the most objective VO director. Formulating your own opinions of an actor before committing to them for a recording session is essential. However, simply having an email or telephone conversation with a prospective performer can reveal a great deal about whether or not that person is right for your recording session.

O'Donnell says, "I strongly believe in the audition process. You get to see if the actor is someone you can direct, get along with, and can understand the character. Also, that's when you can get a feeling of how comfortable they are with the microphone and how their voice will match up with the rest of the cast. One time I hired an actor solely on the recommendation of a talent agent because I didn't have time to bring them in for an audition. Let's just say the description didn't match the performance."

Holding auditions is not necessary in all cases, however. As mentioned before, most voice actors have a demo reel that contains samples of their work. This can allow an excellent assessment of a voice actor's range and abilities without the mutual inconvenience of holding an audition. If you happen to work in California or London, where actors are in generous supply, an audition is an easier prospect than if your developer is based, say, in Slovakia.

Maintain a Portfolio

Establishing a working relationship with good actors is extremely important for writers and directors working on multiple projects. After you are familiar with an actor, you know the actor's tendencies and don't have to sugarcoat your feedback. This leads to a smoother recording process as well as a better end product. Compiling and maintaining a document to keep track of your portfolio of actors is highly recommended for anyone working with voice recordings. This also allows notes to be kept about actors that you choose not to use but you saw potential in.

Maintaining contact can be difficult, however. Voice actors, like any other professional group, experience a great deal of turnover and mobility. The voice of your crack marine may go on to star in the next Hollywood blockbuster, whereas best narrators may find themselves recruited by your cross-town rival. Staying in touch with the actors that you've enjoyed working with makes it much easier to maintain consistent quality throughout your entire body of work.

Preparing Actors

Depending on the type of performers you will be working with, as well as their relative experience level, you may need to do a good deal of coaching to bring out their best performance. This is best done by the director of the recording session, as these exercises will serve the dual purpose of warming up the performers and establishing a rapport between the actors and the director.

Although the best case is to be working with voice actors who are gamers themselves, often your VO talent is not familiar with the medium of videogames. Introducing actors to the unique conventions, rules, and assumptions of videogames is extremely important for them to understand how the final product will be presented.

Sloper says "the best way to prepare a voice actor to record videogame dialogue is to educate them about the context, tell them about the character, and the situation in the game that pertains to the lines that they are about to read. They just need to understand the medium and their motivation."

Assuming the actors are familiar with the medium through which they will be communicating, they should also be introduced to the subject matter that is central to the game. Recording VO for a sci-fi real-time strategy title requires a drastically different treatment and style than VO for a modern sports game. Your actors need to be acutely aware of exactly what type of world their performance will be displayed in.

Varner details his process for familiarizing voice actors with the subject matter. "Always run through an entire script, or manageable sections if you're dealing with a huge script for an entire game, with an actor in one shot and play it back to them. The idea is for them to hear themselves with the full understanding of what their character is doing in a particular scene, how they should be reacting, what pressures are on them, and so on."

After you have introduced your performers to the subject matter and medium within which they will be performing, it can be helpful to have them mentally walk through the setting where the lines take place. Describing the specific conditions under which the VO lines will be played back can help to both lessen any apprehension actors may have about working with an unfamiliar medium and can make it easier for your talent to fully immerse themselves in the roles that they are filling. Tell the actors what world they're in, what role their character plays in the society of the game, and what their character wants to accomplish by saying its lines. This process can be helpful for the writer as well as for the director, as it can reveal holes or inconsistencies in the script, and puts everyone in a unified frame of mind.

Ideally, the notes accompanying the voice actor scripts will provide much of the context to make this possible. Short, carefully constructed references to who the characters are and what they are doing at any given point will provide enormous assistance to the voice actors when they begin recording.

Vocal Warmups

After your talent has been introduced to the subject matter, medium, and any other factors unique to your particular recording session, you need to get their bodies and minds prepared to record. During most natural conversations, humans are in an active state. Whether running through a chaotic battlefield or sifting through a mystic tome in an ancient library, we are in a natural state brought about by physical or mental activity. No matter how professional and experienced, performers in a recording studio are very much out of their natural element. To get the most out of voice actors, the person in charge of the recording session must encourage them to engage in formalized warm-ups.

As Lynne Ransom, a veteran VO actor and director across a multitude of different media, points out, "the goal of warming up is to be alert and relaxed and ready to go with the flow of recording. The director needs to figure out what type of actor they are working with, and then help that actor to maximize the potential of their voice. This can be easier said than done."

Getting voice actors to begin their warmups before reaching the studio can save valuable recording time and shave dollars off your recording costs. Prepping them a few days before your sessions with some basic warmup exercises will pay big dividends when your recording session is underway.

Ransom points out "your actors may need to warm up at home before you head for the studio, because studios rarely have green rooms or other places to relax and prepare. It's really important that the voice actor relaxes the body and facial muscles. If you can give your actor cues to relax these muscles, they are much more likely to have a fuller, more flexible, more resonant voice that can accommodate to the specific needs of your script. Give your actor twenty to thirty minutes to warm up the body, voice, and acting muscles and your talent will do a much better job recording."

In addition, all actors recording dialogue for your game should be able to review the script well in advance of the recording session. Giving your actors time to familiarize themselves with the script, story, and setting of your game means that time in the studio can be spent recording useable material, rather than bringing your actors up to speed.

O'Donnell implores writers to "always have the full script for the actor, not just their lines. Get the script to the actor a day or two ahead of the session."

Like a writer creating game copy, actors do their best work when they are relaxed and prepared. Due to the physical exertion put forth by voice actors however, they also need to focus on warming up the parts of their body that contribute to the creation of vocal speech and sound effects.

Ransom suggests a set of physical exercises that can help your voice actors prepare their bodies for the stresses of an intense recording session:

1. Roll your shoulders, carrying the arms in a circle from the shoulder, back 12 times.
2. Roll your shoulders on the rotator cuff, forward 12 times.
3. Let your head fall to one side and relax your shoulder in the opposite direction. If you are still feeling tense, you can apply slight downward pressure to your head to accentuate this exercise. Take a few deep breaths.
4. Stand up straight and let your head fall to the other side and relax the opposite shoulder.
5. Stand straight and let your torso dangle from your hips, relaxing your arms and letting your head, face, and upper torso relax so that everything is hanging and dangling, relaxing you toward the ground.

"If people do just this much before a session, it's great! The results are definitely noticeable." Ransom also encourages VO directors to send a simple checklist of warmups like these to voice actors before the day.

Naturally, VO recording artists must also spend time preparing their voices for the strain and stress of an intense recording session. This starts with preparing the muscles of the mouth and throat, includes stretching and working out the vocal chords, and results in the performer's voice being "calibrated" and ready for action.

Ransom suggests a few exercises that actors can use to warm up their voices, "Your actors resonate on 'ee' vowels and 'ay' vowels to get their voice placed 'in the mask.' Have them hum a song or two they like or recite some text they know by memory. Whether singing or speaking, they should focus on projecting the sound from the bones and sinus passages around their cheeks and nose."

When the actors are physically ready to perform, they must prepare their "acting muscles." In other words, they must mentally prepare themselves to take on the voice, mannerisms, and eccentricities of an entirely different person. Although this is the single most essential skill an actor has, it is often neglected during formal warmups. Giving your actor a bit of time to ready their skills is essential for recording industry-best VOs.

Ransom advises: "Have your actor identify with the character they will portray by imagining the size, weight, shape, face, mood, and the physical characteristics. The writer or director should give this information, and the actor should fill in the blanks with their interpretation of the role."

Actors will need to prepare for the intricacies and requirements of the specific actions the in-game characters are taking. If the actors haven't seen the script and its notes prior to the recording session, it may be prudent to introduce them to the characters they will be playing during the warm-up session. In this context, the more specific you can be, the better. Although you don't want to spend the entire session talking about the character rather than recording dialogue, repeating this process for each character the actor will be playing is highly desirable.

Ransom suggests a few ways for actors to embrace the characters they will be portraying. "Encourage your actor to identify with the intelligence of the character. How does he think? Is she smart about fighting and moving, but slow in some other way? Is he clever, but lacks confidence? Is she dumb and unreasonably strong? Have your actor describe the character out loud, in a resonant voice, to help get into the character. Have them identify with the mood and motivation of the character. What role does this character play in the whole drama? What does she want? What are his background hang-ups and desires? Does something set her off? Has he just been shot in the foot? Be sure to emphasize that if they are not sure of any of these answers, to consult the director, the writer, or the script for motivation."

One last warning in regard to warming up voice actors: many voice actors are experienced and have their own routines and preferences. It is always worthwhile to ensure that voice actors have everything they need to be comfortable during a session (especially a long one!). A bottle or glass of water nearby is usually a given, but some voice actors have preferences for how they will sit, the position of mikes, and other minor issues. Implement any such request that is reasonable; recording sessions go much more easily if everyone is comfortable.

Even with a warmup, there may be problems during the session, particularly an all-day recording session. If a director finds the actors in a rut, getting them back on track is vital for maintaining a productive recording session.

Ransom points out "the flexibility and fluidity of a voice comes from the way the sound is produced, specifically the way the noise resonates within the nasal passages. If an actor's face gets tense, they can lose this flexibility. If an actor gets in a rut, try asking them to massage their face. Rubbing the chin, cheeks, forehead, along the temples and especially the lower lip will allow the nasal and bone structures to resonate sound appropriately. This system of facial massage can be especially appropriate for older performers who have developed certain habits over a long voice acting career."

Solo versus Group Sessions

Although most voice acting is recorded in solo sessions, there are times to use multiple voice actors in the same session. A particular example of this is when banter and interplay is expected between two characters. For example, scripts requiring two commentators to have an on-air camaraderie (or even rivalry) can particularly benefit from this approach. Even if two voice actors are brought in for the same session, lines must still be recorded separately. The benefit comes not in being able to record as a contiguous take, but in allowing the voice actors to develop a certain rapport between the characters when they are in role.

As a general rule, however, more than two voice actors in a single session will be very difficult to maintain. Although it may seem that you will get better results from having everyone work together, in practice, the problems multiply exponentially with the number of people involved. The majority of games and animated features record dialogue separately, and thanks to the efforts of the writers, actors, and directors involved, the finished result shows no evidence that it was recorded separately.

THE RECORDING SESSION

After the script has been written, the actors prepped, and the equipment readied, the recording session must be well executed, or all the preparation up to this point will be for nothing. This section applies to those writers who are directly involved with the recording session, either exclusively as a writer or as a director, producer, or engineer. This section also gives writers who have not yet been involved a glimpse into an aspect of development they need to understand and may want to get involved in.

The Writer and the Recording Session

Like the overall game-development process, a recording session requires a variety of professionals working together flawlessly for it to be successful. A studio engineer must be present to make sure that the actors' performance is being accurately recorded. A director, who is frequently involved with the writing or design process, should be responsible for coaching the actors and making sure that their performances stay true to the overall feel of the game. A producer may or may not be present to oversee the logistics of the session and ensure that the budget is preserved. Finally, the writer should be present to ensure that the actors accurately portray the core of the script.

Additional professionals may also be present, depending on the specific needs of your game. Sloper details his recording session roster. "Whenever I have a VO recording session, the following people are present: A game designer, a producer, a director, a writer, a sound engineer, a studio engineer (who may be a different person than the sound engineer), and, of course, the actor."

Different sessions will naturally have different people in attendance, but the minimal case is to have at least one person familiar with the game and the script, a director, and an engineer. Although it is possible to work with just two individuals, by having the director be the person who is familiar with the game and script, for example, this is not the best approach. The director will have plenty to do as is and should be free to focus on the directorial role. Furthermore, it is desirable to have a writer (or game designer) make notes onto a copy of the script to record places where the voice actor's recording differs from what is written in the script. In particular, this allows the game's subtitles to be updated in line with what was actually said in the session.

As in other stages of the production process, writers often fill a number of roles during the recording session. Even if a director and producer are present, the writer must be the one who maintains the original vision of the script. Many intricacies, dependencies, and details cannot be communicated by even the most detailed script. The writer is also responsible for making sure these factors are not overlooked during long and laborious recording sessions.

Peschel illustrates one way writers can contribute to the recording process during the session. "Writers can really help by being Johnny-on-the-spot with rewrites. The entire VO production can shut down while a writer produces a rewrite. Writers that are conscious of this are more prepared to make changes on the fly and can be a great asset to a recording session."

Varner gives his take on the writer's role in the recording process: "I think that this varies from studio to studio, although I would definitely prefer writers always being present. A writer can help clear up any mistakes that may be made during the recording session. If the writer has authority to make small edits whenever necessary, you can solve a lot of problems that come up immediately without wasting money and time on a second recording session."

These comments also illustrate the vital importance of annotating a script during the recording sessions. Changes will be made. The notes must accurately reflect those changes to avoid problems later because the paperwork was not adequately maintained.

It is vital to be clear as to who is in charge of a recording session. Depending on the structure of the recording session, this final call may come from the director, the producer, the engineer, or the writer. The choice will depend on the specific experience levels of any given team. However, it is essential to specify who (whether one or more persons) has the final say at the *beginning* of the recording session. This can help prevent personal disagreements from forming and streamline the decision-making process throughout the session.

As Sloper points out, "the amount of control varies based on the skills, personalities, and roles of the people involved as well as their job descriptions. I am a producer/director/designer, so I exercise directorial control when I am at a shoot. However, if I have a superstar designer, and he seems to be doing a fine job helping the actors understand everything they need, then I let him do it. If I'm the designer and the producer and the director and there's no writer there, then I do it all; I'm in charge. But if I've got a control room engineer who is doing perfectly fine, then he's in charge."

Just as you need to rely on your director—unless you are the director yourself—to oversee the recording process, you will need to trust your audio engineer to deliver quality audio recordings; unless of course, you are also the engineer, in which case you need to find the producer of your project and yell at them. Just as you are trained to create an interwoven web of characters and plots, the audio engineer is trained to use every element in the recording environment to optimize the way a recording sounds.

Varner encourages writers present during the recording session to "develop good communication with the audio professional you will be working with. The better the audio guru understands the intended effect and/or motivation of the character in the script, the more accurate results you will be able to get from a recording session."

An important caveat is that because you're placing so much trust in your audio engineer, you should work with an experienced, talented engineer whenever possible. Laing cautions, "Never put a newbie in charge. Direction, engineering, and recording are skills that are not as simple as you would think. I've lost so many good lines because they sounded like a dude was reading them in a tin can."

Each participant in the recording process must be responsible for his own contributions. Writers must ensure the integrity of the script, directors must get the most out of their actors, and engineers must focus on creating the best sound with their equipment. Any divergence from each professional's responsibilities can cause inefficiencies in the overall recording process. Although some divergences are necessary, anticipating and proactively avoiding them is very important.

O'Donnell encourages writers participating in the recording process to "be there but don't direct. Talk to the director and let the director talk to the actor. Actors really like hearing from one person; otherwise, they can easily get confused."

One skill that many veteran writers have developed is the ability to let the director and actors work with the script and improvise where necessary. Writing takes a great deal of time, energy, and personal investment. Accordingly, letting someone who hasn't spent that energy, time, and personal investment come in and make changes can be difficult for some writers to accept.

Laing encourages writers to "not be too picky when working through revisions in the studio. It's important to understand that the writing is out of their hands and in another phase. Writers can get pretty attached to their work at times, which is understandable, but it's more helpful if writers can be available to help revise the script where necessary."

O'Donnell echoes these sentiments: "If you're a great writer, you probably aren't a great engineer and vice versa. Don't try to do everything. If you're a great writer, you might make a great director, but probably not."

As already mentioned, it should always be *expected* that the script will change during the recording sessions, and therefore someone should maintain an annotated version of the script that reflect the edits and spontaneous changes that occur. Never force voice actors to read a script *precisely* as written if the dialogue falls more naturally into another pattern when they read it in character. The only exception to this is if there is some genuine game reason for making the wording match exactly, or if the reading of the line is otherwise materially incorrect in some manner. At all other times, let the process flow naturally. The result will be better than if the script is followed with draconian precisions.

Some writers will prefer to annotate into a laptop or similar device, whereas others will prefer hand annotations on a paper script. Whichever you choose, *always* bring a paper script, even if you don't intend to use it. If your laptop crashes halfway through the recording session, it is infinitely preferable to have a backup on hand, and there are few more reliable media than old-fashioned pen and paper, which will never crash, never run out of power, and are marginally more water resistant than electronic equipment.

Test Runs

One way to preview how a recording will sound—and to prepare your actors for the script they are about to read—is to set up test runs at the beginning of your recording session. Simply have your actors run through their lines, get it on tape, and then listen to it with your actor so you can both see the final product. Experienced, professional performers should be able to adjust for inconsistencies or weaknesses with their initial portrayal of the character. Be careful when working with inexperienced actors, however, as they can sometimes be intimidated when hearing their unedited voice over a rough scratch track.

Varner points out that "in many situations, material recorded during straight test runs has sounded more natural in the end and had much better emotional development than line-by-line recordings. Frequently, you get a lot of good material you can use out of one take. This also gives a good gauge for the how fast the actor should be speaking. While you can sometimes fix an actor that speaks too slowly with some fancy editing, it's much more difficult to try and get dialogue that has been rushed to sound more natural."

Not only can test runs can be very beneficial for introducing your actors to the material with which they'll be working during the session, they can also be a great way to test out the various filters and techniques you'll be using. Like any other part of the recording process, they should be subjected to a rigorous QA process.

Varner shares a near-miss experience regarding test runs: "The biggest mistake that I almost made was recording an entire session at 44.1KHz when I had to turn the voice actors into slobbering orcs. I should have recorded at 192 KHz or at least 96 KHz. Luckily, it was a test run and was never meant to be used as a final cut."

Voice Directors

Sometimes the writer of a script also serves as the director of the voice-recording session. It is usually better to have a separate director, but game development rarely proceeds in ideal conditions. At the very least, writers should be aware of what is involved in directing a session to better understand what their directors do.

After the actors are ready to go, the director must provide them with the proper motivation and context for the performance they are embarking on. The art of human communication is very complex, and many variables can change based on the setting of that communication. For example, there is a distinct difference between speaking a command to a subordinate and requesting backup from a commanding officer, which is not always communicated via the script itself. Accordingly, the writer and director must communicate this information, both through script notation and in-person direction.

Clement gives his advice on how to get your actors into character: "I know it sounds cliché, but the saying is true: 'What is my motivation?' If you write from the perspective of the character at their certain point in time (as opposed to someone who knows the entire sequence of events), the script will likely lend itself to creating characters that players can really identify with."

If you're going to be involved with the recording process, don't be afraid to be unorthodox in your preparation on the studio-side as well. If you are recording a script for a dark, mysterious game featuring vampires, zombies, and other undead baddies, try lighting candles and lowering the lights in the studio to create the appropriate mood. If you're recording an extreme sports game, try playing punk rock music during breaks.

Laing talks about some of the unique challenges he faces as a VO director for sports games: "To effectively convey emotion, you need to get the actor on the right wavelength. Make sure they know the whole story, make sure they read all their lines first, and make sure they're aware of their setting. When recording on-field banter for sports games, I find that I sometimes have to wear out the talent by making them run laps or do jumping jacks while they read their lines."

When the writer and the director are not the same person, it is useful for the writer to agree with the director on how they will interact during the session. For example, when recording is taking place in a separate soundproof area (which it should be), the writer should have a signal to let the director know when to stop the current recording, provide new guidance, and start again. The most obvious statements—"hold on" or "stop it there"—are usually perfectly adequate in this regard. The director can then stop the recording, establish the nature of the problem, convey this instruction to the actor, and then begin the recording of that line again. The important thing is to accept that it is your right and your duty to stop the session if something is wrong.

Keep It Relaxed

One of the most important, yet most frequently overlooked aspects of running a solid recording studio is maintaining a relaxed and comfortable environment that is conducive to improvisation by your talent. Like experienced recording artists, talented voice actors, when they feel free and motivated, can create the "studio magic" that often results in the most memorable lines and most useful assets from your recording session. Enabling this studio magic comes from the combination of an actor's talent, the environment in which the actor is working, and the instruction of the producer or director. Creating a comfortable environment is essential for actors to expand into their full dramatic range.

Varner talks about the benefits of allowing for improvisational exploration during his recording sessions: "I think that the most valuable thing to me has been the abundance of extra material I recorded in VO sessions that I wasn't sure I would ever need. If you have time to do so, it's always a good idea to record things that seem funny, appropriate, or make you think 'hey that's cool! We might be able to use that!' Sometimes those tangents and moments of inspiration become extremely valuable down the road. I always try to keep my mind open to those sorts of things while working on a project, since many times, some of my best material comes from those moments of goofiness or random ideas."

Laing points out that, "I've seen a lot of great things come from allowing an actor a little room to improvise."

O'Donnell agrees, "Voice actors who are adept at improvisation are incredibly valuable and will make your writing brilliant."

Just as improvisation can lead to the intangible studio magic, banter and warm-up takes in between recorded takes can be the most interesting, heartfelt, and high-quality recordings you'll produce from a session.

Laing encourages all directors to "record lots and lots of pickup, extras, and outtakes. You can never have enough to fill in unforeseen blanks."

Actors will frequently experiment with different iterations of the character they are portraying when nobody is watching. These experimentations can reveal different directions in which you can take your characters, as well as extend to what the actor is capable of. Further, today's digital recording processes—combined with very affordable mass storage mediums—mean that you can feel free to record as much extra material as you like. Bottom line: leave the tapes running for as long as you can afford to.

Multiple Takes

Sometimes, a take will sound perfect the first time you hear it, but after you begin reviewing takes, you find out that it doesn't have the right quality or tonality to fit the scene. To combat this, the recording engineer and director should ensure that a number of takes of each line are recorded. Although you don't want to kill your actors with excessive repetition of a single line, due diligence is extremely important in creating high-quality audio for your game project.

Varner highlights the importance of multiple takes: "*Always*, and I mean *always*, record several takes for each line of dialogue. There are always nuances and other aspects of an actor's performance that you don't hear during the session and wish you did. Having the multiple takes can save you a big headache when you listen back to the session a few days later with fresh ears."

Often, this isn't possible because budgets are generally fixed, and you usually only have your voice actors for set slots. If there isn't time for multiple takes, this has to be accepted. Also, some lines simply do not warrant multiple takes. If you are recording 500 barks that are variations on the same theme, there is little value in recording two versions of each. If it transpires that a few dozen fall by the wayside during the recording process for whatever reason, the remaining pool of lines will still be sufficiently viable for the purposes of most games.

A major component of mastering the art of VO recording is determining when your actor has hit a line just right.

Sloper details his process for determining when to try another take and when to move on: "Often the studio engineer, writer, and myself would vote together on whether the line had been delivered well enough by the actor and if we could go to the next line. Everybody's opinions are important to me, since everyone brings something different to the table."

Never be afraid to make a voice actor read a line multiple times, even if you happen to be working with a "big name" established actor who you may find slightly intimidating. Voice actors know that sometimes it takes multiple takes, and no matter how much they swear and curse between takes, they want to get it right. The corollary to this is that some lines transpire to be *impossible* for certain voice actors to read for various reasons. If after a dozen takes, the line is no closer to coming out correctly, it is usually better to provide an on-the-spot rewrite than to continue punishing a voice actor for not being able to render a particular line.

Although determining when to retake and when to move on may seem extremely difficult, sometimes impossible to new VO directors, the skill can be acquired and honed by hearing your game audio implemented in many different games—ideally many different types of games.

Other Technical Considerations

Whether your responsibilities are purely technical or purely creative, certain practices can be applied to your work to reduce many of the unforeseen technical difficulties that can irreversibly damage your product.

The first, and most important, is to maintain adequate backups. "Back up your files, back that backup up, and then back *that* up! I cannot emphasize this enough," says Varner. Nothing is worse than closing out a recording session and realizing with horror that your day, week, or month of recordings have been lost to a cryptic operating system error message. Having an automated off-site backup system, such as an FTP site that your files are automatically uploaded to at set intervals, is the most reliable way to back up your files. However, something as simple as a secondary computer, external hard drive, or a simple USB keychain drive can be a lifesaver as well. The only way to go wrong when backing up VO files is to fail to do so.

Additionally, ensure there are backups for the equipment. More than any other development discipline, the equipment used for recording audio can be fickle and prone to failure at the most inconvenient, embarrassing, and expensive times. The irony of a five-cent adapter failing while your five-grand-an-hour talent is standing by is often lost on the producer and director left standing by while an engineer frantically searches for a replacement.

This includes more than just recording equipment. Clement points out that "the most crucial thing has been having a backup for everything, with regard to everything in the production cycle, such as a backup recording system, backup printers, backup microphones, etc. Even silly little things like headphones, patch cables, or a music stand. They may not seem like a big deal…unless you don't have them. You just want to be sure that when the talent is there and ready to record, you'll be able to."

Maintaining clean air may not be the first thought when approaching a second, but it cannot be overlooked. Actors rely on their voice for their career; accordingly, they are very sensitive about the air they breathe. Although the choice of a recording studio may not always be yours, you should do what you can to select a studio that will make your actors the most comfortable. Where possible, studios should be above ground and should have a high quality air filter running while not recording to maintain a high air quality. You can save money by going with a cheaper basement studio, or a studio in a building with forced air heat, but you may end up losing recording time if actors are coughing, clearing their throats, or having trouble maintaining a consistent vocal tonality.

Finally, save the most strenuous lines until the end of the session. Certain material requires a great deal of strain or physical exertion, and it is unreasonable to expect actors to insert such draining performances in the middle of long scripts.

Peschel cautions that "when recording VO, leave all your death grunts, screams, and other high-intensity recordings for the very end of an actor's booth time. There is nothing worse than watching someone blow out their voice on blood gurgles only to realize *Hey wait... That guy is supposed to be Policeman #2 as well!*"

Particularly demanding tasks may even require a separate recording session. If you expect a voice actor to sing the vocals to a song to be used in game, this must be planned at the end of the recording session at the very least, and ideally in an entirely separate recording session (budget permitting).

After the Session

One of the keys to improving and growing as a writer, as well as a person, is to learn from experience. All too often, writers are forced to move onto another assignment too soon after a VO recording session. If writers take the time to go over their material and compare their original scripts with the final product, they can greatly reduce the amount of time and energy lost on subsequent sessions, as well as produce a higher quality product overall.

One of the most valuable skills writers acquire is the ability to learn and improve upon their skills based on past successes and failures. A popular quote in Aikido teachings is "the master is never afraid to look the fool." To a game writer, this means letting go of the emotional and professional attachment you have to a particular script, take, or style of writing.

When viewing your material, try to avoid thinking about the hours of work that went into that session, the personalities of the actors or director you worked with, or the myriad revisions you went through to get to the recording process. Think solely about the final effect of the words you wrote, how they sound to the player, and how you could have made them better. This can be a difficult, uncomfortable process, but the rewards of enduring such honest self-assessment are both undeniable and significant.

Saving your written and recorded material in an audio "scrapbook" is also a great way to analyze your performance over past projects and your growth as a writer. By being able to compare your written material to your recorded material, you can see how accurately your writing is being translated, as well as assess your progress across projects. Plus, it can be nice to have when you go to apply for that next big promotion.

CONCLUSION

To get the best results from a recording session, preparations must begin from the moment the script is being written. Writers must take into account the limitations of the human voice, use language that is appropriate, and structure sentences that will not turn the voice actors' tongues into pretzels and will allow for appropriate breath lengths. Context must be supplied in character summaries, scene descriptions, and clear and concise voice direction.

Hiring professional voice actors is the most important step toward successful recording sessions; ideally, these actors will have some game literacy and a vocal range that is appropriate to the characters they will be playing. The actors should be suitably prepared and warmed up prior to a recording session. During the session, teamwork between the many participants in the process will ensure the best results, and the writer (or someone on their behalf) must take notes to ensure that discrepancies between the script and the recorded files are adequately recorded.

The recording session for a game script can be a magical experience for a game writer. In the session, what used to be a static collection of words is transformed into people, events, experiences, and emotions. This is often the first point at which writers catch a fleeting glimpse of what the final game will be like, and how the story they have worked upon will be presented to the world. This chapter provides some preparation for the experience, but as with so much in life, there is no substitute for the real thing.

13 Interchangeable Dialogue Content

Ernest Adams

Interchangeable dialogue playback, or *stitching*, is the process of playing short audio files containing fragments of dialogue in such a way that it sounds like continuous speech. A given instance of playback, which for convenience's sake, we'll call a *line*, is usually triggered by some event in the game that causes a character to say something. The game software determines which fragments are needed to create a complete line and plays them back sequentially. By interchanging some fragments for others, the same line can be made to deliver different content; that is, the character can be made to say different things. The software selects which of the audio files is to be played based on data from the game's internal mechanics.

In videogames, stitching is most widely used to create TV-like commentary for sports titles. The commentary describes the action on the field, incorporating data from the game in progress such as the current score and the names of the athletes. This information must be stitched into the commentary to create a credible experience. Stitching is also useful in computer Role-Playing Games (cRPGs), adventure games, computerized versions of TV game shows, and any other game that requires dialogue. However, most of our examples will be drawn from the sports genre, and specifically from *Madden NFL Football,* for which the author of this chapter wrote the interchangeable dialogue audio for many years.

This chapter describes how to write this kind of material and how to create audio recording scripts for the actors or other voice talent who will record it. At the end of the chapter we also discuss a number of technical considerations for recording and editing interchangeable dialogue. However, we don't address how to create the software to perform the actual playback; that has to be done by an audio programmer and depends on the target machine.

CASE STUDY: BRITISH RAIL ANNOUNCEMENTS

Great Britain has a large railroad system with thousands of trains traversing the country every day. The railroad stations display the status of the trains on electronic displays, but they also give audible announcements for the benefit of blind passengers and those not standing near a display. With more than 2,500 stations, it is impractical to use human announcers, who would also be prone to errors. Instead, the stations use an automated audio system in which words are stitched together to make sentences. The following real example announces the arrival of a train bound for Waterloo station:

> The train now arriving at platform five is the eleven twenty-three South West Trains service to London Waterloo, calling at Woking, Weybridge, Clapham Junction, and London Waterloo. This train is composed of eight coaches.

This particular example consists of two English sentences, but it's only one line of dialogue; the two sentences are always heard together and in the order shown. As you can see, these announcements include quite a lot of information that must be stitched together to form a line. Some parts of the line are always the same whenever the announcement is played; we call these parts the *invariant parts*. Other parts change depending on what information needs to be conveyed. These we call the *interchangeable items*. The invariant parts are, in effect, the backbone of the line—the base structure into which the interchangeable items must be inserted.

Here's the example again, divided into its component fragments. The invariant parts of the line are shown in normal text, whereas the interchangeable parts are in boldface:

> The train now arriving at platform / **five** / is the / **eleven** / **twenty-three** / **South West Trains** / service to / **London Waterloo,** / calling at / **Woking,** / **Weybridge,** / **Clapham Junction,** / and / **London Waterloo.** / This train is composed of / **eight** / coaches.

The invariant part of this line, its backbone, is "The train now arriving at platform... is the... service to... calling at...and.... This train is composed of... coaches." This line includes 10 interchangeable items in 8 separate insertions into the line. (One insertion is a list of items.) The interchangeable items are, in order: the platform number, the hour and minute of the intended arrival time, the train operating company name, the final destination, the list of stations along the route, the destination station again, and the number of coaches (cars) that make up the train. Clearly, it would be impossible to record separate announcements for every combination of times, stations, platforms, and so forth.

The system works very well: it's clear, detailed, and unambiguous. However, it doesn't really sound like ordinary human speech. The nouns are spoken with more emphasis than is normal, which helps the passengers to hear them, and there are minuscule pauses between the fragments. The passengers don't mind this, because it's clearer than the mush-mouthed announcements given by harried station managers when something goes so wrong that the system doesn't have an announcement for it. However, our goal in stitching for videogames is to produce speech that is indistinguishable from the real thing.

There's one other point to note about this example. The destination station is given twice, once in the middle of the sentence and once at the end. In normal English speech, the last word of a sentence is inflected downwards; that is, it's usually slightly quieter and spoken in a descending tone. Therefore, the names of all the stations must be recorded twice: once for use in the middle and once for use at the end. This phenomenon is ubiquitous in English, and will be addressed in detail later in the chapter.

IS STITCHING NECESSARY?

Don't assume that every game needs a stitching system. It's a complicated business to design and test one, and stitched dialogue never sounds as good as continuously recorded dialogue. If you can simply play back different audio files for different lines of dialogue, you should. However, as you've seen from the preceding example, this isn't always possible. The two main reasons for doing audio stitching are a shortage of space on your game's distribution medium, and a lack of recording time with your voice actors. Either condition will require that you do stitching rather than record every possible sentence individually.

Shortage of Space

The recorded sentence fragments used to play back stitched sentences naturally take up less space than recordings of every possible combination of sentences. If you're inserting a player's name into a line of game dialogue (for example, "**Bob**, it's your turn. Spin the wheel!"), you may have several hundred names, but not have the space to store that line several hundred times. Storing the one line without the name (the invariant part) and several hundred interchangeable names will naturally take less space on the disc or whatever distribution medium you are using. However, if you only have a small number of interchangeable items, it's less trouble and produces better results to simply record all possible combinations as invariant material. If a character says, "I'd like to buy the blue cloak, please," and the only choices are red, blue, and green, just record all three lines individually.

Lack of Recording Time

You may also need to use stitched material if you have only a limited amount of time to record your voice actors. Even if you have huge amounts of storage space (a Blu-Ray DVD holds 25 GB), it can still be time-consuming for your voice actors to record all the possible combinations in your material. It's also tiring, and you run the risk that the actor will make a mistake with a lot of repetitious material. It's difficult to make the fifteenth reading of a line sound just as interesting as the first one if it only differs by one or two words. Finally, there are cost considerations: if the voice actor is a highly paid celebrity, you simply may not be able to afford to have them do every possible combination of the sentences you have.

Risks of Using Stitching

Stitching is not without its risks, and your team should be aware of them before making a commitment to implementing it. The risks fall into three general categories: aesthetic, technical, and financial.

Aesthetic Risks

The aesthetic risk of stitching is simply that it won't sound right; that no matter how you tinker with a given line in the audio suite, you can't get credible playback. This won't happen with every line, but it could easily happen with one or two, especially if you have large quantities of material. When it does, you have to choose between leaving the line in the game and just letting it sound bad or cutting it out.

You can control the aesthetic risks in two ways. First, have your voice actors record several takes of the each line. The more times you record a given line, the greater the chances are of finding stitching combinations that work correctly. Second, write several different versions of the same line for use in a given game situation. That way if one of the lines simply doesn't work, you will at least have the others to use. This is addressed later in this chapter.

Technical Risks

The technical risks are out of your control as a writer, but you should still know what they are. Audio stitching software must keep track of a large database of information, which the programmers will have to build from your script. This database includes such information as which lines can be played for a given event, which lines have already been played, which interchangeable items can be stitched into a line, and what game data causes a given item to be included. If errors creep into this database, the playback will produce absurd results, playing the wrong line at the wrong time or inserting the wrong material into the line. Furthermore, the software must be able to retrieve the necessary audio data from its storage medium and stream it back smoothly without interruption, while the game itself continues to run. This is seldom a problem when the data is stored on a fast medium such as a hard disk, but it can be tricky when the data is on a slow medium such as CD-ROM or DVD. Your audio programmers should build a proof-of-technology prototype to demonstrate that they can do this on the target platform *before* you write the script or record the voice actors. If you aren't sure that you can make the software work, there's no point in committing yourself to it.

Financial Risks

As we said earlier, stitching can save money if your voice actors are expensive, and you can't afford to pay them to record every possible combination of lines. However, there are also costs associated with stitching. The stitching playback software must be written and tested, and the project will need much more audio editing than nonstitched material requires—depending on the nature of your material, it could be three to five times as much work. Finally, the stitched material will undoubtedly produce a few bugs during the product's final testing, and you will have to budget time to fix these.

TYPOGRAPHICAL CONVENTIONS IN THIS CHAPTER

Before we go into the details of stitching, a few notes on typographical conventions are in order:

If we quote a line of dialogue within a paragraph, it will be surrounded by double quotation marks, thus:

"Drop the gun!"

If the line is in a paragraph by itself, we won't use the quotation marks.

If the line contains interchangeable content, and we list all the possible interchangeable items within the line, we will do so by surrounding the interchangeable items in square brackets and separating the options by vertical bars. The items themselves will be in bold face, as follows:

"Show me the [**watch** | **ring** | **necklace** | **bracelet**]."

If an interchangeable item has too many variants to include them all, we will simply write the item's general description in angle brackets and bold face, like this: "<**quarterback's name**> drops back to pass."

GAME EVENTS

Dialogue playback, whether fixed or interchangeable, is normally triggered by an event in the game. These events may be produced by the mechanics of the game itself, or they may be a response to the player's inputs. If your game includes conversations, many of these events will be choices made by the player about what line he wants his avatar to say, or choices made as a consequence of the game mechanics about what line a NPC should say. Some events will probably also require exclamations outside the context of a conversation—things like "I'm hit!" when a character is wounded, for example. In sports games, the commentary is triggered by events in the match being played. In any case, working with the game designers and programmers, you will create a long list of events that require audio material. These fall into several types, as follows.

Single-Line Events

When something happens in a game that requires a specific line of dialogue, and no other line would be appropriate, we can call it a *single-line event*. When a player selects a line from a menu of dialogue options, for example, the line that he sees in the menu is the line that he should hear. Note that single-line events are not necessarily unique—they may occur multiple times in the game—only that exactly one line of dialogue is required when they occur.

When a player gives an order whose audio always sounds the same ("Open fire!"), or an NPC always responds in exactly the same way ("Aye-aye, sir!"), these are single-line events. Single-line events may still contain interchangeable information, however. When a player character walks into a merchant's shop, the merchant might always open the conversation with the same line: "What can I do for you, [**sir | ma'am**]?" The software still has to insert the correct honorific based on the sex of the character that the merchant is speaking to.

Events that have only one line tend to fall into two categories: those that occur very rarely (or even uniquely in the game), in which case they can have long lines of dialogue, and those that occur very frequently (like "Open fire"), in which case the line *must* be kept as short as possible. If an event occurs neither extremely rarely nor extremely frequently, then it should have several different lines of dialogue for the computer to choose from. We describe this situation in the next section.

Events with Multiple Optional Lines

Sports games tend to be repetitious, with many similar events occurring over and over. The players quickly get tired of hearing the same commentary whenever a particular event occurs. It makes the game sound mechanical and destroys the player's immersion. For each event that occurs with moderate frequency (neither every five seconds, nor only once per game), you should write several lines of commentary and have the computer select one at random when the event occurs. These are *multi-line events.* In *Madden NFL Football,* when a big hit occurs, the game chooses from one of a number of "Maddenisms" to play: "Boom! Where'd that truck come from?"; "He'll remember that number."; "That's how you get on a first-name basis with dirt."; and so on. The more of these you have, the better your game will sound. For sports commentary, we recommend a minimum of five different lines for each event, even ones that are rare, such as an athlete being ejected from the game. For common events, two dozen is not too many. Be sure, however, that all the lines for a given event have the same meaning! If you play a line that is inappropriate for the event that just occurred, the players will notice it immediately.

Ask the programmers to keep a checklist of which lines have been played for a given event. When the event occurs, the software should play one at random from all the unplayed lines and then check it off the list so it won't be played again until all the others have been heard first. When all have been played, it should reset the checklist *except* for the most recently played line, so the players will never hear the same line twice in row.

You can use multiple optional lines for an event in other genres than sports games. When a player chooses a line of dialogue from a menu, and the menu does not quote the line literally, you can create several versions. For instance, if a menu item reads, "Ask about Jane's missing necklace," you can write several different lines and let the software choose one: "What do you know about the missing necklace?"; "Do you know what happened to Jane's necklace?"; "Tell me about the necklace that went missing."; and so on. This adds variety if the avatar has to ask the same question of several characters. It also provides some protection against the risk that one line can't be made to sound right; at least you will have the others to fall back on.

Events That Trigger Long Lines

Sometimes you may have a rare event that triggers a long line—a soliloquy by an NPC, for example. If the event is unique in the entire game—such as uncovering a major plot twist in a story—there's no problem with this, but if the event can occur more than once, you shouldn't play a long line a second time or it will sound artificial (and the player will become annoyed at having to listen to it). The longer a line is, the less often the player should hear it. It's one thing to hear "Yes, sir" or "Cover me!" again and again, but long speeches shouldn't ever be heard a second time unless the player specifically asks for them. If a computer-generated event triggers a long line, you should inform the programmers that the line should only be said once, and then should be silent the next time the event occurs, or play back a different, shorter version from then on. In *Madden,* we designated that certain lines could only be played once per quarter, once per half, or once per game. If the event occurs again within the same time period, the line is unavailable and the software either plays an alternate line (if it's a multi-line event) or remains silent (if it's a single-line event). At the end of each quarter, and at the end of the first half, the software went through and reset the flags on those lines that had already been played so that they could be played again. Those that could only be played once per game were never reset.

Handling Simultaneous Events

Speech takes time, and a speaker can only talk about one thing at once. In a fast-moving sports game, you may find that several things have happened so quickly, the commentary cannot keep up. For the purposes of the playback, these can be considered *simultaneous events.* You will then have to decide which of them the commentator will discuss. To do this, make a hierarchy of event types, so that the high-priority ones get the playback. The programmers will have to implement the hierarchy in software, so be sure to discuss it with them early. Your hierarchy should be sorted by the rarity and importance of the event. In *Madden,* a score has higher priority than everything else because points are scored rather infrequently in American football and a score is very important; it influences the outcome of the game. The next most important event is an injury, followed by a penalty, and then ordinary play commentary. In basketball, where points are scored very frequently, you would probably want to put an injury at the top, followed by a penalty—especially if it requires a free throw—and then a score, and finally ordinary play. Near the end of a close game, however, scoring points should start to be higher priority events.

Interruptions

If the playback is in the middle of a long line when something really important—an event of much higher priority—happens in the game, you may want to interrupt the playback to play a new line that goes with the important event. However, if you do this without any explanation, it will sound unnatural, as if someone simply stopped talking in the middle of a sentence and began to talk about something else. To make the transition, write a series of *interruption lines* that can be selected from at random when the interrupting event occurs. These should be short and generic, so they may be used in any circumstances. "Wow! Did you see that?"; "What in the world?"; "Look out!"; and so on are all exclamations that can legitimately interrupt another sentence and introduce a new topic. They should be recorded with extra emphasis and emotion, to justify the sudden change. After the interruption line has been played, you can then play the line that belongs with the interrupting event.

HOW TO STUDY THE SPEECH SPACE OF YOUR GAME

When writing dialogue for a game, whether interchangeable or fixed, you have to know when the dialogue will be used. Dialogue normally occurs during interactions between characters, but—as in sports games and game shows—it is sometimes used to speak directly to the player *as* a player rather than as a character in the game. For the most part, you won't need to do stitching in mission briefings and tutorial material because it's almost always fixed content. Mission *de*briefings, or summaries after the player has completed a level, however, can be variable because the player either has, or has not, accomplished certain tasks. But the majority of the stitched dialogue in a game will occur during play, not between levels.

Commentary

Sports game commentary requires an enormous amount of stitched material if you want to insert athlete names, team names, scores, and so on. Commentary is a perfect example of the event-driven dialogue described in the next chapter, because almost everything the commentators say will be triggered by something that happens in the game.

To study the speech space of a sports game, you should do two things: listen to real sports matches and read the game's rule book for events that the commentators should talk about. Begin by recording three or four television broadcasts of live matches, and then go back through them and transcribe them word for word. After you have a transcript, you can analyze it to see what kinds of events the commentators speak about and what other remarks they make. You will soon spot general categories of commentary that include interchangeable content: announcements of the score and the amount of time left in the game, discussions about the quality of play by each team (if it's a team sport), biographical and statistical information about the athletes, and, of course, descriptions of ongoing events in the game that include athletes' names. Try to find, or create, a category for every sentence spoken. If your word processor offers a highlight feature, assign a different color to each category, and then highlight every sentence that belongs in that category with the appropriate color. This will enable you to go back through the transcript quickly to find all the sentences that discuss related material and see how they vary from one another.

Most real sports matches only include a subset of all the possible events that can occur in a sport. Many sports have special rules governing rare events, and you'll need to record audio for them too; otherwise, your game will suddenly fall silent when those rare events happen. After you have analyzed the transcripts for three or four typical sports matches, go through the sport's rulebook looking for additional events that you may need to provide commentary for.

Conversations

In nonsports games, you'll need to create stitched dialogue for conversations among the characters (including the avatar if there is one). To begin with, collect all the names and roles of all the characters that will appear in your game. If it's a long game of exploration, like an adventure or role-playing game, there may be dozens, conceivably even hundreds. Now you can classify them according to the amount and type of speaking they will do, as follows:

> **Nonspeaking characters:** These might include animals or monsters that lack the power of speech, people who are only seen in the backgrounds of scenes, and those whose speech will be handled only through text and not audio.
>
> **Characters with limited interactions:** Many cRPGS have a lot of service characters that only do one thing in one location, and their conversation is limited to their job role. Blacksmiths, healers, and shopkeepers seldom have much to say, but what they do say can often benefit from stitching. Put characters in this category that always say the same things regardless of whom they're talking to.
>
> **Characters with many or complex interactions:** This category includes the avatar, the people that the avatar has significant conversations with (including other members of the party and NPCs who have information to offer, in a cRPG), and any other characters that may hold complex conversations in the course of the game. In an adventure or detective game, you may want to allow the avatar to talk to anyone about anything that he already knows about (this requires a token-based system, as described in the next chapter). If that is the case, then all the speaking characters will belong in this category.

Now that you have all the characters divided into categories, you can ignore those in the first; you won't be recording them. The characters in the second category will produce a limited number of events, generated by their job functions; what they have to say is seldom driven by the plot of the game. For them, you can simply write a series of typical conversations associated with the roles they play and then look for the content that will need to be interchangeable.

The characters in the third category require more work because their activities are usually bound up with the plot. You should begin by writing their material as you normally would for unstitched dialogue. If you try to write interchangeable material right from the beginning, you will probably get too caught up in the mechanics. It's more important to get the essence of the interactions down first. After the script is written, go back through it and look for things that need to be interchangeable. Unfortunately, we can't give specific advice about this because it varies enormously from game to game. The things that are most likely to change are particular parts of speech associated with people, objects, or quantities. We address the different parts of speech in detail in a later section.

RECORDING DIFFERENT VOCAL INFLECTIONS

As mentioned in the railroad station example, English uses different vocal inflections for words that appear in the beginning or middle of a sentence and for those that appear at the end. Whether the inflection goes up, goes down, or remains neutral varies with the type of sentence. Therefore, it's not enough to record an interchangeable word just one time; you must record it with all the different inflections that may be required by your material. In this section, we discuss how to record the same word for use in different parts of a sentence and in different kinds of sentences.

Linguists divide sentences into three major categories: declaratives (also called assertions), imperatives (also called commands), and interrogatives (also called questions). In everyday speech, however, there is one more usage with its own vocal quality: responses to questions. We'll look at each category and see how it affects the different inflections we use, and how you need to write for it.

Declaratives

Declaratives are the most complicated form of sentence, and long ones can run on and on. However, you shouldn't need to stitch long sentences except possibly to insert a name. What we're really concerned with is sentences of moderate length that occur fairly frequently. Words at the beginning or in the middle of a declarative sentence usually have a neutral inflection. Words that appear at the end of a sentence are downwardly inflected, which is how we know that the sentence has come to an end. In stitched game audio, these words are almost always nouns: subjects near the beginning and direct or indirect objects at the end. Here are some examples:

Atkins makes the catch.
Atkins and **Williams** were involved in the fight.
The penalty is against **Atkins**.

In the first two cases, the names inserted should have a neutral inflection. In the last case, you'll need a downward inflection for the end of the sentence. This means that for every interchangeable item that can appear at the beginning or middle and at the end of a sentence, you will need to make two recordings. When we first started doing interchangeable dialogue in *Madden,* we even recorded three, distinguishing between the inflection at the beginning and the inflection in the middle of a sentence. Experience showed, however, that they weren't really that different.

Imperatives

Imperatives (commands and orders) tend to be loud, with a verb at the beginning and a noun, if there is one, at the end. An RPG example might be "Give me that [**wand** | **staff** | **amulet**]!" You may be able to reuse the same set of interchangeable nouns in *other* imperatives (for example, "Drop the [**wand** | **staff** | **amulet**]!", but you will almost certainly *not* be able to use them in any other kind of sentence. If you try, you'll get an oddly shouted word at the end of an otherwise normal sentence ("Good afternoon. I'd like to buy an **amulet!**"). Therefore, if you're going to stitch imperatives at all, we strongly recommend that you record all the interchangeable words they will use especially for that purpose so the volume and inflection will be correct.

Interrogatives

Interrogatives (questions) end with a rising inflection in English, and therefore recorded words that are intended to end declarative sentences won't work for questions. You need to make a separate recording of any interchangeable content that ends a question ("Do you know the way to [**San Jose** | **Topeka** | **Hoboken**]?").

For some reason, a number of younger English speakers have, in the fast few years, begun ending declarative sentences as if they were questions. This makes it sound like they're trying to reassure themselves that their listener is actually paying attention, and, used repeatedly, becomes very tiresome ("So we went down to the mall? And we went into J.C. Penney's? And they have these red sweaters?"). You may want to do this if your character is a Valley Girl; otherwise, avoid it like the plague.

Responses

Responses are answers to questions, and much of the time, you can treat them like any other declarative; however, there are exceptions. If the first word of the sentence is the answer that the questioner is looking for, it often gets an extra emphasis ("Who's your best operative for covert surveillance?" "**Wilson** is the one for that job."). You may find that you need to record a separate set of items specifically for this purpose, or the result will sound a little too deadpan.

Responses can also be very short, just a word or two, if the questioner has listed a number of possibilities ("Which will it be, sir, beer, wine, or whiskey?" "[**Beer.** | **Wine.** | **Whiskey.**]"). In this case, the word both begins and ends a sentence at the same time. However, it should still have the downward inflection of the end of a sentence because nothing follows it. The downward inflection indicates that the speaker is finished speaking. You can use the same recordings that you normally use for words that end a sentence, but as always, it's safest to make a special recording for it.

PARTS OF SPEECH

In this section, we'll look at the various parts of speech and consider whether and how they should be stitched. Traditional English grammar defines the parts of speech as nouns and pronouns, verbs, adjectives, adverbs, prepositions, conjunctions, and interjections. We would add articles (*a*, *an*, and *the*) to the list. Many, but not all, of these elements can be interchanged depending on the needs of the game. Conjunctions (*for*, *and*, *nor*, *but*, *or*, *yet*, *so*, *either…or*, and so on) will almost certainly belong to the invariant part of the line and shouldn't be stitched. Interjections (*ouch*, *wow*, *hey*, and similar) will either stand on their own as short lines or belong to the invariant part of a longer line. Greetings and goodbyes are also interjections, and you probably won't need to stitch them into anything else; however, you may want to use them as an invariant with a name stitched on the end ("Good afternoon, **Lady Bracknell**."). We'll go through the remaining parts of speech in detail.

Nouns

Nouns are used as the subjects of sentences and as direct or indirect objects. As objects, they usually fall at the end of a sentence and must be recorded with a separate inflection.

Personal Names

Names are by far the most frequently stitched values in games, especially sports games. There are a number of specialized considerations about stitching names because we don't always call the same person by exactly the same name. Usage depends on genre and cultural context; as we discuss later, manners were different in earlier times. There are also differences when speaking *of* a person and speaking *to* him. Here are some of the options:

Last name without an honorific, e.g. "Jones": Used in sports and military contexts. Bear in mind, however, that two people on a team may have the same last name, and in this case, you'll need to also record a first name-last name fragment to disambiguate them. "He passes to Terence Jones," rather than just "He passes to Jones." Note that in Victorian and earlier times, unrelated male friends used last names rather than first names—first names were for family. It's Holmes and Watson, not Sherlock and John.

Last name with an honorific, e.g. "Mr. Jones" or "Lord Rochester": Used on formal, ceremonious, or public occasions. "Lord Rochester! Tell us the tale of your journey to the land of the giants." Again, in earlier times, people used these more often; a woman would say of her husband, "Mr. Smith and I are going to the ball" rather than "Bob and I," when speaking to strangers.

First name: Used, when appropriate, about or among friends and family members, and now widely used of coworkers and colleagues as well. Informal. "Tell Lancelot if he's not at the Round Table in five minutes we'll start the quest without him."

First name-last name combination: As mentioned previously, you will seldom need to use this unless there is a chance of ambiguity or you need to introduce a character. "Let me introduce you to Susan Roberts." You would never use this when addressing someone directly; it's "Sue" (a nickname), "Susan" (a first name), "Ms. Roberts" (a formal address, mostly used among strangers), or "Roberts" (a military or sporting usage more commonly used among men than women, although this is changing).

Nicknames: Used in cases of close friendship or informality. "Lance! How was the quest?"

Numbers

After names, numbers are the item you're most likely to need to stitch. If your dialogue calls for numerical values to be spoken aloud, you might need hundreds or thousands of versions using fixed audio recordings. With stitched audio, you might need to record hundreds of numbers, but the rest of the sentence can be invariant and you'll only need to have one copy of it.

You should always record multiple sets of numbers for different circumstances. The way we speak numbers varies considerably depending on what we're referring to, and there are more and less formal ways of saying them. For example, in purchasing small quantities of things, people often say, "I'll take a couple of those oranges," or "Give me half a dozen eggs." It would sound stilted and unnatural for a character to say, "I would like to buy six eggs, please." For this reason, you should record a separate set of numbers for each different *type* of usage in your game. That is, you should record different sets of numbers for buying objects and for telling distances or any other distinct usage, such as scores, amounts of money, and so on. Every time a character mentions a particular sum of money ("That'll cost you seventy-three gold" or "The price for that is seventy-three pieces of gold, sir"), the software should stitch in the "money numbers" rather than the "distance numbers" or the "score numbers." Times of day are another special case of numbers; they are so distinctive that we address them in a separate section later on.

You will probably find that some circumstances require only limited quantities, so you won't have to record too many numbers. For example, if the longest distance anybody can possibly travel in your world is 30 miles, you only need to record "distance numbers" from 1 to 30.

Another reason for recording different sets of numbers for different types of items is that we often use informal, idiomatic forms for different kinds of things. Whereas someone might say, "Give me half a dozen eggs," he wouldn't say, "The village of Ashby is half a dozen miles to the north." You don't have to record different numbers for buying oranges and for buying apples because their usage type is the same.

Although idiomatic numbers generally seem more natural, the software shouldn't always use the informal forms, or it will sound stilted after a while. A superior alternative is to choose randomly between "six" and "half a dozen" each time that value is needed when referring to a purchase of objects.

Sports Scores

With scores, you'll have to decide how high is the reasonable maximum possible for the game. Basketball games occasionally go above 100, but almost never over 125, so that's a reasonable maximum. In baseball, it's about 25. In soccer, it's more like 15. Of course, the players may collude to create a situation in which they generate a ridiculous score, but if the game is unable to announce it, that's hardly your fault. (It is always possible to provide a special event for this situation: "The scores today have become ridiculous!")

Broadcasters seldom announce sports scores bluntly or at random times during the game; rather, they announce them in some context. In American football, they announce them after every new score, at commercial breaks, and at other normal breaks in the play such as a time out or the end of a quarter. In basketball, the scores change so fast that they usually only announce them at a break in the action. Part of your job is to figure out when it's appropriate to give the score and in what terminology.

One of the peculiarities of announcing a score is the number of ways broadcasters have of saying "zero." They seldom actually say "zero"; instead, they say, "nothing," "scoreless," or "still not on the board." In tennis, a zero score during a single game is traditionally called "love." In baseball, after the first half-inning is over, the team in the field will not yet have had a chance to score, so the announcer will say, "And after the first half-inning, it's the Pirates three, and the Reds are coming to bat." You should create several variants appropriate to the sport you're writing for.

Distances

In recording numbers to be used with distance, remember that people become less accurate as the numbers get larger. "Las Vegas? Yeah, it's about another hundred miles from here," someone will say, when it's actually 93 miles. If your player needs precision (or the character speaking is a naturally precise type, such as Mr. Spock), you'll want to record every single number that might be used. But for ordinary sloppy conversation, you can round to the nearest 5 on numbers above 30, and the nearest 10 on numbers above 70.

Don't forget to include fractional values for numbers under 1: one-quarter (or one-fourth), one-half, and three-quarters (or three-fourths). Naturally, you'll want to make these idiomatic: "'bout a quarter mile north of here," and so on. Be sure to also record the phrase "less than a mile" (or whatever unit you're using) for characters who are less precise.

Times

Times generally consist of the hour and minute, along with the terms "AM" and "PM." You will need separate insertions for the hour and the minute unless you want to record all 720 possible combinations in a 12-hour day. In military and certain other contexts, you will want to use a 24-hour clock and drop the AM and PM. Note that you can't reuse numbers recorded elsewhere for the minute values from one to nine, because people don't say, "It's eleven-three"; they say, "It's eleven-oh-three."

When telling the time, however, people seldom give exact figures, especially if they're wearing analog watches. They often round to the nearest five minutes, and they leave off the AM and PM, expecting the listener to know that. There are also special usages for the quarter and half hours. For example, in addition to "it's five fifteen," you should also include "it's a quarter past five." You can also use "half past five" rather than "five thirty," and "a quarter to five" rather than "four forty-five." Don't forget to include "noon" and "midnight."

Places

If place names are proper names, such as the names of towns, you can treat them like the names of people; they don't take an article ("**Chicago** is a rough town, mister."). If they're references to things in the landscape, you'll have to treat them more like objects: "Meet me by [**the well** | **the hollow tree**]." You may also have to stitch street addresses, which will require two interchangeable values: one for the number and one for the street name. These, again, will be a special kind of number, because we say, "Seven-thirty-one Maple Street," not "Seven hundred and thirty-one Maple Street."

Compass Points

Compass points occasionally appear in cRPGs when one character is giving directions to another; you'll normally just want the 4 cardinal points plus the 4 ordinal ones (northeast, southeast, southwest, and northwest). Modern-day ships and aircraft use degree designations, for example, "Make your heading ninety degrees" means due east, and this is preferred for military contexts. In earlier times, sailing ships used 64 different named compass points such as "south-southeast" and even "northwest by west a half west." Finding out what these are and what they mean is left as an exercise for the interested reader!

Objects

War games and cRPGs tend to include large numbers of objects: unit types, weapons, magical items, clothing, jewelry, and so on. If characters speak of them, you will need to stitch the names of the objects into their sentences. The names of objects themselves are not intrinsically difficult to handle, but they way they relate to the words around them is. Articles and adjectives complicate matters, and are discussed in more detail in the following section. You will have to record the name of each object in many different combinations: with and without a preceding article, in singular and plural forms, and with inflections for the beginning or middle and for the end of a sentence. You may also want to use contractions. Here's a list of some of the possible variations of the word *sword* in a line:

I'd like to buy a sword. [end of sentence, indefinite article, singular]

I'd like to buy the sword. [end of sentence, definite article, singular]

I'd like to buy five swords. [end of sentence, no article, plural]

I'd like to buy a sword and shield. [middle of sentence, indefinite article, singular]

I'd like to buy the sword and shield. [middle of sentence, definite article, singular]

I'd like to buy five swords and a shield. [middle of sentence, no article, plural]

A sword's no use to me. [beginning of sentence, indefinite article, contraction]

The sword's not any good. [beginning of sentence, definite article, contraction]

If an object is unique, it's best to record its name as a single item, even if the name could be stitched together. Suppose, for instance, that the game includes the armor of a mighty warrior named Dorgon, consisting of pieces called "Dorgon's Helm," "Dorgon's Shield," "Dorgon's Hauberk," and so on. You'll get better results if you simply record these names as individual items, rather than trying to stitch them as "<**name**>'s Helm," and so on. For one thing, the S at the end of "Dorgon's" should really blend smoothly into the S at the beginning of "Shield," and that won't happen if you stitch it.

Articles

In English, articles are the words "a" and "an" (the indefinite articles) and "the" (the definite article). Articles should not be recorded as interchangeable items by themselves, nor treated as part of the invariant parts of a line. Rather, they should be recorded and stored *with* their accompanying noun, as a single fragment, if at all possible. You will need to record nouns both with and without articles and use the different versions in different places. For example, the line, "I want to buy your [**horse**

| donkey | mule | elephant] and a saddle" interchanges various nouns without a preceding article. However, the response does require an article:

"[**The horse** | **The donkey** | **The mule** | **The elephant**] will cost...."

You might think that you can let the word "the" be an invariant beginning to the sentence and simply insert the correct noun after it. However, articles are pronounced differently depending on the sound of the following word. If the first letter of the word following "the" is a consonant or Y-sound, then "the" will be pronounced *thuh*. If the first letter following is a vowel, then "the" will be pronounced *thee*. So in the preceding sample, the nouns should be recorded as thuh horse, thuh donkey, thuh mule, but thee elephant. It's also thuh universe but thee undertaker because "universe" begins with a Y sound.

This also applies to the indefinite article. "A" is used for words beginning with consonants; "an" for words beginning with vowels. Therefore, you should keep the article together with its noun and insert them as a unit in sentences where they are needed:

Richard III: My kingdom for [**a horse** | **a donkey** | **a mule** | **an elephant**]!

It's better to simply record the article with its noun and insert them together rather than try to keep track of which nouns begin with vowels and which don't.

Another reason for keeping an article with its noun is that some nouns don't require articles. If you were to build the article into the invariant parts and then insert a noun beginning with a proper name, the result would be wrong. If Dorgon was the name of a warrior, you wouldn't say, "I have found the Dorgon's Shield." The line should be written as "I have found <**object name**>," and then you can interchange "Dorgon's Shield," "the Sword of Galahad," "an elephant," or "five gold rings and four calling birds," as needed.

However, there is an exception! The rule about keeping an article together with its noun *does not apply* if an adjective comes between them and the adjective is interchangeable. In that case, the form and pronunciation of the article will depend on the adjective. We cover this in the next section.

Adjectives

There isn't a lot of need for interchangeable adjectives in sports games, but cRPGs are another story. Such games include large numbers of objects in great variety, and the variation is often described by adjectives. In English, adjectives are used before the noun but after any preceding article. You will therefore need to record combinations both with and without articles: "red," "the red," and "a red"; "blue," "the blue," and "a blue"; and so on. You can then insert the adjective, with its article as appropriate, in front of the name of any object that it needs to modify. As with objects, remember that the pronunciation of "the" and "an" change depending on the initial letter of the word that follows it.

Adjectives don't always precede a noun; they can also end a sentence, for example, "I want the one that's **red**." If you write such a sentence, you'll have to record a downward inflection for your adjectives.

Pronouns

English pronouns are divided into first- (*I*), second- (*you*), and third-person (*he, she,* or *it*) forms and into various cases: subject (*I*), object (*me*), reflexive (*myself*), and two possessive cases, (*mine* and *my*). Some of these are gender specific, and they're the ones you're most likely to interchange to suit the sex of the character being referred to. A villain might say of your protagonist, "Take **him** to the dungeons" or "Take **her** to the dungeons," for example. You may also need contractions such as *he'll* (contraction of *he will*), he'd (contraction of *he would* or *he had*), *he's* (contraction of *he is*), and of course their feminine forms.

One of the most teeth-grindingly annoying misusages in recent years has been the incorrect replacement of *I* or *me* with *myself,* as in "Sharon and myself went into town" or "He gave the documents to Tom and myself." *Myself* is reflexive; it only applies to things that someone does to him*self,* not to something that someone else does.

If you're planning to use the archaic "thou" and "ye," please be careful to use them properly or your game will sound corny and destroy the player's immersion. Read the Gamasutra webzine article, "Some Thoughts on Archaic Language," for further tips (*http://www.gamasutra.com/features/designers_notebook/20000229.htm*; free registration is required).

You're unlikely to interchange the ungendered forms (*it, its, itself*) of these in the same sentence as the gendered forms unless your sentence refers to animals interchangeably with ungendered nouns. Your villain won't need to say "Take it to the dungeons" unless your hero is sexless. On the other hand, you may have a character say, "I'd like to sell this [**horse** | **armor**]" and the potential purchaser reply, "Very well, let me take a look at [**him** | **her** | **it**]" depending on whether the player was referring to a male or female horse, or some armor.

Prepositions

Prepositions refer to physical relationships between objects. You will only need to interchange prepositions if you're giving details about the placement of objects, and those details can change for some reason. For example, suppose you're making a detective game and the clues are randomized each time it is played. The protagonist is the detective, questioning a suspect about where the suspect found a gun or some other important object. The suspect would need to be able to reply, "I found it [**in | under | beside | on top of | in front of | behind**] [**the bookcase | the wardrobe | the cupboard**]" if those are all the places the gun could be.

Don't Stitch Verbs

For the most part, you shouldn't try to stitch verbs. Verbs describe action, so the line that contains them is likely to be triggered by a related event in the game. A different event should trigger a different line. Rather than try to write one line that allows for interchangeable verbs, it's better to write multiple lines with different verbs in the invariant part, to serve as an anchor for everything else that may be inserted into the line.

Using the detective game example again, imagine that the detective is asking a pathologist how a victim died. Rather than try to make one line that works with any possible combination of events ("[**He | She**] [**fell | took | shot**] [**down the stairs. | off the balcony. | an overdose. | poison. | himself. | herself.**]"), create three separate lines, one for falling, one for taking drugs, and one for shooting:

"[**He | She**] fell [**down the stairs. | off the balcony.**]"

"[**He | She**] took [**an overdose. | poison.**]"

"[**He | She**] shot [**himself. | herself.**]"

This way you're less likely to leave something out of your script by mistake or confuse the programmers and cause the software to accidentally generate nonsense ("She fell poison.").

Verbs also carry emotional meaning, and if you try to interchange them, you may find that the inflection of the rest of the sentence doesn't work properly. Consider the two imperatives, "Chamberlain, summon my imperial wizard!" and "Chamberlain, go get my imperial wizard." The first is more dramatic, to be used on a formal public occasion; the latter is a simple request for something. The speaker's tone would be completely different, so you couldn't interchange "summon" and "go get." Or consider several possible outcomes of a dramatic situation. Suppose that Susan has discovered that Bob has betrayed her, and the speaker is describing what happened when they next met. There might be several variants: she could smack him, shout at him, or ignore him. But if you simply interchange the verbs ("Susan [**smacked | shouted at | ignored**] Bob") the result will lack emotional punch. It would be better to record them as separate sentences with suitable intonation and additional detail:

- "Susan smacked Bob a good one."
- "Susan shouted at Bob for fifteen minutes straight."
- "Susan ignored Bob completely; just froze him out."

WRITING SCRIPTS WITH INTERCHANGEABLE CONTENT

You will need to write two versions of your script, one for the programmers to use and one for your voice actors. We'll describe their formats later in this section. The audio editor will need a copy of both scripts. You should create the version for the programmers first, even though this may seem strange if you're not used to writing for videogames. The reason is that you will make decisions during this process that will affect the recording script used by the talent. The script will be divided into two major sections: the invariant lines and the interchangeable material.

Recording Scripts

To produce a natural result, the recording script that the voice actors will read *must* make grammatical sense—that is, it should be composed of complete, normal sentences even if you will only use parts of them. If you record the invariant part of the line in individual fragments and then try to stitch them together, the result is guaranteed to sound unnatural. The same goes for interchangeable items such as names or numbers. You *must* record each interchangeable item as part of a complete sentence and then cut the extraneous material out afterwards. (However, the sentence doesn't have to be—and often should not be—the same line that it will be inserted into.) The best actors in the world can't put the correct inflection or emotional tone into a sentence fragment if they don't know what comes before or after it.

Writing the Invariant Parts

Begin by creating a list of all the events that will trigger dialogue, whether it contains interchangeable material or not. In a sports game or game show, these will be events in the match; in a story-based game, they'll be conversations and plot points. Group related events together into general categories or by participants in the conversation, and order the groups chronologically through the progress of the game.

In *Madden,* we had events for welcoming the players at the opening of the game, remarks about the teams' and players' performances, weather, injuries, penalties, scores, and all kinds of play-by-play commentary for different kinds of plays, including pass plays, run plays, punts, field goals, and so on. There were about 30 general categories of events and hundreds of individual events. Some were quite specific: the software could detect the difference between a dropped pass, a deflected pass, and an overthrown pass, and then trigger an appropriate line for each. The more detailed you can be, the better your game will sound; but it's more work for the programmers. They will tell you which conditions can be detected by the software and which cannot.

For each event, write one or more lines, depending on whether it's a single-line event or a multi-line event. Then, for each line, ask yourself which of the words in the line might change if the player played through the game a second time. If a word or phrase in the line might change, either because of a player's choice or the internal mechanics of the game, then that item will need interchangeable material. Make a note that the line requires stitching and what category of thing will be stitched into it—the name of an athlete, a type of weapon, an amount of gold, or whatever it may be. However, don't write the actual interchangeable material into the line. Instead, use a *placeholder word* in the place where the interchangeable material goes. Placeholder words will get cut out by the audio editor.

Placeholder Words and Plosives

For your placeholder word (sometimes it's a phrase, but we'll continue to use the term), choose a word that sounds natural in the sentence but, wherever possible, begins and ends with a *plosive*. Plosives are sounds created by the lips or tongue that will create a clean break in the audio stream. T-, D-, K-sounds are best, followed by B- and P-sounds. V-, R-, L-, and F-sounds are not as good, and S-sounds are the worst, as they tend to slur into the preceding or following word.

Suppose the invariant part of your sentence is "…steps up to the free throw line," and an interchangeable name is to be inserted at the beginning of the sentence. Write this as "Trent steps up to the free throw line." The hard T at the end of Trent will create the break you need. If you were to write "Simmons steps up to the free throw line," *Simmons* will slur into *steps*. With numbers, consider using *twenty-eight* as your placeholder word in the sentence; it both begins and ends with T and so will be cut cleanly.

Your placeholder word should, however, make grammatical sense. You don't want to ask your actors to read nonsense, or you'll get an awkward performance. This means that sometimes you will have to use placeholder words that begin with TH-sounds or A-sounds, because the placeholder word will begin with *the* or *a*.

Writing the Interchangeable Items

After you have all the lines written, you can start thinking about what material the stitched lines will need. Here again, you will need to work with the designers. If a game contains 15 kinds of weapons whose names must all be spoken as part of dialogue, the game designers will tell you exactly what their names are. You will then have to write material for the actor to record all the names, in all possible inflections and variations that may be needed by the lines you have written. Remember, however, you can't just record the items by themselves; you must record them as part of a complete sentence, the majority of which will be thrown away. In the interchangeable part of the script, all of the sentence *except* the part you're trying to capture will be placeholder.

The rule about using plosives before and after the item still applies. If you have hundreds of items, these sentences should be as short as possible to cut down on recording time. Here, for example, we're recording the names of weapons with the indefinite article for use at the end of a declarative sentence:

I'll take **a sword**.

I'll take **a mace**.

I'll take **a longbow**.

I'll take **a spear**.

I'll take **an elephant gun**.

The words "I'll take" are the placeholder words, which will be cut off and thrown away by the audio editor. *Take* was chosen because it ends with a K-sound and produces a clean break before the interchangeable item.

It's not a bad idea to use different placeholder content from one line to the next, to keep the recording from becoming monotonous and singsong. Here's the text for recording a group of names at the beginning of a declarative sentence:

Hewitt tips it.

Heyward tackles him.

Hicks can't hold on.

Hiles keeps it.

Hill calls for the flag.

Hilliard kicks it high.

Hitchcock caught it.

Hoard crushes him.

Hobert takes it away.

Hogans catches it.

Group all the interchangeable items by their general usage type: score numbers, time numbers, proper names, and so on. Within those groups, further subdivide them by inflection: beginning of a declarative, end of a declarative, end of a question, end of an imperative, and so on. When dealing with objects and adjectives, you need to create still more subdivisions based on which (if any) articles precede them. In short, keep everything well organized and you're less likely to omit something by accident.

The Actor's Version

The actor's version of the script should be written in a format that the actor is comfortable with. You're trying to obtain a performance that is as natural as possible, so anything that distracts him should be avoided. Don't include any punctuation or formatting that indicates what the placeholder words are. Leave off references to filenames, inserted items, and so on. It should simply look like plain English text.

It's also a good idea to reorganize the actor's version of the script so that he records the interchangeable material directly before or after the invariant lines into which it will be stitched. This way, he's more likely to record it at the same volume and tone of voice, and you have a better chance of stitching it successfully.

Finally, during the recording process, you (or the director) should keep track of how many takes were made of each line and which take sounded best at the time. You can scribble these notes on your own copy of the actor's version of the script as recording is going on. This will make life a little easier for the audio editor later on.

Programmer's Scripts

For production and file-management reasons, it's actually easier to create the programmers' version of the script in a spreadsheet such as Excel rather than a word processor. The spreadsheet serves as a simple database of assets. Write each line on a different row, and group lines together that are optional variants to be played when a multi-line event occurs. Use multiple sheets to divide the text up into pages of a reasonable size. If you need to add information about a line, you can put it in a different column on the same row. For example, you may want to dedicate a column to the name of the audio file that the audio editor will eventually create from the line. You may also need to add special instructions to the programmers, as when a line should not be played more than a certain number of times.

Here's a hypothetical example from a football game. All the lines to be played following a passing play (under ordinary circumstances, not following a score or other high-priority event) are grouped together in the "Passing Plays" sheet of the spreadsheet. This particular event, a dropped pass, is named at the top of the group of lines that can be played when it occurs. The example is shown in Table 13.1; an extra column for the filename should also be used, but it is omitted here for clarity.

Some lines are fixed and require no stitching. In the lines with interchangeable content, the placeholder words are marked in square brackets. The Inserted Item column indicates that the interchangeable content to be inserted in the line is the name of the intended receiver on the passing play, as recorded for the beginning of a sentence. The audio editor will enter the file names into their column when he cuts up the studio recording.

TABLE 13.1   Example of a Programming Script Section for a Dropped Pass

Voice	Text to Be Read	Inserted Item
Rogers	He couldn't hold on to it.	
Rogers	[Trent] couldn't hold on to it.	Receiver name, beginning
Rogers	[Trent] couldn't hold on to that one.	Receiver name, beginning
Rogers	He couldn't quite hang on to it.	
Rogers	[Trent] never really had control of it.	Receiver name, beginning
Rogers	[Trent] never really had possession there.	Receiver name, beginning

CASE STUDY: AMERICAN FOOTBALL

American football is a complex game that can include a large number of different kinds of events. The ball may be kicked, carried, or passed down the field. There are 4 different ways to score points. Each team fields 11 men at a time, and each player has a particular role. At any given time, one team is on offense and one is on defense, with specialist players on the field who are substituted in when possession changes from one team to the other. The position of the ball and the amount of time remaining in the game are essential details that every player must know. The rules are complicated and often broken, sometimes unintentionally. There is a wide variety of penalties for different infractions.

The following are annotated fragments of a recording script for the broadcast commentary in a real videogame about professional American football. The script has been annotated with comments in square brackets and italics, to indicate the purpose served.

Town and Team Names

The objective in this section is to record the names of all the towns and all the team names in a variety of inflections. Teams are referred to by name but also by the hometown or state that they're from, and sometimes both together. The entire script included every possible town and team in the league. Notice that the city or state name is not preceded by the word "the," whereas the team name is. To use them interchangeably within a sentence, the world "the" must be included with the team name.

Welcome to **Tempe, Arizona**, where **the Kansas City Chiefs** have come to take on **the Arizona Cardinals**. *[This records the town name, the full name of one team in the middle of a sentence, and the full name of another team at the end of a sentence.]*

Arizona takes a time out. *[The team's home state at the beginning of a sentence.]*

That's the end of the season for **Arizona**.*[The team's home state at the end of a sentence.]*

It looks like **Arizona** can't make it. *[The team's home state in the middle of a sentence.]*

The Cardinals take a time out. *[The team's name at the beginning of a sentence.]*

That's the end of the season for **the Cardinals**. *[The team's name at the end of a sentence.]*

It looks like **the Cardinals** can't make it. *[The team's name in the middle of a sentence.]*

Score Numbers

The purpose of this section is to record all the possible score values from 100 down to 0, as they would sound when given for the team that's ahead (in the middle of a sentence) and for the team that's behind (at the end of the sentence). Notice that the city names chosen both begin and end with plosives (K for New York, D and T for Detroit), so the numbers can be cut off cleanly.

It's New York **101**, Detroit **100**

It's New York **100**, Detroit **99**

It's New York **99**, Detroit **98**

etc.

It's New York **1**, Detroit **nothing**

It's New York **nothing**, Detroit **nothing**.

Halftime Score Announcement

The halftime score announcement is a multi-line event that occurs when the second quarter ends. In this example, we're recording a number of lines that the software can choose from. We're only interested in keeping the invariant part of the line; the interchangeable material, in boldface, will be thrown away.

At the end of the 2nd quarter it's **tied at three**.

So we've reached the end of the 2nd quarter with **Texas Tech** ahead of **Tennessee**.

That's the end of the 2nd quarter with the score **tied at three**.

So at halftime it's **tied at three**.

We've reached the halfway point with the score **tied at three**.

At halftime **Texas Tech** is ahead of **Tennessee**.

SPECIAL CONSIDERATIONS FOR STITCHING

This section is not about writing per se, but about some of things you need to be aware of as your scripts are recorded and edited. As the writer, it is highly desirable for you to be present during the recording session at least, so you can correct errors as they occur. You don't necessarily have to be present for the editing, but you should supervise the process and, of course, listen to the result.

Recording Sessions

We have already encountered many aspects of the recording session process in the previous chapter. Here, we are considering additional issues to take into account when recording interchangeable audio content.

Beware of Inflection Changes During Recording

If you're going to have the voice actors record long lists of items such as names or numbers, they will have a natural tendency to change inflection as they read to break up the auditory monotony of the task. For example, suppose that you're recording names for the beginning of a sentence. You will, of course, be recording a complete short sentence and then cutting the name off, for example, "Johnson takes it." Normally, "Johnson" and "takes" would be inflected at about the same level of emphasis. However, after about 10 or 15 of these, your actor will be tempted to start emphasizing the name over the rest of the sentence. "*Carter* takes it. *Cogswell* takes it. *Custer* takes it." In the social context of reading a long list of names, it is natural to emphasize the name and deemphasize the rest of the sentence because we've heard the remainder before and it never changes. However, you *can't* let this happen! You *must* require the talent to use the exact same inflection for every single name. Otherwise, when you try to stitch it into some other sentence, you'll get a peculiar sound: "*Carter* gets a base hit" rather than "Carter gets a *base hit.*" Carter is the only person at bat, so his name is less important than what he did.

Brief the voice actors as to the requirements before beginning and specify or allow for breaks after a certain number of lines have been recorded. This will allow the process to unfold more smoothly. If you hear that the emphasis has shifted, stop the session, explain the problem to the voice actor, and then resume.

Keep Recording Conditions Identical

As much as possible, keep the recording conditions identical from one session to another. This means using the same studio and the same voice booth, if possible, but it goes beyond that. To get truly interchangeable audio, you should control as many variables as possible.

Record at the Same Time of Day

Record at the same time of day every day and don't record for too long. Don't start at the crack of dawn, but a reasonable hour such as 9 or 10 AM. Right after people wake up, their vocal cords are still relaxed and their voice is lower than it is later in the day. If you start in those conditions, you'll get material in which their voices are at different pitches, and it won't work when you stitch it together.

Make sure they've had a chance to warm up before they start. Let them do a few vocal exercises or practice takes to get into the flow of things. Give your talent plenty of breaks and lots to drink—you don't want them getting hoarse or dry-mouthed.

Use the Same Equipment

Be sure you use the same audio gear from one session to another: microphones, recording devices, amps, and so on. You would be surprised how a little thing like a different microphone can affect the sound quality. If you're renting time in a voice booth at a commercial studio, try to get the same booth each time and even the same engineer. Make sure the gear is all calibrated the same way at each session; have the engineer note down his settings at the first session and use them at every subsequent one. A good engineer will record a few seconds of "room tone" to find out what background sounds are present; these can be removed from the audio recordings later.

Keep the Voice Actors a Fixed Distance from the Microphone

The voice actors need to remain at the same distance from the microphone all the time. If they get too close, the microphone will start picking up "popped" P's—little explosive bursts when they say the letter P. It will also pick up mouth noises, such as liquidy clicks and slurps, caused by the tongue and other parts of the mouth, that sound rather disgusting. If voice actors move too far away, obviously their recording will be quieter than it should be. You can compensate for this by amplifying it later, if necessary, but that's a time-consuming process and one that's likely to introduce errors; it's better to avoid the problem in the first place. Experienced voice actors will know this.

If your voice actors really have to move around for some reason, you can consider a headset or lavaliere mic, but they aren't as good as proper studio mics. You also risk picking up the sound of their clothing or hair brushing the microphone.

Try Not to Mix Recordings from Different Years

If you're working on an annual product such as a sports game, it's tempting to reuse audio recorded in previous years to avoid having to re-record it. This will save both time and money. Unfortunately, it's very likely to introduce variation in the quality of your recordings, which will stand out when played back stitched together. You may not be able to get the same gear or calibrations as you had before, and people's voices do change slowly with time. If your voice actors are expensive or only available for a limited time, you may have no choice about this. You can check to see if it will work by taking some audio from the first day's recording and stitching it into last year's material.

Editing

Editing interchangeable dialogue audio is a long and tedious process. There are two key considerations. One is keeping track of all the assets—the hundreds of little audio files that will result from cutting up the original studio recording. As editors cut up the original recording, they will need to generate new filenames for all the files. To manage this, you'll need a flexible and user-friendly file-naming convention because at least three different people will deal with the material: you, the audio editor, and the programmer. The name of each file should indicate, at a minimum, who is speaking and what group of dialogue elements it belongs to, such as the invariant parts of a particular conversation, or names to be inserted into the beginnings of sentences. The audio editor should note these filenames alongside the line that they came from in the spreadsheet that goes to the programmers.

The other tricky part of the task is cutting the audio at exactly the right place. The gap between one word and another in normally spoken English is typically only a few milliseconds long. If a word is cut off short or extra space is included by accident, the ear will detect it immediately. This is why it's so important for you to put plosives in the throwaway material at cut points; it gives the audio engineer a clean break.

CONCLUSION

Interchangeable dialogue audio is a powerful tool for the writer. Implemented well, it permits you to create the illusion of natural speech about a variety of content. You can customize the game audio to reflect the player's own decisions and preferences, and you can have characters speak about specific circumstances and events, rather than only making generic remarks. It actually makes your game seem more intelligent.

Making stitched dialogue work properly requires a great deal of planning, hard work in the audio edit suite, and rigorous testing. But the final, polished result is well worth the effort.

14 Dialogue Engines
Chris Bateman

A dialogue engine is the means by which a game speaks. This software mediates the delivery of all dialogue (and monologue) inside the game and is critically important to the game writer. However, in most projects, the writer will have little or no input in how the dialogue engine functions—this will likely be determined by the game designer or someone else in the development team.

In general, writers do not need to understand how the dialogue engine has been implemented; they simply need to know how to write the raw material that the dialogue engine will deliver. That said, understanding the most common forms of dialogue engine makes it considerably easier for a writer to come to terms with the task of providing the dialogue for any game.

TYPES OF DIALOGUE ENGINE

The way that dialogue will be delivered in a game depends on the type of dialogue engine that is implemented, and different games suggest different engines. As a crude generalization, however, all dialogue engines fit broadly into three categories: event driven, topic driven, and dialogue trees.

Event-driven engines trigger dialogue in response to player actions in the game world. They are the most common form of dialogue engine, and the easiest for a writer to work with. Dialogue triggered by an event-driven engine can take many different forms—it may be genuine dialogue between the player and an NPC, it may be narration, or it could be a comment the player's avatar makes as a private monologue.

Topic-driven engines trigger dialogue in response to specific choices the player makes when talking to the NPCs of the game world. Although less versatile than the event-driven approach, topic-driven scripts can be considerably more complicated to write.

Dialogue trees are often the most complicated form of dialogue engine and provide very little advantages over other forms. However, some players are fond of the illusion of expressivity inherent in this approach.

The following sections discuss each approach in detail.

Event-Driven Engines

This is a standard form of dialogue engine in which events within the game-space trigger specific conversations. Most platform games and shooters fit this mold. Although the concept is common enough, there is essentially no standardization as to how individual event-driven engines work, and there is no common script format. Most likely, the writer will be asked to complete a spreadsheet that has been divided up into the different types of events that can occur.

The core of an event-driven approach is the events the game engine can detect. Although in principle the game should know everything the player is doing, in practice, this is not always the case. Instead, certain activities are relatively easy to detect (such as the player's direct activities—pressing a button to jump, for instance), some require some preparation (such as detecting when a player enters a specific area, which may require level designers to place an event trigger at the entrance to that area), and some require extreme efforts to detect (for instance, it is monumentally difficult to detect whether or not the player has understood an instruction they have been given).

Broadly speaking, writers deal with three forms of events. The first are the *player's direct actions,* which are always known; the second are *triggers,* which the level designers for the game will have to position in the game world; and the third are *game state events,* which are inherent to the design of the game. We will discuss each in turn.

Direct Actions

Direct actions describe those activities that result directly from the player's use of the control devices—pushing a button on the controller or selecting a particular menu option, for instance. Rarely do the player's direct actions require dialogue. For instance, if the player's avatar speaks every time it jumps, this will become annoying and repetitive very rapidly (although a collection of short grunts might be acceptable in this context).

An exception to this is when one of the buttons has been defined as a Talk button—but even then, the dialogue that results should be a consequence of the game state and not merely random chatter.

Some menu systems are designed to act as if they are people—such as the shops in cRPG games—and in these cases, some dialogue might be associated with selecting particular options. For instance, buying and selling items may elicit general responses ("that's fine quality merchandise"), and it is not uncommon for the option that exits to have a line of dialogue associated with it ("see you around").

For the most part, however, direct actions are less important than those events that emerge from the game world.

Triggers

Little need be said about triggers, which are generally positioned in the game world by level designers. In essence, a *trigger* can be thought of as an invisible bubble in the game world—when the player enters the bubble, the event is triggered and dialogue (or a cut scene) results.

Game writers need to understand, however, that when their script for a game requires triggers to be specified, this is work that someone else must carry out. Writers need to know the degree of freedom they have in this regard—can they add as many triggers as they need, or should they stick to adding only a small few triggers to avoid making extra work for the development team? The only way of knowing is to ask the development team for its perspective on the matter.

Scripting for triggered events is generally easy, because we know exactly where the player is in the game world. However, some caution must be taken to ensure that the dialogue always makes sense. Game writers generally need to read and understand level design documentation carefully to ensure that any dialogue they write will always make sense.

Suppose for instance that we are specifying dialogue for a trigger that plays when the player first boards a ship. Provided the player can only board via a gangplank, the trigger can be placed upon the gangplank to play when the player first comes aboard ("So this is the famed Silver Rose…"). However, if there is another way for players to get aboard (perhaps they can drop from a nearby crane), the trigger may then apply when the player comes to the gangplank from on deck—the dialogue as written will no longer make sense.

One of the many unique skills a game writer must develop is writing dialogue that always makes sense, regardless of the actions that the player took prior to the dialogue triggering. This is not something that can be taught but rather is something that game writers learn from experience.

Game State Events

Every game has associated with it a vast variety of game states, and the events associated with these game states are always detectable. For example, here is a list of the key game state events that occur in *Pac-man* (Namco, 1980):

- Eat a pellet
- Eat a Power Pill

- Eat a ghost (while under the influence of a Power Pill)
- Killed by a ghost
- Use a passageway to go off the left and come on the right of the maze (or vice versa)
- Clear a maze of pellets

This is pretty much everything that happens in the game states of *Pac-man*, and every one of these could be used hypothetically to trigger dialogue. This wouldn't be a good idea for a small and simple game like *Pac-man*, but it does demonstrate the principles of dealing with game state events. In all the following examples, note that the game of *Pac-man* would be considerably worse if it included dialogue, and the examples serve merely to demonstrate how it *could* be used in this game, not to demonstrate that it *should* be used.

For each game state event, we can either have no dialogue specified, have a single line of dialogue specified, or have multiple (alternative) lines of dialogue specified. Additionally, some events may have different cases that apply, which could be used to specify additional cases. For instance, when Pac-man eats a ghost or kills a ghost, we could vary the line of dialogue spoken according to which ghost is involved. In terms of the *Pac-man* events:

Eating a pellet occurs too frequently for dialogue to be associated with it.

Eating a Power Pill occurs with considerable frequency and may also be too frequent for dialogue to be sensibly employed. Certainly, if dialogue is to be used at this point, it needs to be very short ("Pac-power!").

Eating a ghost is a rewarding moment in the game and a potentially appropriate juncture for dialogue. The writer has the choice here as to whether to have Pac-man supply the line ("Gotcha!") or the ghost ("Dang!"). Because this particular interaction involves two characters, multiple lines of dialogue are probably desirable, so we could specify lines for both Pac-man and the ghosts and choose one at random.

Being killed by the ghost is an annoyance for the player and can only happen up to three times in any given game. It is the reverse of the preceding case, but fewer alternative lines are needed because the event is expected to occur less often. Another argument suggests that the player's death is not a good place for dialogue because the player is likely annoyed at this moment and not receptive to being entertained by a line of speech. (Although failure dialogue may be used to encourage the player rather than add insult to injury—something that's particularly useful when writing for a children's game.)

Using a passageway does not obviously seem like an event that needs dialogue. We could, because it's very easy to detect, but what would we say? "I'm using a passageway" is too dull, and expressions like "Can't catch me!" only make sense if the ghosts are hot on Pac-man's tail (a game state which we cannot test without specifically adding software code to do so).

Clearing the maze of pellets is the goal state and could be a suitable place for a line of dialogue. If something were to be said at this point, it would need to be very short, and we would need to have enough variety for it to repeat only rarely. These two requirements make it hard to imagine what exactly would be said. "Yes!" or "I've done it!" seem to work, but could we really come up with 20 variations on this theme—and even if we did, would any of them be worth hearing?

Looking at this simple game and the game state events associated with it illustrates the kind of questions that must be dealt with when deciding how to use event-driven dialogue in a game.

Often, the writer will be told by the team when and where they want dialogue and how many different lines of dialogue are desired in each case—but this does not preclude the writer from making suggestions as to where additional dialogue could be useful, suggesting different numbers of alternative lines, or pointing out cases where the use of dialogue might be ill advised.

Determining the Number of Alternative Lines

Many event-driven dialogue cases will occur many times during the course of a game, so it is useful to have a means for estimating how many lines of dialogue are needed in any given case.

As a general guideline, for situations in which the player is being rewarded systematically, it is possible to get by with a single line of dialogue—such a line will then become a catchphrase for the game. For instance, when a fish is caught in *Sega Bass Fishing* (Sega, 1998), the game supplies one of three lines—"Aw, Small one."; "Okay, average size—good job!"; and "This one's huge!" As an arcade game, these lines occur often, but it works because they become catchphrases for the game.

In other situations, consider how many times the line will appear in an hour (or whatever a typical play session length will be) and how many times it will occur over the length of the game. The minimum case should be no repeat lines (on average) in any given play session, and the maximum case should be no repeat lines (on average) over the entire length of the game. A good value to choose is the median value in the number sequence, produced by doubling the minimum value repeatedly until it is approximately equal to the maximum value and then selecting the middle value.

For example, consider dialogue in a cake-making game in which cakes take 5 minutes of play to make, the typical play session is 30 minutes, and the whole game is expected to last about 8 hours for a typical player. The lines will be used 6 times per typical play session (12 times an hour) or 96 times in the game as a whole. Therefore, at least 6 and at most 100 line variants will be required. The doubling sequence for 6 reads 6, 12, 24, 48, 96 (which is nearly 100), therefore 24 lines of dialogue (the median value in this sequence) is a reasonable choice. This means the player will likely have multiple play sessions before hearing a repeat line.

Topic-Driven Engines

At one time, topic-driven engines were the most common form of dialogue engine, but with the decline of the classic adventure game, they are now relegated to a secondary status. Nonetheless, both adventure games and many cRPG games use a topic-driven dialogue engine. As with event-driven approaches, there is no standardization as to how topic-driven systems function and no common script format.

A topic-driven system usually has a substantial amount of dialogue, almost all of which occurs between the player character and various NPCs as conversation. Although there are many different approaches, they can be broadly characterized as belonging to one of two different styles. *Character scripts* are the least formal, consisting of custom instructions for each game NPC that can be spoken to, whereas *token-based scripts* provide a more rigorous approach and are ideally suited to adventure games.

Character Scripts

In essence, a character script is simply a set of dialogues between the player's avatar and any given NPC, which is organized according to a set of conditions. The complexity of the game writer's work depends on the complexity of these conditions. If the conditions are already worked out, the job of scripting becomes relatively straightforward, while conversely, if the game writer must compose the conditions, the job can become considerably more complex.

The simplest version of a character script is that each NPC has one line of dialogue that plays when the player talks to the NPC, or (in a slightly more complex version) that each NPC has one line of dialogue for each level, chapter, or act of the game the NPC appears in. Writing game scripts in these situations doesn't require much explanation.

More commonly, some conditional situations occur that cause the dialogue for a character to alter. In these situations, it is important for the game writer to understand the logical elements of programming, specifically the Boolean logic of IF... THEN statements. These will be discussed in more detail in a later section of this chapter.

To demonstrate an example of some basic conditional dialogue in a character script, imagine a game in which the player is on vacation on a tropical island. A tour guide NPC lurks around the hotel to advise the player what he can do; the NPC's narrative purpose is merely to help the player find out all the things he can do in the game world. The conversation the player will have with such an NPC might vary as a result of the following:

- What the player has done previously—that is, the tour guide only mentions things the player has not already experimented with.
- The current game weather. The guide gives different advice on a day with rainy weather than on a clear day.

The character script for this NPC might look like this:

Sunny comments:

Beach: "Have you been for a walk on the beach? It's beautiful there."
Swim: "You should go for a swim today—the weather's perfect!"
Tour: "Don't forget, the archaeological visit leaves from the hotel at noon."

Rainy comments:

Pool: "It may be raining, but you can still go for a swim in the hotel's indoor pool."
Table: "How about a nice game of table tennis?"

It will fall to the game's programmers to make the logic for this script function correctly—the game writer need only provide the lines of dialogue in a suitable form that can be readily understood.

Token-Based Scripts

Some games, and in particular adventure games, have tokens in the game world that are particularly relevant for conversations. These might be the objects that the players have collected in their inventory or a set of topics that describes things the player has learned, as in the notebook from *Discworld Noir* (Perfect Entertainment, 1999), which contained clues about the mysteries the player was investigating. In a token-based script, when the player talks to an NPC, the player selects one of these tokens (objects, clues, and so on), and the NPC responds relevantly to that topic.

Token-based scripts give the player much more control over the dialogue—but at a price. The player may potentially get lost in all the conversational options. For a puzzle-driven game such as an adventure game, this may be acceptable, but for a game with a faster pace, it may not be.

For every token that can be a legitimate conversation topic in a token-based system, *every* NPC *must* have a line of dialogue specified. The exception to this is that some default cases may apply. For instance, a given NPC may have a line of dialogue that says "I don't know anything about that," which plays when asked about something the NPC knows nothing about.

As an example, imagine a game in which the player is a construction worker building a house. Players can pick up many different tools and building materials, and they can talk to the other builders or the foreman to learn about those items. Suppose that all the builders share the same conversation, but the foreman is a separate character, and there are two tools (a saw and a hammer) and two building materials (wood and nails).

The token-based script might look like this:

Foreman

Saw: "Yeah, use that to cut the lumber to size."

Hammer: "Once you've cut the lumber to size, hammer it into place with some nails."

Wood: "That's the lumber; cut it to size, then nail it into place."

Nails: "What's the matter, you ain't never seen nails before?"

Builders

Nails: "Careful with that—you'll have someone's eye out!"

Default: "Ask the foreman about that."

The Default category applies for any of the cases not specified—specifically the Saw, Hammer, and Wood in this instance. In this instance, where there are only four different tokens, you could write all the lines of dialogue—but if there were 50 topics and 100 NPCs, default categories can save the writer from a Herculean labor.

In some cases, a single default category is insufficient to the task. Instead, the game writer can collect related tokens together to provide default responses. An example of this can be found in the *Discworld Noir* script (for those unfamiliar with the game, Lewton is the protagonist of the story, a hard-boiled detective in the film noir tradition):

TOPIC: Milka, Stranger asking questions, Two mysterious passengers, Murders, Selachii Vault, Therma is buried in the Selachii Vault, Scrap of Cardboard, Foreign Label, Torn Matchbook, Matchbook, Azile, Mundy's Murder, Counterweight Killings, Mundy Hung Upside Down and Killed, 3712V, Cargo, Sapphire's Money, Wine Barrels, Varberg Crates, Losing Streak, Secret Meeting, Meeting with Therma, Malachite's Murder, Bestial Attacker, Shipping Order, Fabric, Plaster-encrusted Bandages, Theatre Flyer, Bedmaker and Laundryman, Moss, Perfume, Meeting of the True Believers, List of Names

EVENT: Error1 (*Default Lewton asks about message)

ACTOR: Butler

Sir has many questions, but alas I have few answers.

TOPIC: Mundy, Al Khali, Malachite, Therma, Madame Lodestone, Ilsa and Two Conkers, Horst, Laredo Cronk

EVENT: Error1 (*Default Lewton asks about message)

ACTOR: Butler

Regrettably, sir, I know nothing about that person.

TOPIC: Patrician's Clerk's Murder, Reader of Esoteric Occultism's Murder, Merchant's Murder, Saipha Drowned in a Vat of Wine in the Palace, Mathom was Poisoned in the Widdershins Wing, Gamin Strangled in the Merchant's Guild

EVENT: Error1 (*Default Lewton asks about message)

ACTOR: Butler

I don't know anything about any murders, sir.

TOPIC: Nylonathatep, Octagram of Murders, Sewers, Temple of Anu-anu at Al Khali, Errata, Dead Men's Pointy Boots, Strange Symbol, Sign of the Eel, Eight Great Tragedies, Pendant

EVENT: Error1 (*Default Lewton asks about message)

ACTOR: Butler

Sir would have to consult the library on that.

TOPIC: Lewton's Purse, Crowbar, Back Passage, Envelope, Troll's Tooth, Something in the River, Grappling Iron, Golden Sword, Mundy's Coin, Jewel, Hiding Place, Grapple without Rope

EVENT: Error2 (*Inappropriate topic)

TOPIC: Default

EVENT: Error1 (*Default Lewton asks about message)

ACTOR: Butler

I'm sorry; I cannot assist sir in that matter.

This script was a particularly complex token-based arrangement, consisting of many different topics, many different characters, and conditional elements that varied from act to act. Where the script says "Error1," this means to play the Error1 text for the token that is being used. For instance, the Error1 message for the Foreign Label clue says "Can you read this?" Therefore, if the player selects this item as the topic for conversation, the following exchange results:

Lewton: "Can you read this?"
Butler: "Sir has many questions, but alas I have few answers."

This occurs because the Foreign Label object is listed in the first list of topics; the behavior specified is to play the Error1 message for that object, and then to play the response specified.

Similarly, Error2 is used for objects for which it would be inappropriate to talk to anyone about. For instance, the Error2 message for Lewton's purse reads: "I suppressed the urge to ask for money. I was broke, sure, but I wasn't that desperate." This covers for any objects that would be completely inappropriate for the player to ask people about for any narrative reasons.

While looking at this particular script, it is worth noting the following section:

TOPIC: Mundy, Al Khali, Malachite, Therma, Madame Lodestone, Ilsa and Two Conkers, Horst, Laredo Cronk
EVENT: Error1 (*Default Lewton asks about message)
ACTOR: Butler
Regrettably, sir, I know nothing about that person.

Every character in the game has a default case like this for characters about which they know nothing. Although this made sense in English, it was a problem for translators because in other languages, it is not always possible to make gender-neutral reference such as "that person" or "them." It would have been better if these sections had been organized by gender, as follows:

TOPIC: Mundy, Al Khali, Malachite, Horst
EVENT: Error1 (*Default Lewton asks about message)
ACTOR: Butler
Regrettably, sir, I know nothing about him.

TOPIC: Therma, Madame Lodestone, Laredo Cronk
EVENT: Error1 (*Default Lewton asks about message)
ACTOR: Butler
Alas, sir, there is nothing I can divulge about her.

TOPIC: Ilsa and Two Conkers

EVENT: Error1 (*Default Lewton asks about message)

ACTOR: Butler

Perhaps sir has mistaken me for someone else—perhaps, someone who wishes to help him?

This is the sort of issue that you must be watchful of when dealing with a token-based system such as this.

Dialogue Trees

Despite the name, dialogue trees are seldom true trees but rather converging and diverging chains of conversation. They can be a nightmare to work with, and the benefits they provide are somewhat minimal. Nonetheless, some players greatly appreciate the illusion that they have control over what their character can say, with the consequence that dialogue trees remain important, especially to cRPG games.

Dialogue trees are structured like a choose-your-own-adventure book. They are divided into segments, which are linked to and from different choices that the player is given. This is easier to understand by seeing an example, so what follows is a hypothetical dialogue tree for a conversation between a protagonist who is an insurance investigator and a mechanic in a game based around otherworldly events in a small town (in the manner of an HP Lovecraft story):

M1: You a cop?

> No, I'm a claims adjuster. [go to M3]

> Private investigator. I have a few questions. [go to M2]

> Yeah, I'm a plain-clothes cop. I've got questions for you. [go to M2]

M2: Nah, you're dressed too smart. I reckon you work for the insurers.

> Lucky guess. [go to M3]

> That's for me to know, and you to guess at. [go to M3]

M3: I reckon this counts as an act of God.

> What happened? [go to M4]

> I don't believe in God. I reckon this was an act of man. [go to M3a]

M3a: Yeah, right—you didn't see those lights coming down from the sky—you didn't see those bodies… the blood…. [go to M4]

M4: It was horrible… I don't even want to think about it.

> I'll come back tomorrow. Give you a chance to recover. [go to M9]

I need to know what happened, or we can write off your claim here and now. [go to M5]

M5: I drove up to the farm that night. It was quiet. I mean, dead quiet. Even the cicadas weren't making a sound, and those critters are deafening most nights. [go to M6]

M6: When I got close, the engine just died on me. I started checking the sparks, and then it happened. [go to M7]

M7: Lights, I mean, something glowing, just pouring down from the heavens onto the farmhouse. It was beautiful and terrible and… I don't know. But, when I got to the farm… My God…

This is obviously very difficult for you. I'll come back tomorrow. [go to M9]

Go on. You're just getting to the good bit. [go to M8]

M8: They were lying around outside the farmhouse… I thought maybe a cow had been struck by lightning. But they weren't. They didn't even look human… [go to M9]

M9: I'm sorry… I've never… I just…

This has obviously been hard on you. Get a good night's sleep… I'll see you in the morning. [End]

Pull yourself together, man! I'll come back tomorrow morning—but you'd better not start blubbering when I come back, or you can kiss the insurance money goodbye. [End]

The first thing to note is that although termed a dialogue *tree*, it is actually just a linear conversation with a few branch points that connect to different places inside it. Some sections are only heard by the players if they pick certain options (such as the dialogue in sections M5-M8), but for the most part, this is a relatively straight-forward linear conversation. The reason for this is that while in principle a dialogue tree can allow for a tremendous range of different responses, pragmatically it would be too costly and inefficient to develop all the separate branches of a genuine tree.

In fact, this problem (which is known as the *combinatorial explosion*) is the chief reason that branching structures are not used in dynamic dialogue or dynamic narratives. You only need a few unique branches to be dealing with an intractable volume of options. For instance, a dialogue tree that solicits 1 of 2 choices from the player at 10 separate stages would contain $2^{10} = 1,024$ different conversation segments. Even one such conversation would be a major undertaking to construct!

For this reason, the dialogue tree is something of a sleight of hand used to give the player the illusion of freedom of choice, but in fact the players are just selecting what their character says at each point and mediating a very small number of sub-branches within the conversation.

Commentary Engines

Certain games—in particular, sporting games—use a specific type of event-driven dialogue engine that we call a *commentary engine*. In these cases, the dialogue engine must provide a more or less constant stream of chatter, and therefore attention must be paid not only to what can be detected, but what can be said when nothing is known about the game state.

For instance, although there was no commentary engine in the final released version of *Mashed* (Supersonic, 2004), the game was originally designed with an advanced commentary system that was implemented in prototype but eventually cut to minimize the cost of localization. The brief for this work involved two recognizably northern American commentators describing the race and chatting to each other. The commentary system was designed to be as flexible as possible, to relate commentary to play action, and to avoid repetition. The narrative design of the commentary system involved three types of modular script:

- Track scripts concentrated upon track-specific features.
- Banter scripts provided generic chat for use when lines from the other scripts hadn't been triggered for some time.
- Main scripts detailed common racing events (using an Ident system to stitch racer names to lines for greater variety).

Next, you'll see examples of each of these types of scripts. The commentators are Big Al Farley, ex-racer and lead commentator, and Todd Bleacher, a younger, more professional TV personality.

Note that in the following examples, the \\ mark indicates a comment—that is, something the writer has put in place for the programmer to read, usually because something needs to be done during implementation that the writer has no means of specifying in the script format. The choice of mark for comments was agreed with the programmers prior to the commencement of the scripts.

The first type of script we will examine is the track script, which is particular to certain courses. They consist of a number of different sections, the first of which is the track preview, which plays during the introduction of the course. Because the player needs more information when playing for the first time, the introduction gets shorter the more often it plays:

Track Preview:

Discuss Track Full:

BIG AL (excited): "So, Todd, here we are at Karnak. I'm sweating badly already!"

TODD (**serious**): "I can confirm that, Al. What's this track famous for?"

BIG AL (**pleased**): "The last corner, a hairpin left which I call the Pharaoh's Curse, is especially dangerous!"

TODD (**light-hearted**): "But it does give the option of a tricky short cut to the inside! Will anyone dare take it?"

Discuss Track Short:

TODD (**excited**): "Al and I are at Karnak in Egypt today, racefans! As are the racers!"

BIG AL (**serious**): "Which is useful, as we're here to see a race!"
TODD (**excited**): "Let's see if anyone can pull off that inside route on the Pharaoh!"

Discuss Track Familiar:

BIG AL (**excited**): "Karnak is one of my favorite tracks, Todd!"

TODD (**fond**): "Yes, Al! Egypt—land of mystery, romance, and fatal automotive accidents!"

Additionally, track scripts contain sections of dialogue that relate to specific track features. Each course has three specified features with dialogue relating to the various different ways racers could fail at each corner.

Track Feature A:

First corner—turn left onto narrow straight with cliff drop to right. Slippery ground.

Identify (*may play when approaching for the first time*):

TODD (**tense**): "This is a deceptive left, Al."

BIG AL (**happy**): "The cliff beyond chews racers up, Todd!"

Survive (*plays if all racers survive*):

TODD (**matter-of-fact**): "They all made it."

BIG AL (**disappointed**): "Aw."

Victim (*plays if one racer falls off; examples of Idents can be found later*):

\\ Play TODD Bad ident

\\ If Male then

BIG AL (**amused**): "He's gonna feel that in the morning!"

\\ Else

BIG AL (**amused**): "She's gonna regret that when the hospital bill comes through!"

Multiple victim (*plays if more than one racer falls off*):
BIG AL (**pleased**): "That was a nasty mess!"
TODD (**serious**): "They're driving beyond their limits!"

All victim (*plays if all racers fall off*):
TODD (**serious**): "They dug their own graves, Al."
BIG AL (**amused**): "I'll name that tomb in three!"

Repeat victim some (*plays if someone goes off the corner a few times*):
\\ Play TODD Bad ident
\\ If Male then
BIG AL (**serious**): "He consistently pushes too hard there!"
\\ Else
BIG AL (**musing**): "She really should take that corner easy."

Repeat victim many (*plays if someone goes off the corner repeatedly*):
\\ Play BIG AL Bad ident
\\ If Male then
TODD (**serious**): "He just hasn't worked that corner out."
\\ Else
TODD (**serious**): "She just can't get a handle on that corner."

Slide (*plays if someone slides on the corner*):
\\ Play BIG AL General ident
TODD (**happy**): "A lack of traction plus a cliff... bad combination, Al!"

Multiple slide (*plays if multiple racers slide on the corner*):
TODD (**amused**): "Hey, Al, what has four wheels at dawn, two at noon, and three at dusk?"
BIG Al (**irritated**): "Talk sense, man!"

Banter scripts served the purpose of providing general discussion when nothing is going on that could be commented upon. Although these scripts contained some dialogue for points scored and other generic events (anything that happened with such frequency that the dialogue needed to vary constantly), the core of each Banter script was a sequence of discussions between the commentators with no direct bearing on the race. Each numbered section (01 to 06) plays as soon as a suitable gap in the commentary occurs (the sections were therefore written to make sense even when separated by other dialogue, with all six sections, in the case of the next example, forming an on-and-off conversation between the two characters that takes place throughout the entire race):

Banter Script 2 (of 40):

Banter 01:

BIG AL (**cheerful**): "This is Big Al Farley watching the race with Todd 'Creature Feature' Bleacher!"

TODD (**annoyed**): "Al, please don't call me 'Creature Feature'."

BIG AL (**happy**): "But all commentators need a nickname, Todd!"

Banter 02:

BIG AL (**cheerful**): "What about your nickname, Todd? Any thoughts?"

TODD (**slightly embarrassed**): "I'm happy with my given name, Al."

BIG AL (**cheerful**): "What about Todd 'Pleased to Meetcha' Bleacher?"

TODD (**unhappy**): "I don't think so, Al...."

Banter 03:

BIG AL (**cheerful**): "We've had a few calls about your nickname, Todd!"

TODD (**trying to be professional and failing**): "Oh joy."

BIG AL (**reading**): "'The Toddomatic,' 'Winter White Bleacher,' 'The Toddminator,' 'The Wrath of Todd'...."

TODD (**sick**): "Gee, thanks, race fans. You made my day."

Banter 04:

TODD (**plotting**): "If I need a nickname, Al... what about 'Big Todd'?"

BIG AL (**confused**): "But I'm Big Al, Todd! We can't be Big Al and Big Todd!"

TODD (**cheerful**): "Hmmm.... Maybe you're right...it does sound kind of egotistical."

Banter 05:

BIG AL (**confused**): "What's wrong with 'big' as a nickname, anyway?"

TODD (**matter-of-fact**): "You're not big, Al. You're actually quite small."

BIG AL (**plaintive**): "I'm Big Al Farley! Call me Big Al, Todd!"

Banter 06:

BIG AL (**hurt**): "Why won't you call me Big Al, Todd?"

TODD (**exasperated, professional voice on the last sentence**): "Jeez, okay Al, you're big. You're watching the race with Todd and Big Al."

Finally, the Main scripts were used for general events, and also Idents, which are used whenever a particular racer needed to be named. Idents were provided for both commentators, in a good, neutral, and bad form—according to how well the individual person was racing. Subsequent lines could then follow the Ident, meaning that the commentators could comment on all racers without each comment line having to be recorded six times. The following example demonstrates the Ident system:

Idents:

Big Al Good ID:

\\ 1 line per driver Red:

BIG AL (**excited**): "Red's showing his grit, Todd!"

Bluejay:

BIG AL (**excited**): "I'm impressed by Bluejay today!"

Melon:

BIG AL (**excited**): "Look at Melon go!"

Shadow:

BIG AL (**excited**): "Shadow's in the zone, Todd!"

Pink:

BIG AL (**patronizing**): "Aw, check out plucky little Pink!"

Gold:

BIG AL (**excited**): "And... look at Gold!"

All this complexity was required to assure that the commentators would always have something that they could comment about. In many sports, the state of play is rigidly defined, and therefore the categories for which dialogue can be used are clearly defined. Even so, the task of defining the commentary for any such game is one of the more complex propositions that any game writer will face. However, the project's game designer will usually design the commentary engine, and the game writer need only complete the lines of dialogue for a commentary script. That being said, the number of lines involved can be astronomical, and therefore writing a commentary script is in general a mammoth undertaking.

TEXT-ONLY ENGINES

In the West, we now expect almost all games to use recorded dialogue, but this is not universally the case. Many cRPG projects are still allowed text-only dialogue, if only because the sheer volume of dialogue is prohibitively expensive to record. Although the bias is definitely skewed toward recording all dialogue, text-only engines are cheaper and can be more versatile. The cost savings can be significant because not only is the cost of preparing the game in the native language reduced, but the cost of localization is dramatically reduced as well.

Text-only engines have other benefits that make them worth considering:

■ You can make changes to the script throughout the production process. In a recorded dialogue game, after the audio files are recorded, it can be difficult (in some cases impossible) to get "pickups" recorded to make corrections to the game.

■ You can make dynamic changes such as text string insertions (discussed later) as much as is needed—allowing for the players to name their own character (for instance), which is not possible in a speech-recorded game without resorting to a text-to-speech engine, which is an expensive and not very convincing solution at the time of writing.

■ Animation costs for lip synching to animations become irrelevant.

Often, even in a game with text-only dialogue, speech is still recorded for cut scenes. This hybrid approach is a reasonable balance—giving the adaptability and cost-savings of the text-only approach, while still including some recorded dialogue to aid in the player's sense of immersion into the game world.

Game writers usually will not have any involvement in a decision as to whether to record all speech or to use text alone. However, as a general guideline, if more than 10,000 lines of speech are required for a game, or 3,000 lines if the game is anything but a flagship AAA title, it is worth suggesting that all or part of the game script would be better rendered as text alone.

DYNAMIC ELEMENTS

When a script contains dynamic elements, it will inevitably become more complex than a static script. The following sections discuss the most common ways in which dynamic material might be involved in a game script and provide some basic notation related to the way programming languages are written. When game writers specify dynamic material in this way, they are in fact writing very simple code in a pseudo-programming language. The programming team must then implement this pseudo-code in the genuine programming language of the game.

We will look at three specific cases—the use of conditions and flags to provide simple yes/no switching, the use of cases and states to provide more complex logical structures, and finally the use of inserted text strings.

Conditions and Flags

The simplest dynamic elements relate to having lines of dialogue that are only played under certain conditions. Logical conditions (using Boolean logic) are used to determine whether or not the text should be played or omitted, and the variables that these conditions are based upon (Boolean variables) can be referred to as *flags*. Basically, a flag can be either FALSE (off) or TRUE (on). Generally speaking, flags begin set as FALSE, but the initial conditions can be specified otherwise.

The basis of a condition is to use IF… THEN statements to control whether a line plays. The basic form is

```
IF (flag) THEN [line of dialogue]
```

This plays the line of dialogue if flag is set to TRUE. Alternatively:

```
IF (NOT flag) THEN [line of dialogue]
```

This will play the line of dialogue if flag is set to FALSE (the logical operator NOT inverts the condition of the flag). There is also the operator ELSE, which is used to chain IF… THEN conditions together to create further conditions:

```
IF (flag1) THEN
        [line of dialogue]
ELSE
```

```
        [alternative line of dialogue]
```

Or:

```
IF (flag1) THEN
        [line of dialogue]
ELSE
        IF (flag2) THEN
                [alternative line of dialogue]
        ELSE
                IF (flag3) THEN
                        [another alternative line of dialogue]
```

The indentation in the preceding example represents one way of formatting such nested conditional statements for clarity, although this is by no means universal.

Using conditions and flags allows for lightly dynamic variation in dialogue. For example, suppose we have a character script in which the player character is talking to a shopkeeper. There are barrels outside the shop in question, and the player may have smashed these (all players seem drawn to smashing barrels, perhaps because so many games train them that there are rewards for doing so). We could add a line to the "goodbye" part of the character script to draw attention to this fact:

Goodbye:

```
"See you next time!"
IF (barrels) THEN
    "And try not to break any more of my barrels-they're expensive!"
```

This might become annoying if it plays every time the player exits, so we might prefer to include a flag so that it only plays once:

Goodbye:

```
"See you next time!"
IF (barrels AND once) THEN
{
    "And try not to break any more of my barrels-they're expensive!"
\\ set once to FALSE
}
```

The logical operator AND allows multiple conditions to be included. Note also the addition of the curly braces—{ and }—to denote the scope of the conditional statements when multiple lines are to be included.

As a second example, consider the hypothetical tropical island vacation game described earlier in this chapter. In this, we had a section of script that was intended to vary according to which activities the player had already tried and according to the weather. The following represents the script, including the Boolean logic required to make it work. First, we must define the flags and their initial conditions:

Sunny : \\ This is TRUE if it is sunny or FALSE if it is raining.

Beach: \\ Defaults to FALSE, becomes TRUE if player has been to the beach ever.

Swim: \\ Same as preceding, but for swimming.

Tour: \\ Same as preceding, but for the archaeological visit.

Pool: \\ Same as preceding, but for the indoor pool.

Table: \\ Same as preceding, but for the table tennis.

The script segment itself then becomes:

```
IF Sunny THEN
{
    IF (NOT Beach) THEN
        "Have you been for a walk on the beach? It's beautiful there."
    ELSE
    IF (NOT Swim) THEN
        "You should go for a swim today—the weather's perfect!"
    ELSE
        IF (NOT Tour) THEN
        "Don't forget, the archaeological visit leaves from the hotel
        at noon."
    ELSE
        "Have a nice day!"
}
ELSE \\ it is Raining
{
    IF (NOT Pool) THEN
        "It may be raining, but you can still go for a swim in the
        hotel's indoor pool."
    ELSE
    IF (NOT Table) THEN
        "How about a nice game of table tennis?"
    ELSE
        "Don't let the rain get you down!"
}
```

At this point, the complexity of the script has become noticeably convoluted, and the game writer is practically programming! It is also somewhat questionable that the conditional approach is appropriate in this instance. Certainly, the game writer could have left the script in the bare bones form that it was originally pre-sented, as the programmers could have been comfortably left to implement the game logic (which they would likely do in a far more elegant fashion than the spaghetti of the preceding conditions!).

Cooperation with the game programmers responsible for implementing the script is vital when any dynamic elements are to be included, and broadly speaking the game writer will need to negotiate with the programmers concerning the script format they prefer, as there are currently no formally specified script formats in use within the games industry.

Cases and States

Whereas conditional statements allow for single yes/no decisions to be made dynam-ically in the script, *cases* allow for greater variety. The essence of a case statement is variables that can have multiple values. For instance, suppose that we have a variable "Die" that can have a value of 1, 2, 3, 4, 5, or 6. These values are the states of this vari-able. We can then have a case statement to distinguish between the different six cases:

CASE

       1: "You rolled a 1!"
       2: "You rolled a 2!"
       3: "You rolled a 3!"
       4: "You rolled a 4!"
       5: "You rolled a 5!"
       6: "You rolled a 6!"
END

We can also include a Default case, when it is useful. Suppose, for instance, that the player wins the die roll on a 5 or a 6:

CASE

       5, 6:   "You win!"
       Default: "You lose!"
END

This is identical to:

CASE

       5, 6:   "You win!"
       1, 2, 3, 4: "You lose!"
END

Default cases are extremely useful when the number of cases becomes prohibitively complex and is good practice in general terms whenever this sort of case-based logic is to be used.

For instance, consider a speaking signpost in a fantasy game. The player can approach the signpost from the north, south, east, and west. Suppose that there is a castle to the north, a swamp to the south, a forest to the east, and the cavern of despair to the west. We can specify some dialogue in a case statement format to remind the player what is in each direction. The state given is the direction the player has arrived from, and therefore all other directions are described:

```
CASE
    North:
    "Welcome! Dead ahead you will find the swamp, while to your left is
    a lovely forest. Or, if you are feeling adventurous, why not try
    the Cavern of Despair to your right?"
    East:
    "Greetings! To your right is the castle, and to your left is swamp.
    Dead ahead is the dreaded Cavern of Despair… I get woodworm just
    thinking about it!"
    South:
    "If you're headed to the castle, go straight ahead, otherwise the
    forest is to your right and to the left… well, let's just say I
    wouldn't go there without some anti-depressant enchantments."
    West:
    "Hey, did you just come from the Cavern of Despair? You must be
    some hero… or did you just take one look at it and then turn tail
    and run?"
END
```

As a second example, consider a system in which the greeting that a player receives from a certain NPC varies according to the mood of the NPC—Friendly, Neutral, or Hostile:

```
CASE
    Friendly: "Greetings!"
    Neutral: "Hello."
    Hostile: "What do you want?"
END
```

This sort of approach can allow for NPCs that feel more believable. However, it may be inappropriate to use this approach with recorded dialogue because it may become necessary for all dialogue for any given character to be recorded for all three states (Friendly, Neutral, and Hostile), which can become exceedingly complex.

Cases and states allow for highly dynamic variations in dialogue—but at a cost in complexity that can add considerably to the development time of the script and to the time and cost required for testing the game. However, they are much easier to work with than nested conditional statements and are worth considering for scripts where this sort of dynamic variation in dialogue is useful.

Inserting Text Strings

In text-only engines, *text strings* allow for dialogue to be composed in an ad hoc fashion, from the basic insertion of the player character's name to entirely procedural paragraphs as used in its simplest form in *Elite* (Firebird, 1987). The topic of procedural text is really beyond the scope of a book on game writing because it is largely a programming problem, but the use of text strings is a method that game writers would do well to learn.

In essence, any script that allows for text string insertion will specify a format in which text strings can be specified, for example $name could be used to specify the name of the player character. Any number of different text strings could be used, for instance $rank (for the player's current rank), $ship (for the name of the player's ship), or $pet (for the name of the player's pet).

Additionally, if the player is allowed to vary the character's gender, it may be necessary to have text strings for pronouns—for example, $he and $him, which would resolve as "he" and "him" for male characters and "she" and "her" for female characters. Consider the following extract from a hypothetical fantasy game:

Castellan: "What's $he doing here?"
Player: "$He has a name, Castellan. Call me $name, or call me $rank."
Castellan: "I don't trust you, $rank $name. I never have."
Player: "Doesn't matter to me whether you trust me or not."

Assuming the player is a female Captain named Salia, this would appear to the player as follows:

Castellan: "What's she doing here?"
Player: "She has a name, Castellan. Call me Salia, or call me Captain."
Castellan: "I don't trust you, Captain Salia. I never have."
Player: "Doesn't matter to me whether you trust me or not."

This neatly demonstrates the advantages of a text-only approach—it allows the text to be dynamically generated on the fly containing elements that are personal to the player. Many players will doubtless use the system to give themselves silly names, but no matter—if it gets the player laughing, it gets an emotional response, and that in some respects is the goal of any creative writing.

CONCLUSION

At the current time, all dialogue engines are based around prewritten scripts. Even the most dynamic dialogue in use is still constructed by hand by a game writer or a game designer working in the role of a game writer. Similarly, stories are plotted "by hand"—no one has yet produced a "plot engine" of any note. However, advances in technology that are on or just beyond the horizon have the potential to completely change the nature of game writing.

We are primarily waiting for higher quality text-to-speech engines to support the same kind of variety in audio as we can currently achieve in text. After we have these, it will become theoretically possible to eliminate the distinction between text-only and recorded dialogue—but this is still in the distant future. Although text-to-speech engines have become reasonably advanced, they still lack the nuance and expressivity of a human voice, and solutions to these problems do not even exist in theory at this time.

By the time we have text-to-speech systems that are sufficiently advanced to render the voice actor obsolete (or at least, to give the voice actor some competition), we are likely to also have AI systems that can compose dialogue semantically—creating the illusion of independently thinking characters. This too lies far beyond our reach at the moment, but there can be little doubt that at some point in the future something akin to this will be possible.

It follows that game writers of the future might no longer have the role of a composer of dialogue but might instead take up the role of a narrative engineer. Rather than composing individual dialogue, they might create individual characters with motivations and quirks and combine these with a framing situation of circumstances and events, from which a narrative can be allowed to emerge organically.

Perhaps, however, the traditional role of a game writer will not be lost. After all, the success of theatre, TV, and film did not affect the popularity of books. It is likely that no matter how advanced our narrative engines might become in the future, there will still be a place for the game writer to exert some authorial influence and produce narratives that have the rigidity of a traditional noninteractive narrative but the freedom of play inherent to games.

Fanciful thoughts of narrative engines aside, we have only just begun to explore the realm of game writing. As games become more recognized as an art form and become accepted into culture (as inevitably must happen), game writers will gradually earn the respectability that they currently lack and become a valued addition to the diverse roles that cooperate to produce these strange and wonderful experiences we call games.

By understanding the many different ways that a dialogue engine can be constructed, game writers gain an insight into the infrastructure that supports their art, and by learning to design them, a game writer crosses into the ill-defined borderlands between game design and game writing. Although it is by no means necessary that they do so, by having at least some understanding of the design of dialogue engines, game writers take some responsibility for how the narrative will be conveyed to the player. In the final analysis, this is the true role of the game writer—to influence and guide the manner in which a game conveys its narrative—and it can only grow in importance as games become more and more relevant to our modern cultures.

Glossary

AAA game: any game that has been developed with sufficient budget and emphasis on production values to be considered of the highest quality in comparison to other games developed at the same time.

agency: the capacity for a player to effect meaningful changes in a *game world* (q.v.) or the illusion therein.

archetype: a particular narrative role, or a strongly defined recurring theme in character role. This may refer to a particular system of archetypes, as per Jung or Campbell, or refer more generally to patterns in the use of characters in storytelling.

avatar: another name for the *player character* (q.v.) or game world representative.

backstory: the history of events prior to commencement of the story.

bark: a colloquialism referring to a short interjection in a game script context (e.g., "ow" or "argh!").

barrier: a feature specifically designed to mediate player progress, usually by blocking egress until the player acquires the mechanism to nullify or bypass the barrier.

bible: in screenwriting, a document that describes the principal characters and details of the particular setting; in essence, a reference document for a certain *IP* (q.v.).

branching: in interactive stories (q.v.), this refers to a form of plot in which there are certain points where the story can proceed down alternate paths, thus creating many different paths and outcomes in the *story-space* (q.v.).

breadcrumbing: laying a trail that the player can follow in order to complete the game. It may be a trail of items or a narrative trail, such as comments from *NPCs* (q.v.), which direct the player's attention.

camera case: any scene that may be created through camera movements within the game world, possibly also using stock (rather than purposely created) animations for character movement.

casual gamers: a subset of game players who generally devote less time and money to playing videogames than *hardcore gamers* (q.v.). Casual gamers tend to prefer less complicated games that can be played in short sessions.

character: any individual in any story can be considered a character, although if the character in question shows no sign of personality, they can be considered an *icon* (q.v.).

characteristics: in the context of characters, an element of a character's background.

cinematics: in-game movies, generally consisting of multiple *cut scenes* (q.v.) and often using *FMV* (q.v.),—especially in the context of the opening sequence of a game (the opening cinematic). The term is sometimes used as a direct synonym for cut scene.

closed story: a story with a conventional structure—a beginning, middle, and an end—as opposed to an *open story* (q.v.).

code: generally speaking, this refers to lines written in a programming language, specifically the software that runs a game.

color dialogue: text used solely to enhance the sense of authenticity and the richness of a narrative *setting* (q.v.).

combinatorial explosion: a problem in *branching* (q.v.) stories that results from the mathematically large number of outcomes that result from having many branches.

contiguous structure: a means of structuring a game so that the environment consists of a set of *domains* (q.v.) that are seamlessly joined together from the player's perspective, also referred to as a world.

continuous structure: a set of *levels* (q.v.) that are seamlessly joined together from the player's perspective.

cRPG: computer Role-Playing Game, as opposed to a tabletop role-playing game. See also *role-playing game* (q.v.).

cut scene: a short movie presented to the player at specific points in the game. Cut scenes may be *in-engine* or *FMV* (q.q.v.) There is a certain ambiguous middle ground between *in-engine* cut scenes and *scripted events* (q.q.v.).

dialogue: conversational text, sometimes delivered by a *voice actor* (q.v.), otherwise written in text. Although the term dialogue historically refers to conversation between two people, the term is often stretched to include monologue and narration.

dialogue engine: software that mediates the delivery of dialogue, text, and narrative material to the player.

dialogue tree: a complex type of *dialogue engine* (q.v.) in which speech is structured as a branching tree of conversation options, often in a recombinant form to avoid the *combinatorial explosion* (q.v.).

direct actions: actions the player takes directly using the control devices.

domain: a hermetic "mini-world" that forms a part of a game. The distinction between a *level* (q.v.) and a domain is largely subjective, but related chiefly to the manner of presentation. A domain represents an area that can be traveled to and explored; a level may refer to a much smaller and simpler component of the game-space.

domain structure: a means of structuring the game environment so it is arranged as a set of *domains* (q.v.).

emergent narrative: synonym for *implicit narrative* (q.v.).

event-driven: a common type of *dialogue engine* (q.v.) in which speech is triggered by events that occur in the game world.

FMV: Full Motion Video; a type of *cut scene* (q.v.).

forced failure: a situation in which the player has no choice but to accept failure as the outcome because the narrative demands it. This occurs most often when a game requires the death of an *NPC* (q.v.) or the plot requires the player to lose a plot device for narrative reasons.

formal narrative: storytelling delivered solely by prescribed methods with no variation of content as in other approaches, such as *interactive narrative* or *interactive story* (q.q.v.).

FPS: First Person Shooter; a common videogame genre.

Freytag's triangle: a method of analyzing plots derived from Aristotle's concept of unity of action, proposed by the German critic Gustav Freytag.

funneling: providing assistance to a player (especially through dialogue and narrative) to lead them back to the *game spine* (q.v.).

game literacy: knowledge of the typical conventions of how a videogame works. This can include understanding game-specific concepts, such as bosses, and the capacity to anticipate how a game will function based on prior experience of other games in a related genre.

game mechanics: the mathematical and logical specification of the game's underlying behavior.

gameplay: any and all the activities undertaken by a player with any given game.

game-purpose: of a character, the reason for the character in terms of *gameplay* (q.v.) as opposed to *narrative purpose* (q.v.).

game-space: the locations, states, and conditions of the game.

game spine: a sequence of actions that allows a player to progress through the core game materials and reach the end of the game. It is of particular relevance to narrative-driven games.

game state event: an event associated with a key element of a game's design.

game world: all the locations of a particular game, especially when seen as a *contiguous structure* (q.v.).

gating the story: a technique by which a game is modeled as a series of challenges that players can undertake in any order, and linear story progression is then mapped to the outcome of these modular challenges.

golden path: the optimal route through a game. It differs from the concept of a *game spine* (q.v.) only in that the golden path is assumed to be the route of least resistance and maximum reward.

hardcore gamers: a subset of game players for whom playing games is an important part of their lifestyle. Hardcore gamers include those who buy and play many different games, and those who spend many hours playing games each week. Also known as core gamers.

Hero's Journey: a template derived by Joseph Campbell from examining multiple mythological sources, which can be used as a framework for constructing certain types of story.

high-level story: a synonym for *story* (q.v.) that is used as a counterpoint for *immediate-level story* (q.v.).

hotspot: a point in the game world where the avatar can interact with the world in a meaningful way.

HUD: head-up display; referring to any information that is overlaid on the game screen for the player's reference.

icon: in the context of game narrative, a very simple form of game character that is representational but lacks emotional definition or depth.

IF: *interactive fiction* (q.v.).

immediate-level story: a description of the experience that an individual player has of playing the game itself, quite apart from any story that is embedded within the game.

immersion: a state of mind where a person is completely absorbed in what they are doing. In the context of games, immersion can result from suspension of disbelief or from a high degree of engagement with the current activity.

implicit narrative: the interaction of elements within the game systems to develop events that may be interpreted by the player as story. Also known as emergent narrative.

in-engine: a term referring usually to *cut scenes* (q.v.), and denoting that they are created using the same software as is used for the interactive gameplay.

infodump: relevant narrative information delivered to the player rapidly by the use of terse dialogue or a *cut scene* (q.v.).

in-game artifacts: objects in a world that contribute directly or tangentially to the narrative, either by providing exposition (usually in text) or by having some referential or symbolic relevance.

interactive fiction: a genre of games (previously known as text adventures) in which the game world and all the player's interactions therein take place in text.

interactive narrative: a form of narrative in which the players' actions can affect the delivery of the narrative content, while the underlying plot (or story) remains unchanged.

interactive story: a story in which the player actions have direct consequences for the story as a whole. See also *branching* and *parallel paths* (q.q.v.).

interchangeable dialogue playback: a technical term for *stitching* (q.v.).

interchangeable items: in *stitching* (q.v.), this refers to the components of a *line* (q.v.) that will differ according to what information is to be conveyed.

interruption line: a piece of dialogue suitable for interrupting a longer line of dialogue without the resulting conversation playback sounding unnatural.

invariant part: in *stitching* (q.v.), this refers to sections in a *line* (q.v.) that do not change; in essence, the backbone upon which the stitched line is constructed.

inverted pyramid: a technique in writing in which salient points are placed at the beginning and are gradually expanded and clarified in a series of more detailed sections.

IP: intellectual property; in the context of games, the *characters, setting* (q.q.v.), and other details associated with a particular brand.

kisses with continuity: references to tangential details in the source narrative or *setting* of a *licensed game* (q.q.v.), included with the purpose of cementing the game's sense of authenticity.

levels: in the context of this book, this term is used to refer to discrete areas for play, as opposed to *continuous structures, domain structures,* and *contiguous structures* (q.q.v.).

licensed game: a game developed with a world and *setting* taken from an existing *IP* (q.q.v.), usually an IP originating outside of games.

licensor: a person or organization who grants a license for the use of a particular *IP* (q.v.).

line: a line of dialogue. This may be a line of dialogue to be displayed in text, a line of spoken dialogue, or a line of dialogue composed from separate audio files by *stitching* (q.v.), in which case, it may consist of multiple sentences.

localization: the process of adapting a game into other languages or cultures.

MMORPG: massively multiplayer online role-playing game; essentially, an online *cRPG* (q.v.) that supports a few hundred players at a time. See also *role-playing game* (q.v.).

multi-line events: an occurrence in a game for which there are multiple specified *lines* (q.v.) that can occur in response.

narrative: the methods by which the story materials are communicated to the audience.

narrative design: the process by which the delivery of story materials in a game is planned out.

narrative engine: a hypothetical game engine capable of composing narrative dynamically at the plot and character level.

narrative purpose: the role a character possesses in terms of the plot or story, as opposed to the character's *game purpose* (q.v.).

noninteractive sequence: a *cut scene* or *scripted event* (q.q.v.).

nonlinear: referring to a game or story in which the content is delivered according to a structure that is not sequential. In general terms, this means the game or story has some variability into the sequence of events.

NPC: non-player character; game character that the player cannot and does not control. Historically, it is a legacy term from tabletop *role-playing games* (q.v.), but it remains in frequent usage.

open story: a type of story in which there is no predefined conventional narrative structure, and often no end point, such as campaigns in a tabletop *role-playing game*, a *cRPG*, or a *MMORPG* (q.q.v.).

parallel paths: in *interactive stories* (q.v.), a form of *branching* (q.v.) in which separate story paths are recombined at certain key story points, thus keeping the path of the narrative more tightly constrained.

placeholder word: a word used in a recording script that is intended to be replaced with other words through the process of *stitching* (q.v.).

player agency: see *agency* (q.v.).

player character: the character that the player controls in a game, sometimes abbreviated to PC. Although the term *avatar* (q.v.) is seeing increasing usage, player character remains popular in part because of its historical roots in tabletop *role-playing games* (q.v.) and in part because it more clearly refers to a *character* (q.v.) and not a game element.

plosives: sounds created by the lips or tongue that will create a clean break, especially T-, D-, and K- sounds.

recording session: time spent recording lines of dialogue by a *voice actor* (q.v.), usually in a recording studio.

role-playing game: any game in which the player is provided or creates a specific persona, and which a core element of play rests in how the player approaches the task of playing this role. Often abbreviated to RPG, the term is also applied to any videogame with game mechanics that resemble archetypal tabletop role-playing games such as *Dungeons & Dragons* (TSR, 1974). In this book, *cRPG* (q.v.) is used to make this distinction.

scripted events: an event within a game that uses the game engine for narrative purposes, but falls short of being considered an *in-engine cut scene* (q.v.) by virtue of leaving the player in control or by only wresting control from the player briefly as in a *camera case* (q.v.).

script immunity: a property bestowed upon certain characters so that they are not permitted to die under any circumstances.

setting: the world that a story takes place within. The term covers all aspects of this world, including the metaphysics (such as whether the world follows contemporary physics, some type of retro-physics, a hypothetical science-fiction physics, or a more fantastical metaphysical context such as magic).

single-line event: an occurrence in a game that requires a single *line* (q.v.) in response, such as a response to selecting a menu item.

spectacle: in Aristotle's *Poetics*, a term that includes *setting* (q.v.), sets, and special effects.

spine: see *game spine* (q.v.).

stitching: combining short audio files containing fragments of dialogue to make it sound like continuous speech.

story: the set of events driven by or affecting a certain set of characters (or character archetypes), which combine to provide a coherent narrative framework. By this definition, the same story can be used for many different *narratives* (q.v.).

story arc: the flow of a continuous story through multiple events or episodes.

story-space: the possible events and occurrences in the narrative level of a game.

storytelling vehicle: any method by which narrative content can be delivered to the player directly or indirectly, including *dialogue, cut scenes, in-game artifacts* (q.q.v.), and more indirect methods such as the layout or appearance of game locations.

talent: short for voice talent, a synonym for *voice actor* (q.v.).

text-only engine: this term describes *dialogue engines* (q.v.), which use text to deliver dialogue, not audio files.

text string: a short element of text, such as the *player character's* (q.v.) name, which can be inserted into text-based dialogue on an ad hoc basis.

theme: the underlying center of attention of a narrative, usually in terms of the focus of its ideological, moral, or intellectual content.

tokens: in the context of *dialogue engine* (q.v.), a token is a game object or a predefined topic that can be used to elicit dialogue from *NPCs* (q.v.).

topic-driven: a type of *dialogue engine* (q.v.) in which speech is triggered in response to choices the player makes about what they want to discuss with the *NPCs* (q.v.).

traits: in the context of characters, an element of a character's personality.

trigger: a specific physical area in the game world that will produce an action (often dialogue or a cut scene) when the avatar enters this predefined space.

voice actor: a person who records specific *dialogue* (q.v.) for specific characters.

voice direction: instructions intended to provide context to a voice actor. Often, this can be simply the emotional tone of a line of dialogue.

voice-over: narration that is played without the speaking character being visible.

writers' guide: a synonym for *bible* (q.v.).

References

[BBC05] BBC Creative Research & Development Research Paper, *Gamers in the UK: Digital play, digital lifestyles*, December 2005.

[Booker05] Booker, Christopher, *The Seven Basic Plots: Why We Tell Stories*. Continuum, 2005.

[Campbell49] Campbell, Joseph, *The Hero with a Thousand Faces*. Bollingen, 1949.

[Coleridge1817] Coleridge, Samuel Taylor, *Biographia Literaria: Biographical Sketches of my Literary Life & Opinions*. Rest Fenner: London, 1817.

[Csikszentmihalyi91] Csikszentmihalyi, Mihaly, *Flow: The Psychology of Optimal Experience*. Harper Perennial, 1991.

[Ekman03] Ekman, P., *Emotions Revealed*. Times Books Henry Hold and Company, 2003.

[ELSPA04] ELSPA White Paper, *Chicks and Joysticks: An exploration of women and gaming*. Available online at *http://elspa.co.uk/assets/files/c/chicksandjoysticksanexplorationofwomenandgaming_176.pdf*, September, 2004.

[Field99] Field, Syd, *The Screenwriter's Workbook*. Dell, 1988.

[GameVision04] GameVision Europe, *European Consumer Intelligence Report*. Available online at http://*www.gamevisioneurope.com*, Spring, 2004.

[Henderson97] Henderson, Mary, *Star Wars: The Magic of Myth*. Spectra, 1997.

[IGDA04] IGDA Whitepaper, *Accessibility in Games: Motivations and Approaches*. Available online at http://*www.igda.org/content/reports.php*, June, 2004.

[Ray03] Graner Ray, Sheri, *Gender Inclusive Game Design: Expanding The Market*. Charles River Media, 2003.

[Vogler92] Vogler, Christopher, *The Writer's Journey: Mythic Structure for Storytellers and Screenwriters*. Michael Wiese Film Productions, 1992.

Index